Series Editors:

Jan Broekhoff, PhD
Michael J. Ellis, PhD
Dan G. Tripps, PhD

University of Oregon
Eugene, Oregon

The 1984
Olympic Scientific
Congress
Proceedings
Volume 9

Sport and Disabled Athletes

Claudine Sherrill
Editor

Human Kinetics Publishers, Inc.
Champaign, Illinois

Library of Congress Cataloging-in-Publication Data

Olympic Scientific Congress (1984 : Eugene, Or.)
   Sport and disabled athletes.

   (1984 Olympic Scientific Congress proceedings ;
v. 9)
   Bibliography: p.
   1. Sports for the handicapped—Congresses.
2. Wheelchair sports—Congresses.   3. Special
Olympics—Congresses.   I. Sherrill, Claudine.
II. Title.   III. Series: Olympic Scientific Congress
(1984 : Eugene, Or.).   1984 Olympic Scientific
Congress proceedings ; v. 9.
GV565.O46 1984 vol. 9   796 s   85-18112
[GV709.3]   [796'.01'96]
ISBN 0-87322-014-5

Managing Editor: Susan Wilmoth, PhD
Developmental Editor: Susan Wilmoth, PhD
Production Director: Sara Chilton
Copyeditor: Kristen LaDuke-Gallup
Typesetter: Sandra Meier
Text Layout: Janet Davenport
Cover Design and Layout: Jack Davis
Printed By: Braun-Brumfield, Inc.

ISBN: 0-87322-006-4 (10 Volume Set)
ISBN: 0-87322-014-5

Printed in the United States of America

10 9 8 7 6 5 4 3 2 1

Human Kinetics Publishers, Inc.
Box 5076, Champaign, IL 61820

Contents

Series Acknowledgments

The Congress organizers realize that an event as large and complex as the 1984 Olympic Scientific Congress could not have come to fruition without the help of literally hundreds of organizations and individuals. Under the patronage of UNESCO, the Congress united in sponsorship and cooperation no fewer than 64 national and international associations and organizations. Some 50 representatives of associations helped with the organization of the scientific and associative programs by coordinating individual sessions. The cities of Eugene and Springfield yielded more than 400 volunteers who donated their time to make certain that the multitude of Congress functions would progress without major mishaps. To all these organizations and individuals, the organizers express their gratitude.

A special word of thanks must also be directed to the major sponsors of the Congress: the International Council of Sport Science and Physical Education (ICSSPE), the United States Olympic Committee (USOC), the International Council on Health, Physical Education and Recreation (ICHPER), and the American Alliance for Health, Physical Education, Recreation and Dance (AAPHERD). Last but not least, the organizers wish to acknowledge the invaluable assistance of the International Olympic Committee (IOC) and its president, Honorable Juan Antonio Samaranch. President Samaranch made Congress history by his official opening address in Eugene on July 19, 1984. The IOC durther helped the Congress with a generous donation toward the publication of the Congress papers. Without this donation it would have been impossible to make the proceedings available in this form.

Finally, the series editors wish to express their thanks to the volume editors who selected and edited the papers from each program of the Congress. Special thanks go to Claudine Sherrill of Texas Woman's University for her work on this volume.

Jan Broekhoff,
Michael J. Ellis, and
Dan G. Tripps

Series Editors

Series Preface

Sport and Disabled Athletes contains selected proceedings from this interdisciplinary program of the 1984 Olympic Scientific Congress, which was held at the University of Oregon in Eugene, Oregon, preceding the Olympic Games in Los Angeles. The Congress was organized by the College of Human Development and Performance of the University of Oregon in collaboration with the cities of Eugene and Springfield. This was the first time in the history of the Congress that the event was organized by a group of private individuals, unaided by a federal government. The fact that the Congress was attended by more than 2,200 participants from more than 100 different nations is but one indication of its success.

The Congress program focused on the theme of Sport, Health, and Well-Being and was organized in three parts. The mornings of the eight-day event were devoted to disciplinary sessions, which brought together specialists in various subdisciplines of sport science such as sport medicine, biomechanics, sport psychology, sport sociology, and sport philosophy. For the first time in the Congress' history, these disciplinary sessions were sponsored by the national and international organizations representing the various subdisciplines. In the afternoons, the emphasis shifted toward interdisciplinary themes in which scholars and researchers from the subdisciplines attempted to contribute to cross-disciplinary understanding. In addition, three evenings were devoted to keynote addresses and presentations, broadly related to the theme of Sport, Health, and Well-Being.

In addition to the scientific programs, the Congress also featured a number of associative programs with topics determined by their sponsoring organizations. Well over 1,200 papers were presented in the various sessions of the Congress at large. It stands to reason, therefore, that publishing the proceedings of the event presented a major problem to the organizers. It was decided to limit proceedings initially to interdisciplinary sessions which drew substantial interest from Congress participants and attracted a critical number of high-quality presentations. Human Kinetics Publishers, Inc. of Champaign, Illinois, was selected to produce these preceedings. After considerable deliberation, the following interdisciplinary themes were selected for publication: Competitive Sport for Children and Youths; Human Genetics and Sport; Sport and Aging; Sport and Disabled Individuals; Sport and Elite Performers; Sport, Health, and Nutrition; and Sport and Politics. The 10-volume set published by Human Kinetics Publishers is rounded out by the disciplinary proceedings of Kinanthropometry, Sport Pedagogy, and the associative program on the Scientific Aspects of Dance.

Jan Broekhoff,
Michael J. Ellis, and
Dan G. Tripps

Series Editors

Preface

Elitism in sport is no longer limited to the able-bodied. In *Physical Activity: Human Growth and Development* Kenyon and McPherson (1973) stated that "athletes who have reached a level of competition at or near a national standard are arbitrarily labeled elite performers" (p. 314). Deaf athletes have competed internationally since 1924; physically disabled athletes have done so since 1952. Special Olympics, Inc. provided mentally retarded persons their first international competition in 1968. Depending upon one's perception of "at or near a national standard," it seems reasonable to consider the top 3% to 5% of each country's disabled athletes as elite. Some use wheelchairs, some make the best of limited sensory input, and some compensate for missing limbs, severe perceptual-motor deficits, or abnormal reflex activity and muscle tone. Qualifying standards for able-bodied athletes are not attainable in some sports by disabled persons. But whoever ruled that the criteria for elite performance must be identical for all human beings? Performance differences between genders have long been recognized in the establishment of qualifying times and distances in sports for the able-bodied. Likewise, athletes of widely varying body weights are permitted to achieve elitist standings in boxing and wrestling through a universally accepted classification system. The innovation of classification systems, based on degree of disability and/or functional ability, permits disabled athletes with a broad spectrum of individual differences to compete against one another and to achieve recognition as elite performers.

The year 1984 is memorable in the history of sport for disabled athletes in that several firsts occurred. Of the several Olympic Congresses held since 1925, the 1984 International Scientific Congress held in Seattle, Oregon, was the first to include research and discussion sessions on sport for disabled athletes. This proceedings, as an outcome of the International Scientific Congress, is thus the first book to be published on the international sport movement for disabled athletes. This volume includes papers of 19 presentations made at the International Scientific Congress as well as 9 additional papers developed to provide comprehensive coverage of the history, philosophy, and current status of sport for *all* elite athletes with disabilities.

The contents of the book are organized in seven parts: History and Philosophy, Sport Classifications for Equalizing Competition, Exercise Physiology Research, Biomechanics Research, Sport Sociology and Psychology Research, Applied Research, and Appendices. Although little research in these areas currently exists, it is hoped that this content will stimulate additional scientific and philosophic inquiry by investigators in many countries and that findings will be ready for dissemination in 1988 at the next International Scientific Congress in Korea.

It is not possible, however, to fully understand chapter 1 and succeeding chapters, nor to observe sport events of disabled persons without an introduction to the many and varied systems for equalizing competition. The brief descriptions included in the 1984 International Games for the Disabled program guide are in the appendix along with an explanation of the system used with spinally paralyzed athletes. It should be noted that Roman numerals are used for classification of spinally paralyzed athletes, whereas Arabic numbers denote classifications for other disability groups. In a meeting on research at the 1984 International Games for the Disabled, sport classification was voted the topic most in need of research. Of importance, also, is the responsibility of all researchers to fully describe populations and samples studied in terms of sport classifications as well as of specific disability.

I wish to express my appreciation to the 41 writers who contributed to this book, to our editor, Sue Wilmoth, and to Rainer Martens, our publisher, who understood our dream of elitism in sports for all human beings, regardless of disability. A thank you, also, to Stan Labanowich for serving as the organizer and chair of the section on sport and disabled athletes at the 1984 International Scientific Congress.

Claudine Sherrill
Editor

The 1984
Olympic Scientific
Congress
Proceedings
Volume 9

Sport and Disabled Athletes

PART I

History and Philosophy

1

Training and Fitness Programs for Disabled Athletes: Past, Present, and Future

Robert Steadward and Catherine Walsh
DEPARTMENT OF PHYSICAL EDUCATION AND SPORT STUDIES
UNIVERSITY OF ALBERTA, EDMONTON, CANADA

Sport for physically disabled people is a relatively recent addition to the modern day sport scene. In fact, it was only 37 years ago that the late Sir Ludwig Guttmann staged the first sport competition for the physically disabled in Stoke Mandeville, England, with only 16 competitors participating. Since these first games in 1948, sport for physically disabled athletes has grown immensely. But sport for the disabled is still a mere fledgling caught within the superstructure of modern day sport. Throughout its short history, sport for disabled athletes has struggled to equate itself with the so-called "normal" realm of sport. Unfortunately, however, this rapid growth has not been accompanied by a similar worldwide development in coaching and training methods for these athletes. As a result, research and training centers are needed not only to provide disabled athletes with a place to train for their specific events but also to conduct research projects and to provide coaches with the most recent information on training the disabled athlete.

In the 1968 Canadian National Wheelchair Championships, a Class V male athlete won the 1500 m in a time of 8:33.2. The winning time of Classes II and III combined was 9:23.8. Unfortunately, track events beyond 100 m for paraplegics did not appear internationally until the 1976 Torontolympiad.

At the 1976 Torontolympiad, Randy Wix completed the Men's Class V 1500 m with a winning time of 5:12.80. The Class IV winner, David Kiley, finished in 5:15.50. The 1500 m was not offered for Class II and III competition (see Figure 1).

In 1980, in Arnhem, Holland, Mel Fitzgerald of Canada set a new world and Olympic record in the Class V 1500 m event. His time of 4:17.00 was almost 1 minute under the 1976 Olympic record. Brad Parks of the United States similarly bettered the previous Class IV Olympic record by half a minute with a time of 4:46.40. Once again the 1500 m was not offered for Class II and III competition (see Figure 1).

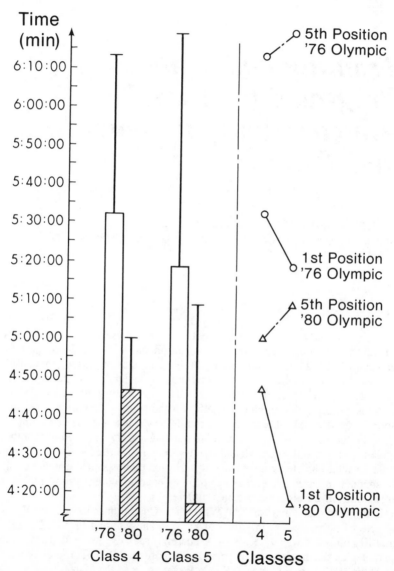

Figure 1. Wheelchair track—men 1500 m.

At the 1983 Variety Village Classic in Toronto, Canada, six athletes (Class II–V) broke the 4-minute mark in the 1500 m. The results were as follows:

D. Westley	(V)	3:57.2
G. Kerr	(II)	3:58.1
M. Fitzgerald	(V)	3:58.1
A. Viger	(III)	3:58.3
R. Hansen	(IV)	3:58.4
G. Murray	(III)	3:58.9

Marathons, unofficially introduced in 1975 for wheelchair athletes, demonstrated more than a dramatic improvement in performance (see Figure 2). Similarly it has been shown that female wheelchair athletes have enjoyed

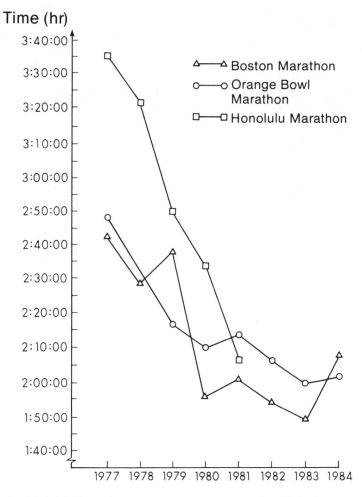

Figure 2. Wheelchair marathons—winning times (men's division)

the same achievements (see Figure 3). Although the overall performaces of the athletes for the various events have improved significantly over the years, very little difference exists between the paraplegic classes (see Figure 4).

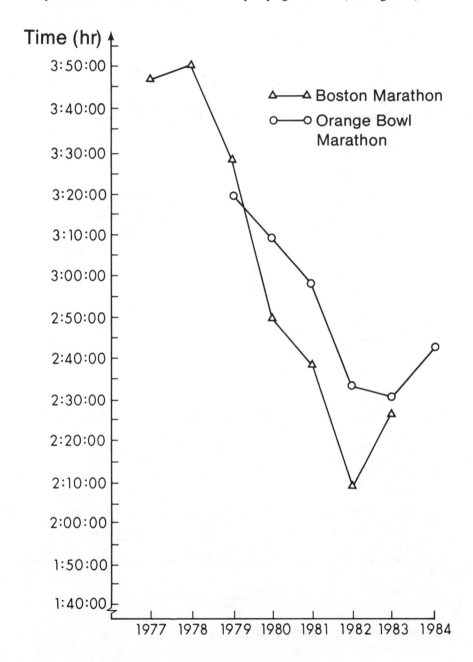

Figure 3. Wheelchair marathons—winning times (women's division)

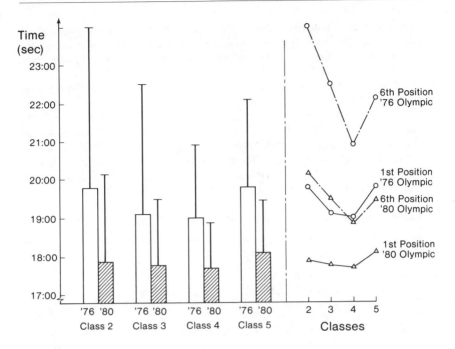

Figure 4. Wheelchair track—men 100 m

What can be expected at the 1984 World Wheelchair Games and the 1984 International Games for the Disabled? What should one look forward to in 1988? Will performances continue to improve at a rate similar to those demonstrated in the Men's 1500 m over recent years? To what can these improvements be attributed?

The purpose of this paper is to review the developments in training and fitness programs for the physically disabled athlete over the years, to identify present efforts to improve the fitness and performance levels of the disabled athlete, and finally, to make some predictions about the future of sport and fitness for the physically disabled athlete.

In the Past

It was mentioned before that sport for the disabled had its roots in England, at the Stoke Mandeville Hospital, as a result of the work completed by the late Sir Ludwig Guttmann. The large numbers of disabled veterans returning from World War II provided new impetus to the idea of sport as an aid to the remedial treatment and rehabilitation of disabled persons. Until then, the efficacy of sport as a rehabilitative mode for paralyzed people had not been tested.

In early 1977, the Spinal Injuries Centre of the Stoke Mandeville Hospital was opened, and sport was introduced for war veterans, who, in the past, had been considered outcasts of society and hopeless invalids with a short duration of life. Sir Ludwig experimented with punchball exercises, darts, and snooker from a wheelchair; then he introduced the first competitive team sport of wheelchair polo followed closely by basketball.

These experiments along with the concept of using sport as a clinical treatment were the beginning of a systematic development of competitive sport for paralyzed people under the auspices of the International Stoke Mandeville Games Federation (ISMGF). On July 21, 1948, the first Stoke Mandevill Games for the Paralyzed opened with only 16 ex-members of the British Forces—14 men and 2 women. It was a demonstration to society that sport is not exclusively the prerogative of the nondisabled; men and women with spinal paraplegia can become sportsmen and sportswomen in their own right.

Table 1. Participation changes at wheelchair competitions

Year	Place	No. of competitors
1948	Stoke Mandeville	16
1949	Stoke Mandeville	61
1950	Stoke Mandeville	110
1951	Stoke Mandeville	126
1952	Stoke Mandeville (International)	130
1953	Stoke Mandeville	200
1954	Stoke Mandeville	250
1955	Stoke Mandeville	280
1956	Stoke Mandeville	300
1957	Stoke Mandeville	360
1958	Stoke Mandeville	350
1959	Stoke Mandeville	360
1960	Olympics (Rome)	400
1961	Stoke Mandeville	240
1962	Stoke Mandeville	320
1963	Stoke Mandeville	363
1964	Olympics (Tokyo)	390
1965	Stoke Mandeville	390
1966	Stoke Mandeville	360
1967	Stoke Mandeville	370
1968	Olympics (Tel Aviv)	750
1969	Stoke Mandeville	450
1970	Stoke Mandeville	415
1971	Stoke Mandeville	430
1972	Olympics (Heidelberg)	1000
1973	Stoke Mandeville	550
1974	Stoke Mandeville	560
1975	Stoke Mandeville	630
1976	Olympics (Toronto)	1700
1980	Olympics (Arnhem)	2500
1984	Olympics (New York)	3000
1984	Olympics (Stoke Mandeville)	1000

In 1952 the Stoke Mandeville Games became the first annual international sport event for disabled athletes when a team of paralyzed ex-servicemen from Holland went to England. These competitions are currently taking place annually in England. Every fourth year they also take place somewhere else—if possible, in the country and place of the Olympic Games for the nondisabled.

The first Olympic Games for the Physically Disabled were held in Rome in 1960, where 400 wheelchair competitors from 22 countries joined in friendly competition. In 1968 the Olympics took place in Tel Aviv, Israel, because the committee in Mexico was unable to organize the Games for the disabled athlete. In 1972, 1000 competitors from 45 nations participated in Heidelberg, Germany, and in 1976 in Toronto, Canada, 1700 amputee, blind, and spinal paralytic sportsmen and sportswomen participated together for the first time.

The addition of blind and amputee athletes to the 1976 Olympic competitions made it necessary to form the International Sport Organization for the Disabled (ISOD), an international umbrella organization for all disabled. However, as time went on, ISOD became the international organization only for the amputees, disabled skiers, and les autres. 1980 was another milestone. Because Russia was unable to organize the Olympics for the Disabled, the citizens of Arnhem, the Netherlands, hosted the Games, which included cerebral palsied athletes for the first time. Now the Games had more than 2500 competitors from over 40 countries. With the addition of blind, amputee, and cerebral palsied athletes, additional international sport movements developed, such as the International Blind Sports Association (IBSA) in 1981 and the Cerebral Palsy-International Sports and Recreation Association (CP-ISRA) in 1978.

On December 6, 1981, in Paris, France, the ISOD General Assembly recommended that ISOD propose the creation of a Cooperative Committee with three representatives each from CP-ISRA, IBSA, ISMGF, and ISOD. As a result, the first Cooperative Committee met on March 11, 1982, in Leysin, Switzerland. During this first meeting the committee agreed to the following terms of reference: (a) Three representatives from each of the four international sport organizations, (b) will cooperate in matters of joint interest like multidisabled sport events, (c) will formulate an organizational structure for future cooperation with the individual international sports organizations, and (d) will maintain a joint calendar of sport events. The Cooperative Committee also discussed the steps necessary to finalize an organizational structure of an umbrella federation.

In 1983 the Cooperative Committee developed into a more formal organization and changed its name to the International Coordinating Committee (ICC). This committee requested that the four member organizations each draft a proposed set of bylaws and a constitution. These constitutions were circulated to the various international sport organizations during the spring of 1983. At this time the Canadian Federation of Sport Organizations for the Disabled (CFSOD) reacted to the ICC developments and constitutions by submitting a position paper on June 1, 1983 (see Appendix A). The ICC is still a fledgling organization that requires a great deal of work and organization in order to ultimately develop into an effective umbrella association representing all sports for disabled athletes and participating nations of the world.

Over the years the increase in the number of sports was not without growing pains. As indicated earlier, it was not until after the 1980 Summer Olympics in Holland that the sport technical and medical committees permitted athletes in Class II and III to race in distances of over 400 m. Similarly, quadriplegics, until 1981, could not compete internationally in track events longer than 200 m. While basketball, swimming, and archery have been practiced by disabled athletes for some years, only recently sports such as tennis, wheelchair rugby (murderball), volleyball, and winter skiing have been made popular. These changes came about as a result of pressure from athletes, coaches, and scientists of the various countries.

As evidenced by the increase in number of participants as well as number of events, sport for the disabled has obviously grown very rapidly. Its increase, however, have not only been in quantity but in quality as well. But in its infancy, sport provided a fundamentally new concept and, it was believed to play an important role in the rehabilitation of people with spinal injuries.

What therapeutic benefits could be derived from sport that remedial exercise alone was not providing? Guttmann (1976) and others (Jackson & Frederikson, 1979; Lipton, 1970; Rosen, 1973; Weiss & Beck, 1973) believed that sport's great advantage over formal remedial exercise lay in its overall training effect on the neuromuscular system. Sport was considered invaluable in restoring the disabled person's strength, coordination, and endurance. During the 1940s sport and training programs were prescribed and administered by medical doctors, nurses, and therapists. Because of the therapeutic nature of the programs, the intensity of the prescribed exercise was limited and the resultant performance by the athletes were reflective of this level of work.

Status of Sport for the Disabled Today

In today's world, sport for the disabled is much more than therapy. It is a means by which the disabled athlete can attain a high level of physical fitness. Sport is also a motivational force that assists athletes in preparing and achieving their maximum potentials. It also develops a competitive spirit, self-discipline, and self-respect. Sport is a vehicle for enhancing the quality of life and for increasing a person's opportunities, options, and experiences. It also provides opportunities for high-level competition with fellow athletes and for the achievement of athletic goals. The physically disabled athlete today is an athlete, not a patient.

But how did sport for the disabled grow and develop from what it was in 1948 to what it is today? What factors have contributed to the improved performances by disabled athletes, and what ingredients are required to continue the increase in the athletic performance of disabled athletes?

First, National Research and Training Centres for the Physically Disabled like the one established in 1977 in the Department of Physical Education and Sport Studies at the University of Alberta, Edmonton, Canada, and Variety Village, Toronto, Canada, need to be established. These centres provide the environment, facilities, and equipment so physically disabled athletes can train and condition for their specific sports. Also, the centres have the location and programs necessary to train and certify staff and coaches interested in prescribing programs in order to improve the athletic performance of their athletes.

In addition, it is the function of the centres to assess and evaluate the present fitness and performance level of each athlete. Based on this information, specialists design and implement a comprehensive, individual, prescriptive training program specific to each athlete's sport. It is also important to build-in monitoring systems for recording progress. Each assessment should be described in terms of what was tested, how it was tested, the results, and what they mean in terms of training. A further function of the research and training centres is to provide a focal point for research into instrumentation, test protocol, establishment of normative data, and the quality of exercise necessary to elicit optimal improvements of performance. As a result of the functions described, the research and training programs, as well as other additional information, needs to be disseminated to workshops, seminars, conferences, newsletters, pamphlets, and technical manuals.

More specifically, changes in wheelchair design and improvements in training methods, coaching, and research all have contributed significantly to the growth in sport for disabled athletes.

Wheelchair Design

One of the greatest contributors to the improvements in athletic performance over the years has been the wheelchair. Originally, athletes utilized their everyday chairs for all sports—basketball, table tennis, track and field, archery and so forth. Today, wheelchairs are being designed to suit not only the specific needs of each sport but also the needs of each individual athlete. Prior to embarking on designing a new wheelchair, however, a few considerations should be taken into account:

1. The history of the development and design of wheelchairs.
2. The rules governing the design and limitations imposed on the wheelchair.
3. The material required for the frame and the seat.
4. The design of the frame and the seat.
5. The wheels and rims, including their size and position on the chair.
6. The anthropometric dimensions of the athlete and his or her lesion level.
7. The sport.

In basketball, tennis, and wheelchair rugby (murderball), for example, chairs are built with stability, agility, and speed of movement in mind. Lightweight chairs, such as those manufactured by Quadra or Motion-Design, provide the athlete with an opportunity to be more efficient than in the past.

The wheelchair has changed dramatically for track events. Over the years, the standard Everest and Jennings chair has evolved into a sleek, lightweight machine. Large 70 cm (27 in.) racing wheels, small handrims ranging from approximately 11 to 15 inches in diameter, seat positions that place the athlete's center of mass low to the ground, large front wheels ranging from 12 to 16 inches in diameter, and highly personalized, molded seats are some of the features that are now commonplace on a wheelchair track. Today's chairs have been designed to be lightweight but strong in order to allow maximal force application.

Wheelchairs for the field athlete have seen only modest changes over the years. Higher backs with curved hand bars, for example, have assisted in improving trunk stability, while an overall increase in chair weight has resulted in greater chair stability. Although these changes have not been as spectacular as those implemented by the track athlete, they have helped to enhance the performance of field competitors. In the future, the rules governing the strapping of the legs of the competitor in field events need to be reviewed. This may affect the overall performance as well as the performance between the various classes.

Developments in the area of wheelchair design have been accompanied by similar improvements in other equipment utilized by the disabled athlete. Prosthetic devices for the amputee athlete, for example, have undergone major developments over the past several years. Lighter, stronger, and better-fitting prostheses today have enabled the amputee athlete to achieve higher performance levels. Improvements in equipment such as ski sleds, weight training devices, and indoor wheelchair ergometers have all helped to improve the performance of the disabled athlete.

Training Methods and Coaching Certification

The improvements in athletic performance that have been displayed by disabled athletes over the years can also be attributed to improved training. Undoubtedly, the disabled athlete today trains more than his or her counterpart of the past. Similarly, the quality of training today far surpasses that of years gone by. This has been witnessed by the sophisticated assessments and individually prescribed training programs that are available for and compiled on each athlete. Also, the disabled athlete has had considerable exposure to able-bodied sport clubs and programs.

The caliber of coaching has also helped to improve the quality of training and performance of the disabled athlete. While in the past many of those who coached disabled athletes were medical professionals, today's coach, with a background in physical education and sport, has the knowledge, expertise, and experience required to work with these athletes.

In Canada, the CFSOD and the national sport governing bodies for each disability, together with the National Coaching Certification Program, are attempting to further improve the caliber of coaching by ensuring that all coaches of disabled athletes are certified. While the program for coaches of nondisabled athletes has been in existence for about 10 years now, it has only been in the past year that additional programs and certification for coaches of disabled athletes have been available. Presently, coaches are becoming certified to coach the disabled in table tennis, archery, swimming, and basketball. Work is now completed to include track and field in the certification program.

The result of the above efforts has been an improved quality of coaching for disabled athletes. With individualized training programs designed and supervised by well-trained coaches, disabled athletes are now performing at levels far greater than expected.

Research

Research has also played a major role in improving performances of disabled athletes. Without the keen interest, devotion, and commitment of our colleagues from around the world like Coutts (1983), Davis (1981), Dreisinger (1982), Gass (1979, 1981), Glaser (1979, 1980), Kofsky (1981), Shephard (1978), Taylor (1979), Wicks (1976, 1977, 1983), and Zwiren (1975, 1977), sport for the disabled would still be where it was years ago.

But a terrific lack of instrumentation and test protocol still exists, and much of the data are rare and incomplete. Most of the research from 1945 to 1975 relating to sport for disabled people was conducted from a historical perspective. This included such topics as the value of sport for the disabled, the history of sport for the disabled, and sport classification (Guttmann, 1976; McCann 1980, 1981). It was primarily descriptive in nature and documented the needs, abilities, processes, and developments. Extensive objective assessments were virtually nonexistent.

Today, strategies must be found to answer the following questions:

1. Does training have an effect on the disabled?
2. What are the most appropriate tests to assess the disabled athlete's present level of performance?
3. What equipment should be used?
4. Do we have any standard protocol?
5. How do we interpret the results?
6. Can we compare a disabled and nondisabled athlete? Are the same principles of training employed?
7. Can we establish any normative data?
8. What about the severely disabled athlete?

Sport for the disabled is obviously a fertile area for research studies and available information is beginning to increase.

Research has shown that it is possible to elicit positive training effects in physically disabled individuals. Improvements in such components as muscular fitness (strength, power, and endurance), maximal oxygen consumption, body composition, and flexibility have been documented by various researchers with differing results (Dreisinger & Londeree, 1981; Davis, Kofsky, Kelsey, & Shepard, 1981; Gass & Camp, 1979; Gass, Camp, Davis, Eager, & Grout, 1981; & Glaser, Foley, Laubach, Sawka, & Suryaprasad, 1979; and Glaser, Sawka, Brune, & Wilde, 1980). Studies have also demonstrated that different training protocols will result in a variety of training responses (Dreisinger & Londeree, 1981; Coutts, Rhodes, & McKenzie, 1983; and Davis, 1981). Such information is valuable to coaches and athletes interested in selecting the best training method for their particular sports.

Various methods for testing the performance of disabled athletes have been devised through research. Today's disabled athlete can be assessed in the area of cardiovascular fitness by using one of several methods. Blind and upper body amputees can, for example, be tested on a treadmill or a stationary bicycle (Dreisinger & Londeree, 1982; Davis, Kofsky, Kelsey, & Shepard, 1981; Glaser, Sawka, Laubach, & Suryaprasad, 1979; Glaser, Sawka, Brune, & Wilde, 1980; Wicks, Lymburner, Dinsdale, & Jones, 1977; Wicks, Oldridge, Cameron, & Jones, 1983). Athletes who are confined to wheelchairs are tested on an arm ergometer or on a variety of wheelchair ergometers, each one having the capability of offering varied resistance.

The assessment of muscular fitness of disabled athletes is still in its infancy. Techniques to assess muscular fitness range from hand dynamometers and cable tensiometers to the more modern techniques using the cybex Isokinetic Dynamometer and Hydragym equipment.

Body composition has traditionally been predicted by means of skinfold measures or underwater weighing techniques. These same techniques have been used for the disabled, but the accuracy of the predictions are questionable since the formulas are derived from nondisabled populations. Therefore, in some instances total skinfold measures are used without making percent fat predictions. Work done at the Research and Training Centre for the Physically Disabled in Edmonton, Canada, illustrates this. But with the aid of these and other tests, coaches are now better provided with a means of monitoring their athletes' progress.

Research has also been a tool for analyzing the technical components of many sport skills. Over the past several years researchers have been interested in the analysis of various skills practiced by disabled athletes. For example, recent studies have evaluated the technique utilized by wheelchair athletes in both basketball and racing. Through biomechanical analyses, both the coach and the athlete have been provided with the technical information necessary to enhance athletic performance (Steadward, 1979).

Three recent studies have been completed in the Research and Training Centre for the Physically Disabled in Edmonton. One study (Steadward, 1979) recorded multiple internal measurements (EMG) from subjects moving in a wheelchair. The researchers were interested in analyzing the muscles involved in pushing a wheelchair. In order to accomplish this they had to design an artifact-free EMG system that permits the recording of EMG potentials from several different muscle sites simultaneously while the subject is free to move. They also had to design a method to objectively synchronize and correlate EMG potentials and image movement through high speed cinematography. And finally, they analyzed the action of selected muscles involved in pushing a wheelchair.

The second experiment (Steadward, Koh, & Byrnes, 1983) was designed to analyze the wheelchair pushing pattern of elite, physically disabled athletes. They were interested in the drive and the recovery phase of the wheelchair racing stroke, as well as joint movements and muscular activity during the complete pushing cycle.

A third project (Walsh, Marchiori, & Steadward, 1984), related to the previous experiments, has just been completed. With the rapid advances in wheelchair design, they were interested in investigating the effects of nine wheelchair seat positions on maximal linear velocity in wheelchair sprinting.

These three studies will have and have had a tremendous effect on the design of wheelchairs for the disabled athlete and have provided valuable information related to the technique of wheelchair racing.

The improvements and developments that have taken place in disabled sport have been tremendous. They are, however, far from complete. In the years to come it is expected that training will continue to improve, wheelchairs and other equipment will be further refined, and researchers will continue to provide valuable information. As a result, the performances of disabled athletes undoubtedly will continue to improve.

The Future of Sport for Disabled Athletes

The future of sport for disabled athletes rests, not only in the hands of research and technology but also in the development of junior athletes and in the development of an effective international governing body. Within the past few years a great deal of attention has been given to junior sport development. Today's young athletes will undoubtedly benefit from the developments that have already taken place in the areas of coaching and equipment design. Their sport careers will be enhanced by well-designed wheelchairs, excellent facilities, well-planned programs, and knowledgeable coaches; the results will obviously be positive.

With the current interest and opportunities for the young disabled athlete, it is expected that for the 1988 World Games for the Physically Disabled the number of competitors will increase to well over 4000. That is 10 times the number of competitors that participated in the first Olympic Games for the Physically Disabled in Rome.

Continued improvements in the performances of disabled athletes can also be enhanced by governments and national sport organizations. For athletes to perform to their full potentials it is necessary that they be given the opportunity to train on a full-time basis. In many countries financial government assistance through grants and bursaries is available to able-bodied athletes to offset living expenses. In Canada, elite disabled athletes have also been provided with the same benefits that have been extended to their able-bodied counterparts. This has undoubtedly helped to improve the opportunities, programs, attitudes, and ultimately the performances of disabled athletes. But additional steps can still be taken.

The establishment of more National Training Centres would permit national teams to train as units, would provide for consistent assessment techniques, and would further enhance the caliber of disabled sport. The appointment of Certified National Coaches would similarly be a positive step toward improving the performances of elite disabled athletes. These things, however, can only take place through the initiative of colleges, universities, and national sport governing bodies and with the financial backing of governments. It is expected that in the years to come this will become a reality. Disabled sport will once again leap ahead.

Training and fitness programs for disabled athletes have indeed come a long way since Sir Ludwig Guttmann first introduced sport for the physically disabled in the early 1940s. Not only have the number of participants and the number of sports increased dramatically, but the quality of performance has similarly improved. Highly specialized equipment, educated coaches, individualized training programs, well-equipped training facilities, ongoing research, the establishment of junior sport programs, and athlete assistance programs have all contributed to this improved performance.

Sport for disabled athletes is, however, still growing. Although many accomplishments have been achieved over the past 40 years, the list of developments that have yet to take place is endless. Perhaps 40 years from now wheelchair races will be more than exhibition events in the able-bodied Olympics. Perhaps sport for the disabled will one day have a permanent place in able-bodied competitions.

References

Coutts, K.D., Rhodes, E.C., & McKenzie, D.C. (1983). Maximal exercise responses of tetraplegics and paraplegics. *Journal of Applied Physiology, 55,* 479–482.

Davis, G.M., Kofsky, P.R., Kelsey, J.C., & Shephard, R.J. (1981). Cardiorespiratory fitness and muscular strength of wheelchair users. *Canadian Medical Association Journal, 125,* 1317–1323.

Davis, G.M., Shepard, R.J., & Jackson, R.W. (1981). Cardiorespiratory fitness and muscular strength in the lower-limb disabled. *Canadian Journal of Applied Sport Sciences, 6,* 159–177.

Dreisinger, T.E., & Londeree, B.R. (1982). Wheelchair exercise: A review. *Paraplegia, 20,* 20–34.

Gass, G.C., & Camp, E.M. (1979). Physiological characteristics of trained Australian paraplegic and tetraplegic subjects. *Medicine and Science in Sports and Exercise, 11,* 256–259.

Gass, G.C., Camp, E.M., Davis, H.A., Eager, D., & Grout, L. (1981). Effects of prolonged exercise on spinally injured subjects. *Medicine and Science in Sports and Exercise, 13,* 277–283.

Glaser, R.M., Foley, D.M., Laubach, L.L., Sawka, M.N., & Suryaprasad, A.G. (1979). An exercise test to evaluate fitness for wheelchair activity. *Paraplegia, 16,* 341–349.

Glaser, R.M., Sawka, M.N., Brune, M.F., & Wilde, S.W. (1980). Physiological responses to maximal effort wheelchair and arm crank ergometry. *Journal of Applied Physiology, 48,* 1060–1064.

Guttmann, L. (1976). *Textbook of sport for the disabled.* Oxford: H.M. & M. Publishers.

Jackson, R.W., & Frederikson, A. (1979). Sports for the physically disabled: The 1976 Olympiad (Toronto). *American Journal of Sports Medicine, 7,* 293–296.

Labanowich, S. (1978). Psychology of wheelchair sports. *Therapeutic Recreation Journal, 12,* 11–17.

Lipton, B.H. (1970). Role of wheelchair sports in rehabilitation. *International Rehabilitation Review, 21,* 25–27.

McCann, C.B. (1980). Medical classification—art, science, or instinct. *Sports 'N Spokes, 5,* 12–14.

McCann, C.B. (1981). Does the track athlete need medical classification? A possible effect of wheelchair design. *Sports 'N Spokes, 7,* 22–24.

Rosen, N.B. (1973). The role of sports in rehabilitation of the handicapped. *Maryland State Medical Journal, 22,* 35–39.

Royer, D. (1979). The applications of aerobic and anaerobic training to wheelchair athletes. In R.D. Steadward (Ed.), *Proceedings of the First International Conference on Sport and Training of the Physically Disabled Athlete* (pp. 80–96). Edmonton: The University of Alberta.

Royer, D., & Taylor, A.W. (1981). Utilisation de biopsies musculaires et d'études enzymatiques dans la planification de programme d'entraînement pour des athlètes d'élite en fauteuil roulant. In J.C. DePotter (Ed.), *Activités physique adaptées* (pp. 195–196). Bruxelles: Editions de l'Université de Bruxelles.

Shephard, R.J. (1978). Handicapped athlete. In R.J. Shephard (Ed.), *Fit athlete* (pp. 183–188). Oxford: Oxford University Press.

Steadward, R.D. (1976). Technique analysis—Wheelchair racing. In R.D. Steadward (Ed.), *Proceedings of the First International Conference on Sport and Training of the Physically Disabled Athlete* (pp. 118–131). Edmonton: The University of Alberta.

Steadward, R.D. (1979). Research on classifying wheelchair athletes. In R.D. Steadward (Ed.), *Proceedings of the First International Conference of Sport and Training for the Physically Disabled Athlete* (pp. 36–41). Edmonton: the University of Alberta.

Steadward, R.D. (1980). Analysis of wheelchair sport events. In H. Natvig (Ed.), *Proceedings of the First International Medical Congress on Sports for the Disabled* (pp. 184–192). Oslo: Royal Ministry of Church and Education, State Office for Youth and Sports.

Steadward, R.D., Koh, S.M., & Byrnes, D.P. (1983). *A descriptive analysis of the competitive wheelchair stroke*. Manuscript submitted for publication.

Taylor, A.W., & Mcdonnell, E. (1979). Skeletal muscle biopsy technique aids Canadian wheelchair athletes. *The Cord, 13*, 18.

Taylor, A.W., Mcdonnell, E., Royer, D., Loisell, R., Lush, N., & Steadward, R. (1979). Skeletal analysis of wheelchair athletes. *Paraplegia, 17*, 457, 460.

Walsh, C.M., Marchiori, G.E., & Steadward, R.D. (1984). *Effect of seat position on maximal linear velocity in wheelchair sprinting*. Manuscript submitted for publication.

Weiss, M., & Beck, J. (1973). Sports as part of therapy and rehabilitation of paraplegics. *Paraplegia, 11*, 166–172.

Wicks, J.R., & Jones, J.C. (1976). comparison of wheelchair and arm ergometry in spinal cord injury subjects. In F. Landry & W.A. Orban (Eds.), *Proceedings of the International Congress on Physical Activity Sciences* (pp. 447–454). Quebec City: Editeur Officiel du Quebec.

Wicks, J.R., Lymburner, K., Dinsdale, S.W., & Jones, N.L. (1977). Use of multistage exercise testing with wheelchair ergometry and arm cranking in subjects with spinal cord lesions. *Paraplegia, 15*, 252–261.

Wicks, J.R., Oldridge, N.G., Cameron, B.J., & Jones, N.L. (1983). Arm cranking and wheelchair ergometry in elite spinal cord-injured athletes. *Medicine and Science in Sports and Exercise, 15*, 224–231.

Zwiren, L., & Bar-Or, O. (1975). Responses to exercise of paraplegics who differ in conditioning level. *Medicine and Science in Sports and Exercise, 7*, 94–98.

Zwiren, L., Huberman, G., & Bar-Or, O. (1977). Cardiopulmonary function of sedentary and highly active paraplegics. *Medicine and Science in Sports and Exercise* (Abstract), *9*, 58.

Appendix A

Position Paper on the International Disabled Sport Situation

In the past few months the Canadian Federation of Sport Organizations for the Disabled (C.F.S.O.D.) has been extremely encouraged by the increased cooperation that has been demonstrated by the members of the International Co-ordinating Committee (I.C.C.). This new spirit of mutual understanding and consideration is bringing us much closer to the long overdue establishment of an international umbrella organization.

Canada presents a working example of how many systems (classifications schemes) can function together effectively without the loss of organizational autonomy. Specifically, our national structure encompasses one umbrella group (the Canadian Federation of Sport Organizations for the Disabled) and five individual sport governing bodies, four of which are organized based on disability (the Canadian Amputee Sports Association, the Canadian Blind Sports Association, the Canadian Wheelchair Sport Association and the Federation of Silent Sports of Canada Inc.), and one organization which is sport specific (the Canadian Association for Disabled Skiing). Like many countries, Canada has been and remains very concerned about our need to relate to a cooperative *yet supreme*, administrative body at the international level. Unquestionably, sport for the disabled has developed to a level of excellence where the long-term competitive needs of our international athletes are dependent on one voice that can provide a coordinating authority for disabled sport development.

On that same basis, the Canadian Federation of Sport Organizations for the Disabled would make the following statements:

1. Canada applauds the International Coordinating Committee's intention to declare themselves as the international organization governing sports for the disabled. Specifically, the Canadian Federation of Sport Organizations for the Disabled supports an international umbrella organization mandated to oversee the organization and control of both the Olympic Games and Multi-Disability World Championships. This organization should govern such areas as:
   (i)   international bidding policies and procedures;
   (ii)   detailed agreements with both Olympic Games and World Champion-ships Organizing Committees;
   (iii) the enforcement of international rules; and
   (iv)   the preparation of international event calendars.
2. In the formation of such an organization, the autonomy of the International Stoke Mandeville Games Federation (I.S.M.G.F.), the International Sports Organization for the Disabled (I.S.O.D.), the Cerebral Palsy International Sports and Recreation Association (C.P.I.S.R.A.) and the International Blind Sports Association (I.B.S.A.) must be respected. (Our constitution reflects a similar statement of autonomy, as this notion was a guiding prin-ciple in the formation of the Canadian Federation of Sport Organizations for the Disabled. As such, member organizations have only gained from working together in areas of common concern).
3. The Canadian Federation of Sport Organizations for the Disabled fully en-dorses the International Coordinating Committee's intention to establish a medical commission. The issue of classification is one that has become increasingly more complex over time. Recognizing the aforementioned, Canada's medical personnel have recommended the establishment of a national medical bureau which would undertake associated research and investigation. The Canadian Federation of Sport Organizations for the Disabled is anxious to follow the International Coordinating Committee's leadership through the medical commission, and we look forward to a cooperative working relationship with the International Coordinating Com-mittee on this important matter.
4. The Canadian Federation of Sport Organizations for the Disabled is ex-tremely anxious to join 'the proposed Confederation of International Sport Organizations for the Disabled.' We would suggest that this organization

consider in their constitution a special class of membership from individual countries such as Canada, where that country has an organization paralleling 'the proposed Confederation.'

5. All International Disabled Sport Groups should hold membership in 'the proposed Confederation of International Sport Organizations for the Disabled.' With this in view, the International Committee of Silent Sports (I.C.S.S.) should be encouraged by the International Coordinating Committee to participate in their discussions.

6. Finally, after reviewing the International Olympic Committee's proposal, the Canadian Federation of Sport Organizations for the Disabled looks favourably upon the details of Mr. Samaranch's offer. Philosophically, the use of the Olympic Rings and the opportunity to stage demonstration events at the able-bodied Olympics should be considered as a great historical moment in our continuing attempt to access the Olympic Movement.

   Practically speaking, the long term strength and development of Sports for the Disabled would be significantly influenced by official International Olympic Committee patronage and their associated fiscal support. The Canadian Federation of Sport Organizations for the Disabled interprets this gesture *as the beginning to a series of ongoing discussions* with the International Olympic Committee, and on that basis; the Canadian Federation of Sport Organizations for the Disabled must endorse the International Olympic Committee proposal as *'the first but not final'* inroad for the world's disabled athletes' acceptance into the Olympic Movement.

As the cost of international participation and competition continues to escalate, it becomes more and more difficult for Canada to access the required financial support from private and public sources when we are unable to demonstrate a systematic approach to World Championships and Olympic Games. This being the case, the need for the 'proposed confederation' becomes increasingly more urgent if Canada is to maintain its present level of involvement in future international events.

As partners in the international sport mosaic, we must work together to provide disabled athletes around the world with a professionally coordinated approach to the provision of international competitive opportunities. The Canadian Federation of Sport Organizations for the Disabled understands that as of June 10, 1983, each of the four organizations will have prepared a paper on the future organization of the International Coordinating Committee. The Canadian Federation of Sport Organizations for the Disabled would be very pleased to receive those proposals under consideration by the individual organizations to aid us in our understanding of this international concern and we trust that every effort will be made to bring the 'proposed confederation' into fruition as soon as possible.

Finally, Canada would encourage *all member countries of international sport bodies* to react to the position presented within this paper by contacting the International Coordinating Committee.

Respectfully submitted by:

The Canadian Federation of Sport
Organizations for the Disabled
Ottawa, Canada

2

Social and Psychological Dimensions of Sports for Disabled Athletes

Claudine Sherrill
TEXAS WOMAN'S UNIVERSITY
DENTON, TEXAS, USA

Since the turn of the century we have seen many signs of rapid human evolution, foreshadowings of transformation, as one supposedly unsurpassable physical limitation after another has been surpassed. There are few more satisfying confirmations of human potentiality than those found in the records of the modern Olympics. (Leonard, 1974, p. 279)

For the many individuals who viewed the International Games for the Disabled (IGD) in New York from June 17–29, 1984, George Leonard's treatise on the ultimate athlete has taken on new meaning. The 1800 athletes who competed in these Games demonstrated that, beyond a doubt, human intentionality is the most powerful evolutionary force on this planet (Leonard, 1974, p. 285). The ultimate athlete can be anyone, disabled or able-bodied, who demonstrates the capacity to dream, the unwaivering intent to be the best, and the willingness to pay the price of long, hard, and strenuous training. The purpose of this paper is to discuss selected social and psychological dimensions of sport for disabled athletes. Although the intent is to encompass all disabilities, much of the content necessarily reflects the beliefs and concerns of athletes with whom the author is personally acquainted. This paper is based on interviews of over 300 elite disabled athletes during 1982 to 1984, an analysis of selected problems confronting these and other disabled individuals, and a review of available psychosocial research on disabled athletes. The people interviewed included approximately 200 cerebral palsied athletes, ages 17 to 59, and 100 blind athletes, ages 17 to 60. The mean ages of the two groups were 26.82 and 25.64 respectively.

Problems Confronting Disabled Athletes

Problems identified by disabled athletes were the same as those experienced by other disabled people and by minority groups in general: stigmatization, stereotyping, and prejudice (Eisenberg, Griggins, & Duval, 1982; Gliedman & Roth, 1980; Wright, 1960, 1983). Problems of equal opportunity, particularly in regard to access of equipment/facilities, knowledge and skills, friends to train/workout with, and availability of coaches, were common to most athletes. Almost all saw sports as a means of affirming their competence, thereby seeking to focus attention on their abilities rather than their disabilities.

Stigmatization

Stigmatization refers to special treatment directed toward people perceived as different. First conceptualized by Goffman (1963), stigma theory defines *stigma* as an undesired differentness, an attribute that is perceived as discrediting, a failing, a shortcoming, or a handicap. Underlying stigma theory is a fear of individuals different from oneself, the equating of differentness with inferiority and/or danger, and the belief that people with stigmata are not quite human and thus need not be accorded the same acceptance, respect, and regard that we give others. Most athletes with disabilities at one time or another have experienced stigmatization. Many perceive sports as a way of fighting this prejudice and gaining increased acceptance. Illustrative of their beliefs concerning the values of sport in this regard are the following:

> A lot of people feel sorry when they see a disabled person. But when they see what a disabled person can do in sports, it helps them understand what he [she] can do in everyday life—things like crossing a street, entering a store, doing a job. I mean, I might not get a job I'm fully qualified for simply because an employer sees me with my crutches. People are MAKING us disabled just by not giving us a chance to extend our abilities. This is our chance to extend our abilities. This is our chance to show what we can do.—Dean Houle, cerebral palsied weightlifter. (Rosner, 1984, p. 4)

> . . . Part of the motivation for the 1984 International Games for the Disabled is to help bridge the gap of prejudice and ignorance that surrounds the disabled. It isn't going to be one panacea, but it demonstrates the possibilities and involvement of handicapped people in various factions of life . . . Each athlete will do the best he/she can. It will be a symbol of ability in disability.—Cynthia Good, cerebral palsied horseback rider. (Robbins, 1984, p. 4)

Stereotyping

Stereotyping refers to conceptualizing and/or treating people the same without regard for their individuality. Stereotypes are assigned primarily to people and groups about which little is known; they may be good or bad; the problem is that they depersonalize. Generally stereotypes are learned from authority figures (parents, journalists, textbook writers) and tend to be more rigid than beliefs developed on one's own (Triandis, 1971). The broader the categories used in stereotyping, the less likely they are to be accurate.

Athletes with disabilities unanimously indicate the desire to be perceived and treated as individuals and/or as members of specific sport classifications rather than to be globally conceptualized as wheelchair users or paraplegics or blind people. Yet much of the general public, as well as some professionals, still often perceive all disabled people as the same. Textbooks still refer to CPs (cerebral palsied people) rather than to Classes 1-8, to blind rather than Classes B1, B2, B3, and to spinally paralyzed rather than Classes 1A, 1B, 1C, 2, 3, 4, 5. Why not? The nature of prejudice is such that all blacks look alike, and all Orientals look alike. Feminists think all males are the same; macho men think all women are, in some way, sex objects. Small wonder then that much of the public thinks all sport events for disabled people are Special Olympics and that professionals wear their Special Olympics shirts and caps to a track meet for cerebral palsied athletes and think they are dressing appropriately.

A sense of identity, pride, and cohesiveness among people with disabilities has developed with the advent of sports for disabled athletes. The growing allegiance to sport organizations in many ways seems to resemble the loyalty that people of different ethnic groups feel for their roots. Many athletes, therefore, are resisting the "melting pot" concept of being integrated with athletes from other organizations. To them, being stereotyped as a cerebral palsied athlete carries more pride and offers more personalization than being broadly stereotyped as a disabled athlete.

Evolution of personal and organizational identity inevitably leads to conflict over ownership of such terms as wheelchair sports, paraplegics, and quadriplegics. Whereas in the past wheelchair sports evoked a mental image of spinally paralyzed and amputee athletes, this stereotype is no longer accurate. Approximately half of the cerebral palsied athletes in the United States use wheelchairs, as do many of les autres competitors. In cerebral palsy sports Class 1, 2, and 6 athletes and Class 3, 4, and 5 athletes are designated as quadriplegic and paraplegic, respectively. Yet the terms *paras* and *quads* continue to be used by the International Stoke Mandeville Games Federation (ISMGF), National Wheelchair Athletic Association (NWAA), and National Wheelchair Basketball Association (NWBA) as exclusively theirs. Illustrative of this is the *Sports 'N Spokes* summary of Team USA to the 1980 Disabled Games in Holland.

> The United States teams consisted of 60 paraplegics (and quads too), 16 amputees, 50 blind, and 24 cerebral palsy. Total athletes at the games were 1055 paraplegics, 447 amputees, 341 blind, and 122 cerebral palsy. (Crase, 1980, p. 8)

Prejudice

Athletes with disabilities wish to be judged on self-actualization (i.e., optimal development of sport ability through long, hard training) rather than physical appearance and/or aesthetics of movement. Both stigmatization and stereotyping, however, often lead to discrimination. Research shows that a hierarchy of stigmatized disabilities exists in the minds of both able-bodied and disabled people (Eisenberg et al., 1982; Tringo, 1970). Sensory disabilities are the least stigmatized; physical handicaps that impair mobility and/or physical attractiveness are next; and mental conditions that affect rationality, self-control, and responsibility are the most stigmatized. People with less-stigmatized disabilities often are quite prejudiced against individuals who are more stigmatized (Hunt, 1966). Thus many sensory impaired and physically disabled athletes express considerable prejudice toward Special Olympians. They feel that mentally handicapped people cannot be athletes in the same sense that physically or sensory impaired individuals can; moreover, they strongly oppose their Games being held at the same time and place as the Special Olympics. Their reasons, of course, are complex. Some are hostile about the unevenness of media coverage and disproportionate share of fiscal and other resources. Others are concerned about the spread phenomenon (i.e., the possibility that the general public will generalize mental retardation stereotypes to their physical disabilities) if multidisabled games are conducted. This same type of reasoning may help to explain why spinally paralyzed athletes in 1984 chose to hold their quadrennial international games at a different site from that of amputee, blind, cerebral palsied, and les autres athletes. The issue of multidisabled versus disability-specific games, approached historically, may offer some insight into the complexity of current psychosocial dimensions of sport for disabled athletes.

The 1984 international events for disabled athletes, conducted in New York and at Stoke Mandeville respectively, have increased the visibility of many psychosocial problems and have broadened the public's consciousness of sports potential, thus improving the public's attitude toward people with disabilities. Many issues remain to be resolved; misconceptions remain to be corrected; and images remain to be shaped. What role is research playing in this drama?

Psychosocial Research on Disabled Athletes

Much has been written about the psychosocial values of sport for disabled people, particularly in relation to rehabilitation (Guttmann, 1976a, 1976b; Jochheim & Strohkendl, 1973; Lipton, 1970; Stafford, 1939; Weiss & Beck, 1973). Many of the primary sources on this topic appear in languages other than English. In the United States, George Stafford, physical education professor at the University of Illinois, was advocating sport for disabled students in the 1930s. Little research, however, can be located to substantiate claims concerning the values of sport competition specifically for disabled people and/or describe disabled athletes. In the section that follows, research is reviewed under the broad topics of motivation theory, participation theory, and social learning theory.

Motivation Theory

Motivation theory has long been recognized as important in the rehabilitation of disabled people (Shontz, 1978) as well as in physical education and sport competition. Studies in this area include attitudes toward physical activity (Kennedy, 1980; Cooper, Sherrill, & Marshall, 1985), reasons for competing (Cooper, 1984), perceived contributions of sport and professionalized versus nonprofessionalized value orientations (Sherrill, Rainbolt, Montelione, & Pope, 1984).

Two research studies have focused specifically on attitudes of disabled athletes toward physical activity as measured by semantic differential instruments based on Kenyon's conceptual model for characterizing physical activity (Kenyon, 1968). Kennedy (1980) examined attitudes of 84 spinal cord injured and amputee athletes in a regional meet of the NWAA, whereas Cooper et al. (1985) investigated attitudes of 170 competitors in the Fourth National Games of the National Association of Sports for Cerebral Palsy. Neither study showed significant differences in attitudes between subjects classified as I-III and IV-VI (Kennedy) and as 1-4 (nonambulatory) and 5-8 (ambulatory) (Cooper et al., 1985). Kennedy reported a significant difference between athletes disabled before and after their 17th birthdays, $F = 5.12$, $p < .05$, with mean scores for those disabled later in life higher for each of the six attitude subdomains. Table 1 permits a visual comparison of the findings of Kennedy and Cooper et al. with those of Alderman (1970), who studied 136 able-bodied athletes in the 1967 Pan American Games; no other research on able-bodied adult athletes could be located.

Table 1. Means on attitude subdomains for able-bodied athletes (Alderman), spinal cord injured and amputee athletes (Kennedy), and cerebral palsied athletes (Cooper et al.)

Attitude subdomains	Alderman	Kennedy		Cooper et al.
		After age 17	Before age 17	
Aesthetic	43.24	43.35	39.28	47.0
Social	40.21	40.78	40.19	47.6
Fitness	39.15	43.14	41.47	46.9
Catharsis	36.10	40.95	39.21	46.4
Vertigo	35.14	36.78	35.92	41.5
Ascetic	29.38	36.30	36.26	41.4

The rankings of the six attitude subdomains are similar in the three studies; athletes are considerably more positive toward aesthetic, social, fitness, and catharsis subdomains than toward thrill and long, hard training. Cooper et al. reported a significant difference between means of the first four and last two subdomains; comparable statistical comparisons were not made by Alderman and Kennedy. Table 1 also shows that cerebral palsied athletes had more positive attitudes toward each subdomain than other groups; without a test of significance, however, this difference must be conceptualized with caution. In order to determine why elite CP athletes ($N = 145$) participate in sports, Cooper (1984) administered a paired comparison instrument that required subjects to choose between 55 pairs of reasons (i.e., 11 reasons each paired against every other reason). The most frequently chosen reasons were

1. challenge of competition,
2. fun and enjoyment,
3. love of sport,
4. fitness and health,

5. knowledge and skill about sport,
6. contribution to team, and
7. team sport atmosphere.

Although the means of these ranks were different, Friedman analysis of variance of ranks and ad hoc tests revealed no significant differences among these seven major reasons. A significant difference was apparent, however, among each of these seven reasons and the four reasons that were ranked as least important:

1. liking for other team members,
2. travel,
3. liking for coach, and
4. status.

Sherrill et al. (1984) investigated values that national-level cerebral palsied athletes ($n = 201$) and blind athletes ($n = 100$) believed they were deriving from sports participation. Table 2 presents the findings that resulted when

Table 2. Means and rankings of six areas in which adult athletes feel sports have made a contribution to their lives

Sports participation outcomes	CP athletes ($n = 201$)	Blind athletes ($n = 100$)
Fitness	2.71 (1)	2.56 (1)
Socialization/friendships	3.14 (2)	2.98 (3)
Self-concept/mental health	3.27 (3)	2.97 (2)
Interesting/exciting use of leisure time	3.66 (4)	4.13 (5)
Tension release/relaxation	4.11 (5)	3.85 (4)
Motor skills	4.15 (6)	4.31 (6)

Note: A rank of 1 denotes the area of greatest contribution.

athletes were directed to rank six areas from 1 (most valuable) to 6 (least valuable) with no tie rankings.

Professionalized versus nonprofessionalized value orientations toward sports of disabled athletes also was explored by Sherrill et al. (1984). Subjects were classified as having professionalized orientations if their main goal in sport was winning and were classified as having nonprofessional orientations if their main goals were playing well, having fun, or playing fairly. Of the 201 cerebral palsied and 100 blind athletes, 21% and 18%, respectively, indicated a professionalized value orientation. For most athletes, playing as well as they could and having fun were more important than winning. For cerebral palsied athletes no significant difference existed between professionalized and nonprofessionalized orientations between genders; for blind athletes, however, significantly more males than females indicated winning as their main goal, $X^2 (1) = 6.48, p < .05$. For cerebral palsied athletes a significant difference existed between nonambulatory and ambulatory athletes on professionalized value orientation, $X^2 (1) = 7.21, p < .01$, with more nonambulatory athletes than ambulatory athletes indicating winning as their main goal. For blind athletes no significant difference existed among visual classifications (B1, B2, B3) on professionalized and nonprofessionalized goal orientation.

Participation Theory

Participation theory in physical education has generally been implicit (not formally stated, but assumed) rather than subjected to rigorously designed experimental research. Descriptive research utilizing multiple regression and/or discriminant analysis techniques to determine the values of sport has been reported by Szyman (1980) and Hopper (1982). Research approaching the benefits of sport through a comparison of disabled and able-bodied athletes includes work on selected personality traits (Monnazzi, 1982) and on mood states and anxiety (Henschen, Horvat, & French, 1984; Mastro, 1985; Mastro & French, 1985).

Szyman (1980) conducted the most comprehensive study of the socio-psychological values of wheelchair sport to date. Subjects included people with traumatic quadriplegia, traumatic paraplegia, cerebral palsy, and postpolio who were eligible for NWAA sports in four midwestern universities. Ages ranged from 18 to 46 years, but 72% of the sample were ages 18 to 24. Sample size was 125 and 75, respectively, for Phase I and II of the study, with a 60/40 male/female percentage in both phases. The independent variable was participation in wheelchair sports. In Phase I of the study four variables were examined: self-concept as measured by the Tennessee Self-Concept Scale (Fitts, 1965), leisure attitudes as measured by the Slivkin-Crandall Leisure Ethic Scale (Slivkin & Crandall, 1978), well-being as measured by the Delighted-Terrible Scale (Andrews & Withey, 1976), and physical health as measured by the Cornell Medical Index (Brodman, Erdman, Lorge, & Wolff, 1949). Pearson product moment correlations between these measures ranged from $-.38$ to .51, with the highest relationship between self-concept and leisure attitudes.

In Phase II, a cross-legged panel design was used to determine whether wheelchair sports participation caused high scores on self-concept, leisure attitudes, well-being, and physical health or whether these variables were the cause of sports participation. The results indicated that leisure attitudes and well-being caused participation rather than vice versa; self-concept and participation were almost equally divided on cause/effect; and no significant positive correlation existed between physical health and participation.

Monnazzi (1982) investigated the hypothesis that athletic activity has an influence on selected personality traits (anxiety, phobia, obsession, somatization, depression, and hysteria) as measured by the Middlesex Hospital Questionnaire. Subjects were 22 paraplegic athletes with a mean age of 28.81 years and 19 paraplegic nonathletes with a mean age of 34.57 years. The two groups included 1 and 3 females respectively. The two groups were more-or-less matched according to the level of spinal lesion and the cause of disability, but the average number of years lapsed since the trauma was 10.22 and 5.68 for athletes and nonathletes respectively.

Inferential statistics were not presented; instead, tables and profiles indicated means for visual inspection of the two subject groups and two normative samples drawn from the literature. Paraplegic athletes more closely paralleled able-bodied people than paraplegic nonathletes on all personality traits except obsession, defined as "increased scrupulosity; in other words it is a personality trait that urges them to more scrupulously take care of their person" (Monnazzi, 1981, p. 91). Monnazzi indicated that the high obsession score may also reflect a deep-seated conflict within the athletes for not giving sufficient attention to their bodies at the time of their accidents. Little difference (6.05 and 6.13) existed between the two paraplegic groups on hysteria, and scores on this trait were similar to those of the able-bodied. Monnazzi reported that these findings confirm his hypothesis. He concluded that the practice of sport by people with paraplegia attenuates anxiety, phobia, somatization, and depression, which seem to characterize disability and help them become more like the able-bodied population.

The Profile of Mood States (POMS, McNair, Lorr, & Droppleman, 1971) and the State-Trait Anxiety Inventory (STAI, Spielberger, Gorsuch, & Lushene, 1967) have been used with spinal cord injured, polio, and amputee athletes (Henschen et al., 1984) and with blind athletes (Mastro, 1985; Mastro & French, 1985). POMS measures six psychological moods: tension, depression, anger, vigor, fatigue, and confusion. Able-bodied athletes have been shown to manifest an Iceberg Profile on POMS (i.e., above average scores on vigor and below average scores on the other moods). Henschen et al. (1984), in a study of 33 male NWAA athletes, reported that disabled athletes also manifest the Iceberg Profile, demonstrating "an even more ideal psychological profile than did able-bodied athletes" (p. 123). The one exception to this generalization was anger, which disabled athletes possessed to a higher degree than would be expected on the Iceberg Profile. STAI measures two types of anxiety: (a) state, the type that fluctuates with mood and setting; and (b) trait, the type that is more-or-less permanently embodied in the personality. Wheelchair athletes scored average on state anxiety ($M = 41$) and low on trait anxiety ($M = 34$), thereby demonstrating similarity to able-bodied athletes (Henschen et al., 1984). In a study of 33 blind male international competitors, Mastro and French (1985) reported that their subjects were similar in both state and trait anxiety to sighted athletes.

Social Learning Theory

Social learning theory (Bandura, 1969; Kenyon & McPherson, 1973) has been applied to the study of sport socialization of disabled athletes by Kennedy (1980); Hopper (1982); Sherrill et al. (1984); Sherrill, Pope, and Arnhold (1985); and Sherrill and Rainbolt (1985). Additionally, Ruckert (1980) examined the relative difference of selected social agents.

Sport socialization of disabled athletes appears to be different from that of able-bodied athletes. Whereas family and school are overwhelmingly the most important sport socialization agents in the lives of able-bodied athletes, friends and community agencies are the prime stimulators of sport involvement among physically disabled athletes. Blind athletes, in contrast, accredit school as being the most influential, with family and friends about equal as sport socializers.

Ruckert (1980) reported findings of a poll of athletes from 18 countries who participated in the 1980 International Games for the Disabled. Responses to the question, Who stimulated you to become involved in sports? were as follows: themselves, 29%; disabled friends, 27%; able-bodied friends, 27%; family, 9%; and physician, 8%. The sample for this study included primarily spinal cord injured and amputee athletes as evidenced by causes of disability: accident, 53%; disease, 23%; and birth, 23%.

The Kennedy Hopper Sport Role Socialization Inventory (Kennedy, 1980; Hopper, 1982) was used to assess sport socialization in two studies of spinal cord injured and amputee adult athletes. This instrument included four items each on the influence of the family, school, peer group, and community. The total possible score for each social system was 16. Kennedy (1980) reported a significant difference between the mean for peer group (11.38) and the means for community (9.48), school (9.33), and family (9.27), $F = 64.37, p < .01$. For his 84 subjects, Kennedy reported that the severity of disability and the age of onset of disability were not significant factors in sport socialization. Hopper (1982) reported for his 87 subjects the same means for peer group, community, school, and family as Kennedy. In Hopper's research, however, the sport socialization overall score was only one of seven independent variables examined in relation to involvement in sport (age, gender, severity of disability, sport socialization score, duration of sport involvement, financial outlay on sport, and personal commitment to sport). Of these seven variables, only one (age, $r = -.28$) was significantly related to high athletic aspiration (i.e., international competition as opposed to national or regional). Multiple regression analysis was used to explain the variables contributing to athletic aspiration. Age, financial outlay, and duration explained 22.1% of the variance; sport socialization score, severity of disability, personal commitment, and gender explained only 1.4%; and 76.5% of the variance remained unexplained.

Selected questions from the Disabled Athlete Sports Inventory (Sherrill et al., 1984) were used to investigate the relative importance of sport socialization agents of 100 blind and 201 cerebral palsied athletes, with mean ages of 25.64 and 26.82 years, respectively. To permit visual comparison with the findings of Kennedy (1980), the percentages of athletes who answered PE teacher, peers/friends, family, or others (i.e., community) as the one factor that most influenced their becoming interested in sport were converted to ranks. These are presented in Table 3.

Findings for cerebral palsied athletes were broken down by wheelchair versus ambulatory classes because sport socialization agents were significantly dif-

Table 3. Rankings of most important sport socialization agent for spinal cord injured and amputee (NWAA), Blind (USABA), and cerebral palsied (NASCP) athletes

Socialization agent	NWAA	USABA	NASCP	
			1–4	5–8
Peers/Friends	1	3	2	3
Community	2	4	1	1
School	3	1	4	4
Family	4	2	3	2

Note: Community includes agencies, recreation centers, and other nonschool settings.

ferent, X^2 (5) = 11.39, $p < .04$. Family and peers/friends were the second and third most important agent for ambulatory athletes, whereas the reverse was true for wheelchair users.

Summary Concerning Research on Athletes

Except for a few studies with very poor research designs, this review encompasses all of the work published on the psychosocial dimensions of sport for disabled athletes. Obviously a great need for research still exists in this area; yet few professionals in adapted physical education and therapeutic recreation seem to consider competitive sport for disabled people as part of their responsibilities. At the 1984 International Games for the Disabled, fewer than 10 U.S. university teachers and/or leaders in these areas were in attendance. Likewise the general public did not express the interest in the Games hoped for by the athletes.

Spectators and Sports for Disabled Athletes

A weakness of the 1984 International Games for the Disabled was the paucity of spectators. True, the stands were often filled, especially for the team sports (CP wheelchair soccer, blind goal ball, and amputee volleyball), but they were filled with the athletes themselves. Considering that spectators had to pay admission fees for all events (a requirement relatively new in disabled sport), perhaps the athletes and the media should have been satisfied with the able-bodied turnout. They were not, however. Repeatedly, disappointment was expressed by athletes concerning the lack of spectators. In contrast, IGD administrators pointed out that approximately the same number of spectators were in attendance at the New York games as at the 1976 and 1980 games; they did not perceive small attendance as a problem. Research is needed concerning spectators: who comes, why, and what enjoyment and/or benefits do they derive? Whether or not people choose to watch the competition of disabled athletes has significance both for the problems discussed earlier in this paper (stigmatization, stereotyping, prejudice) and for research.

Sherrill et al. (1984) asked 100 blind and 200 cerebral palsied elite athletes Does the person(s) you live with attend your sport meets and practices? Thirty-one percent of the blind athletes and 21% of the CP athletes answered "never"; 40% and 31% of blind and CP athletes, respectively, checked "sometimes"; and 30% and 36% blind and CP athletes, respectively, responded "a lot" or "almost always." Consider a moment how many able-bodied elite athletes, if asked this question, would answer no, their family never attended their sports meets and/or practices. Why do family members not attend? Why are so few able-bodied people in the stands? Can we assume, if offered the opportunity to view disabled sports on television, that most able-bodied sport enthusiasts will prioritize their time to include such viewing?

Some people have inferred that spectators watch sports of disabled athletes in different ways and for different reasons than they watch sports of the able-bodied. Recently Jim Mastro, a doctoral student at the Texas Woman's University as well as a Class B1 blind international gold medalist, was challenged to respond to the following statement in regard to the present and future status of disabled games as a spectator sport:

> To be visibly handicapped, one might say, is to possess a body that does not emit social cues in the way normal bodies do. It is to speak a social language that most ablebodied individuals do not understand. (Gliedman & Roth, 1980, p.20)

Mastro's response was to compare the status of disabled athletes today with that of women in the late nineteenth century. He pointed out that Baron de Coubertin, organizer of the first modern Olympic Games in 1896, did not approve of "women perspiring in public, assuming positions he deemed ungainly, and appearing in public riding horses, skiing, or playing soccer" (Spears, 1981, p. 83). De Coubertin's feelings were similar to those of many American physical educators in the 1890s who believed that women were not suited physically or socially to athletics. During the years from 1886 to 1928, when women were denied inclusion in the Olympics, the female gender was ideally characterized, at least by men, as modest, chaste, pure, obedient, domestic, and submissive. The idea of women publicly competing in sport not only repulsed much of the general public but was contrary to the philosophy of Olympism as beauty. Accepting ancient Greek thought that only the male body could be both athletic and beautiful and that only the movement of males could meet the Olympic criterion of an aesthetically pleasant image to watch, the first, as well as subsequent, International Olympic Committees (IOCs) denied women the right to compete. As recent as 1981, IOC was described as neither fostering nor assisting in the expansion of women's sports, at least in comparison with men's sports (Spears, 1981). Today the historic underrepresentation of women in the Olympic Games is considered evidence of prejudice and/or a lack of awareness and caring. Beauty is in the eye of the beholder is a well accepted concept. Most people today believe that female athletes meet the Olympic ideal of beauty in body, intellect, and spirit as well as male athletes.

Will the general public ever behold the body and/or movement of an amputee, blind, or cerebral palsied athlete and see it as beautiful and thus worthy to be included in the Olympics? The Greeks did not see beauty in any physical form unless it was healthy and whole. Even the classic textbook by Rathbone (1959) on corrective physical education and a forerunner of contemporary-adapted physical education books did not include illustrations of physically disabled people; instead, it was illustrated with ancient Greek sculptures, each beautiful and worthy of serving as a model. But what of the human beings whose souls, as well as training regimes, can resemble those of the ancient Greeks but whose bodies can not? Will the best within each sport classification of every recognized disability group ever be included in the Olympics, esteemed and applauded by the general public? Many disabled athletes, as well as professionals in adapted physical education and therapeutic recreation, hope so. Others emphasize that the issue should not be participation in the Olympics versus the Games for the Disabled. It is basically the principle of everyone giving his or her best—the athletes as well as the spectators whose perceptions and beliefs will continue to shape sport and influence life.

References

Alderman, R.B. (1970). A sociopsychological assessment of attitude toward physical activity in champion athletes. *Research Quarterly, 41*, 1-9.

Andrews, F.M., & Withey, S.B. (1976). *Social indicators of well-being*. New York: Plenum Press.

Bandura, A. (1969). Social-learning theory of identification process. In D.A. Goslin (Ed.), *Handbook of Socialization Theory and Research* (pp. 213-262). Chicago: Rand McNally.

Brodman, K., Erdman, A.J., Jr., Lorge, I., & Wolff, H.G. (1949). The Cornell medical index: An adjunct to medical interview. *Journal of American Medical Association, 140*, 530-534.

Cooper, M. (1984). *Attitudes toward physical activity and sources of attraction to sport of cerebral palsied athletes*. Unpublished doctoral dissertation, Texas Woman's University, Denton.

Cooper, M., Sherrill, C., & Marshall, D. (in press). Attitudes toward physical activity of elite cerebral palsied athletes. *Adapted Physical Activity Quarterly*.

Crase, N. (1980). The Olympics for the disabled. *Sports 'N Spokes, 6*(3), 8-12.

Eisenberg, M., Griggins, C., & Duval, R. (Eds.). (1982). *Disabled people as second-class citizens*. New York: Springer Publishing Co.

Fitts, W.H. (1965). *Tennessee self-concept scale manual*. Nashville, TN: Counselor Recordings and Tests.

Gliedman, J., & Roth, W. (1980). *The unexpected minority*. New York: Harcourt Brace Jovanovich.

Goffman, E. (1963). *Stigma: Notes on the management of spoiled identity*. Englewood Cliffs, NJ: Prentice-Hall, Inc.

Guttmann, L. (1976a). *Spinal cord injuries: Comprehensive management and research*. Oxford, England: Blackwell Scientific Publications.

Guttmann, L. (1976b). *Textbook of sport for the disabled*. Oxford, England: Alden Press.

Henschen, K., Horvat, M., & French, R. (1984). A visual comparison of psychological profiles between able-bodied and wheelchair athletes. *Adapted Physical Activity Quarterly, 1*(2), 118-124.

Hopper, C.A. (1982). Socialization of wheelchair athletes in sport. *Dissertation Abstracts International, 43*, 1976A. (University Microfilms No. 84-235, 7242)

Hunt, P. (Ed.). (1966). *Stigma: The experience of disability*. London: Chapman.

Jochheim, K., & Strohkendl, J. (1973). The value of particular sports of the wheelchair-disabled in maintaining health of the paraplegic. *Paraplegia, 11*, 173-178.

Kennedy, M.J. (1980). *Sport role socialization and attitudes toward physical activity of wheelchair athletes*. Unpublished master's thesis, University of Oregon, Eugene.

Kenyon, G.S. (1968). A conceptual model for characterising physical activity. *Research Quarterly, 39*, 96-105.

Kenyon, G.S., & McPherson, B. (1973). Becoming involved in physical activity and sport: A process of socialization. In G. L. Rarick (Ed.), *Physical activity: Human growth and development* (pp. 303-322). New York: Academic Press.

Leonard, G. (1974). *The ultimate athlete*. New York: Viking Press, Inc.

Lipton, B. (1970). Role of wheelchair sports in rehabilitation. *International Rehabilitation Review, 21*.

Mastro, J. (1985). *Psychological characteristics of elite male visually impaired and sighted athletes*. Unpublished doctoral dissertation, Texas Woman's University, Denton.

Mastro, J., & French, R. (1985). Sport anxiety and blind athletes. In C. Sherrill (Ed.), *Sport and disabled athletes*. Champaign, IL: Human Kinetics.

McNair, D., Lorr, M., & Droppleman, L. (1971). *Manual for profile of mood states*. San Diego, CA: Education and Industrial Testing Service.

Monnazzi, G. (1982). Paraplegics and sports: A psychological survey. *International Journal of Sports Psychology, 13*, 85-95.

Rathbone, J. (1959). *Corrective physical education* (6th ed.). Philadelphia: W.B. Saunders.

Robbins, D. (1984). Benefits of competition. *World Class Newsday Commemorative Edition, Long Island News*, p. 5.

Rosner, D. (1984). Only athletes need apply. *World Class Newsday Commemorative Edition, Long Island News*, p. 3.

Ruckert, H. (1980). *Olympics for the disabled: Holland 1980 commemorative book*. Haarlem, Netherlands: Stichting Olympische Splen.

Sherrill, C., Pope, C., & Arnhold, R. (in press). Sport socialization of blind athletes: An exploratory study. *Journal of Visual Impairment & Blindness*.

Sherrill, C., & Rainbolt, W. (in press). Sport socialization of cerebral palsied athletes: An exploratory study. *Adapted Physical Activity Quarterly*.

Sherrill C., Rainbolt, W., Montelione, T., & Pope, C. (1984). *Psychosocial studies of blind and cerebral palsied elite athletes*. Unpublished research paper, Texas Woman's University, Denton.

Sherrill, C. Rainbolt, W., Montelione, T., & Pope, C. (1985). Sport socialization of cerebral palsied and of blind elite athletes. In C. Sherrill (Ed.), *Sport and disabled athletes*. Champaign, IL: Human Kinetics.

Shontz, F. (1978). Psychological adjustment to physical disability: Trends in the theories. *Archives of Physical Medicine and Rehabilitation, 59*, 251-254.

Slivkin, K., & Crandall, R. (1978). *The importance of measuring leisure attitudes*. Paper presented at the meeting of the National Recreation and Parks Association, Miami, FL.

Spears, B. (1981). Tryphosa, Melpomene, and Nadia: The IOC and women's sport. In J. Segrave & D. Chu (Eds.), *Olympism* (pp. 81-88). Champaign, IL: Human Kinetics.

Spielberger, C., Gorsuch, R., & Lushene, R. (1967). *State-trait anxiety inventory*. Palo Alto, CA: Consulting Psychologists Press.

Stafford, G. (1939). *Sports for the handicapped*. New York: Prentice-Hall, Inc.

Szyman, R.J. (1980). The effect of participation in wheelchair sports. *Dissertation Abstracts International, 41*, 804A-805A. (University Microfilms No. 8018209)

Triandis, H. (1971). *Attitude and attitude change*. New York: John Wiley & Sons, Inc.

Tringo, J. (1970). The hierarchy of preference toward disability groups. *Journal of Special Education, 4*(3), 295-305.

Weiss, M., & Beck, J. (1973). Sport as part of therapy and rehabilitation of paraplegics. *Paraplegia, 11*, 166-172.

Wright, B. (1960). *Physical disability—A psychological approach*. New York: Harper & Row.

Wright, B. (1983). *Physical disability—A psychosocial approach*. New York: Harper & Row.

3

Sport for Disabled Australians: Future Directions, Problems, and Prospects

Jeffrey O. Miller
CUMBERLAND COLLEGE OF HEALTH SCIENCES
LIDCOMBE, AUSTRALIA

In Australia the future for expanding the opportunities available in sport for disabled people could be very promising. A plan is urgently required to guide development and assure the government that its continued investment is merited and effective. This paper presents a development strategy which utilizes and is consistent with the results of two recent surveys conducted by the National Committee on Sport and Recreation for the Disabled (NCSRD). This strategy utilizes the powerful social and political circumstances provided by three elements: (a) Australia's pervasive interest in sport, (b) the legacy of the 1981 International Year of Disabled Persons (IYDP), and (c) the demography and history of Australia. Without some assessment of these elements the growth strategy proposed will lack relevance.

The Social and Political Milieu

In Australia sporting excellence is acclaimed and is pursued with vigor. Historically the wish and will to win is something of a legend. Sport has developed as a vehicle to enhance self-esteem, generate national pride, and demonstrate self-sufficiency. The disabled athlete subscribes to, and in fact needs to be, part of this phenomenon and a "good sport." Sport provides a powerful social vehicle in which to base any growth strategy.

The IYDP in Australia raised the expectations of disabled people but also revealed a general lack of opportunity for them to exercise choice and independence. It heightened awareness of the restrictions that disabilities impose and defined the political opportunity attending that increased awareness. *Access* and *integration*, with their many meanings, were the key issues in Australia. They were used effectively to embarrass a complacent public and politicians. As in most instances of generalized application of an excellent slogan, however, the particular application suffered from its generality. The access issue for sport has focused on the physical barriers rather than the real barriers that relate to attitude and perception which deny disabled people opportunities to participate in sport and recreation. In the short term, integration of disabled and nondisabled athletes is neither sought nor favored. In the long term it could be a worthy objective.

But is integration attainable or even necessary? Australian disabled sport groups reject artificial or pseudointegration. Their view is not in accord with the general view of the IYDP on integration. For a government anxious to rationalize all funding programs for sport, there must be some temptation to use the cliché of *integration* to consolidate funding for all sport under one allocation. In the past this approach has disadvantaged disabled sport. Thus the thrust of the position preferred by Australian disabled sports groups must be argued cogently and with some finesse. The case can be explained and argued by reference to a basic social dilemma posed by Mills (1970), who distinguishes between problems and issues. A *trouble* is a private matter whereas an *issue* is a public matter. An issue transcends the local environment of the inner life and cuts across many social groups and organizations. When a private problem does this it becomes a public issue, which attracts government attention. In 1981 Miller's (Miller, 1981) approach was used to focus the attitude of the Australian population on the needs of the disabled community. The goal is to increase the sensitivity of the public as well as the government to the needs of disabled sportsmen. Disabled sportsmen's private problems of access, training, coaching, applied research, aids, mobility, and international competition must become issues that will gain public attention and support. The government must be convinced that disability and its attendant problems are public issues and not solely private matters. This is the challenge and legacy of the IYDP.

Australia has a land mass approximately equivalent to China or that of the United States. It has a population of only 14 million, mainly concentrated in metropolitan cities. Australia's future is linked to the Asian-Pacific region; yet its culture is still Western-European-oriented and -dominated. Cooperation between Australia's various states and the federal government has been determined by political allegiance rather than by national priority. Any growth strategy must recognize both Australia's demographic and political realities if it is to be accepted. It must be both robust and sensitive.

A Growth Strategy

Four facets are identified: (a) a comprehensive national sports plan; (b) a network of applied research and assessment centers; (c) access to suitable training and coaching facilities; and (d) an effective "peak" national organization with the authority to influence national and international decisions affecting disabled sport in general. Only two of these will be discussed because of space restriction. Those not addressed—a national plan and access—while important, are relatively obvious in their delineation. The cooperative network and the peak organization merit attention because they provide an Australian solution to what is also an international problem.

If we are serious about the notion of individual excellence and of maximizing the opportunities available to the elite disabled athlete, it follows that an applied research effort to assist excellence must be part of any comprehensive plan of sport development. This research must be capable of rapid and effective translation to the elite performance level as well as to new sport participants. The requirement for an applied research initiative was highlighted by the recent NCSRD survey (1984) of elite disabled athletes. This survey revealed that, of 126 disabled athletes having national rankings (90%) and world rankings (65%), only 15.5% had access to scientific assessment facilities and programs. The majority stated its interest in securing access to such information and advice. It voiced its need to have access to these facilities on a basis of decentralization. It also emphasized the need for recognition of disabled people's special needs for vocational, social, health, and psychological support.

In Australia we have a unique opportunity to involve higher education institutions in a cooperative relationship. Because this sector is fully funded by the federal government, a particular opportunity exists to initiate a comprehensive approach to applied research in sport sciences without inhibiting the freedom and autonomy of individuals or institutions. The heavy investment in equipment and facilities provided by federal funding in all higher education institutions argues for a cost-benefit approach and provides an opportunity to share existing facilities and resources for community benefit. In 1983 the NCSRD conducted a national survey to establish the location and range of facilities and the expertise for research in the sports sciences. Based on this survey and consultations with disabled sportspeople, one higher education center in each state can be identified to join a collaborating network of applied sport science research centers.

The NCSRD survey (1984) also revealed that a small group of institutions have already developed sound research programs and counseling activities. They can provide the basis for the future organization if the funding is provided.

One peak body presently operates for disabled sport in Australia—the Australian Sports Council for the Disabled (ASCD). It has five members: Australian Paraplegic and Quadriplegic Sports Federation, Australian Deaf Sports Federation, Australian Blind Sports Federation, Amputees Sporting Association of Australia, and the Australian Disabled Skiers Federation. However, each of these national organizations prefers to be treated (for government financial support) separately from the ASCD, and each makes direct application for support in its own name. They also retain their own disability-specific international links.

At the moment, no national sport group exists that represents and develops the interests of the intellectually handicapped. For a number of reasons there has been an unwillingness to include the intellectually handicapped in the disabled sport fraternity.

If the disability-specific view prevails in Australia, it is difficult to consider the viability of one authoritative national peak body. While the need to form an effective national peak organization for the disabled is recognized, the authority of that body, vis-a-vis established specific national and international disabled sport organizations, is yet to be determined. It is likely that the future pattern of a national organization in Australia will reflect an affiliation of national sport groups that will agree to combine for fund-raising purposes and discussion of common issues; but they will not vest authority in a peak body to speak for them on any issue related to their disabilities or to government on their behalf. They will continue to reject pseudointegration. A recent national consultation convened by the NCSRD in March 1984 clearly reaffirmed this view. What about the relationship between peak disabled and nondisabled sport organizations? A clear expression of the attitude of disabled sport organizations on the above issue is revealed by the recent decision of the ASCD not to join the Confederation of Australian Sport (CAS) or its newly created subcommittee for the disabled. However, it is clear that the future organization of disabled sport will be affected by changes at the national level in funding and policies developed and implemented by the new Australian Sports Commission.

What about the international scene? From an Australian viewpoint it seems fair to typify the prevailing international-level organization as being somewhat patriarchal and European dominated. For Australians, a perceived restriction of the opportunity to participate effectively in decision making, at all levels of the international scene, may lead to the development of a structure based in the Asian and Pacific Region, perhaps modeled on the Far Eastern and South Pacific Games (FESPIC) approach which is already firmly established.

In 1982 the four main international organizations for sport for the disabled met and agreed that cooperation was desirable and possible, as long as there was mutual respect for each others' autonomy. They agreed to form the International Coordinating Committee for Disabled Sports (ICCDS). This development is commendable; however, if ICCDS is to be a strong international organization, then organizations for the deaf and the intellectually handicapped must have the chance to be incorporated to provide credibility for ICCDS's role and function. ICCDS has declared itself to be *the* international organization for sports for the disabled and the representative of sports for the disabled on the level of the United Nations and the International Olympic Committee. The democracy of such an action, as viewed by the bulk of disabled people, is a topic worth exploring at another time.

These recent international moves should emphasize the point to our Australian groups that if autonomy can be respected a powerful advantage can be derived from forming an authoritative peak body. Bearing in mind these factors of national and international importance, what of the future for disabled sport and the model outlined?

Conclusion

Australian disabled sport will be increasingly characterized by better organization and fund-raising structures, a willingness to experiment and innovate, and a strong junior development program. Through a coincidence of activity by advisory groups (such as the NCSRD), the good work of disabled sport groups, the increasing sensitivity of government, and the gradual understanding of disability by the community at large, an environment has been created that will support growth. A national policy may be implemented with the awareness that resources have to be used for the benefit of all. Signs show that the government will expand its assistance to disabled sport at all levels and will fund programs providing access to recreational opportunities. In the short to medium term, the government will have to continue its role as a positive facilitator. Gradually the private sector may perceive commercial advantage and altruism to be compatible partners. They could then become more enthusiastically involved in promoting and sponsoring disabled sportspeople.

It is fitting to conclude this paper by reference to a recent policy document prepared by the NCSRD (1983) and submitted to the Minister for Sport, Recreation and Tourism for his action. In the introduction to that document the following statement was made:

> Our unconditional acceptance of the rights of disabled people to participate in activities, freely chosen, on a basis similar to that now accorded to their non-disabled peers, becomes the basic philosophical statement. From such a position the principles of access, choice, equality, dignity and compassion derive meaning and relevance in the particular context of sport and recreation. (NCSRD, 1983, p. 1)

This epitomized the growth strategy developed in this paper. It is supported by the opinion of disabled athletes and provides a sound basis for our future development. Any strategy that seeks to accommodate these various facets must indeed be robust and run the risk that this very quality may make it insensitive to the subtle variations of major themes which in turn may be *the* important themes for disabled people. However, it is a risk that must be taken. The model is reasonable and is ready for implementation. Government initiative, time, and commitment, coupled with an effective national organization, will determine the outcome.

References

Mills, C.W. (1970). *The sociological imagination.* Middlesex, England: Penguin Books Ltd.

Miller, J.O. (1981, August). The place of recreation and sport in programmes for the disabled. *Disabled Persons: Access to Enhancement of Living and Contributing Citizenship Through Education and Technology.* International Year of Disabled Persons Seminar conducted by the Commonwealth Department of Education and the United Nations Education, Scientific and Cultural Organisation's Centre for Education, Research and Instruction, Melbourne, Australia.

National Committee on Sport and Recreation for the Disabled. (1983). *Policy statement.* Canberra, Australia: Department of Sport, Recreation and Tourism.

National Committee on Sport and Recreation for the Disabled. (1984). *Report on status of the elite disabled athlete in Australia and tertiary institution involvement in sports science for disabled people.* Canberra: Department of Sport, Recreation and Tourism.

4

Sports for Disabled U.S. Citizens: Influence of Amateur Sports Act

Karen P. DePauw
WASHINGTON STATE UNIVERSITY
PULLMAN, WASHINGTON, USA

Kenneth S. Clarke
UNITED STATES OLYMPIC COMMITTEE
COLORADO SPRINGS, COLORADO, USA

United States athletes with disabilities, with the exception of deaf individuals, had virtually no opportunities for sport competition prior to World War II (DePauw, 1984). From 1957 to 1981, several national sport groups organized themselves according to each disability and established relations with their respective international counterparts. Each promoted its own programs with little interaction or communication with other sport groups. After the enactment of PL 95-606, The Amateur Sports Act of 1978, however, the sport for the disabled movement took a different approach. The purpose of this paper is to describe the effect of the Amateur Sports Act upon that movement.

Amateur Sports Act of 1978

Events over the last 10 years have significantly changed the image of the sport for the disabled movement. In 1975 President Gerald Ford formed the President's Commission on Olympic Sports; the commission's report on the status of Olympic sports and related topics, published in 1977, formed the basis for the Amateur Sports Act of 1978. Due to the nature of the times, the issue of equity surfaced during the formation of this legislation. The Education for All Handicapped Children Act of 1975 and the Rehabilitation Act of 1973 brought equal opportunity for handicapped individuals to the forefront. Thus provisions for equal opportunity for women, individuals of racial and ethnic minorities, and handicapped individuals were specifically addressed within the Amateur Sports Act.

PL 95-606, The Amateur Sports Act of 1978, was signed into law on November 8, 1978. The purpose of this Act was "to promote and coordinate amateur athletic activity in the United States, to recognize certain rights for U.S. amateur athletes, to provide for the resolution of disputes involving national governing bodies, and for other purposes." (Amateur Sports Act of 1978, 36 U.S.C., p. 371). The result was the reorganization of the United States Olympic Committee (USOC) and a renewed commitment to amateur athletes of the United States (Clarke, 1984).

Structure of the USOC

The USOC originally offered four types of membership, all of which continue today. Group A members are the national governing bodies (NGBs) for the respective Pan American and Olympic Sports. Each sport has its own autonomously incorporated national governing body. Group B members are the multiple sport organizations such as the YMCA, Armed Services, and the NCAA. Group C is for single-sport-affiliated organizations that are pursuing acceptance as Pan American and/or Olympic sport, while Group D members are the respective State Olympic Committees that are organized primarily for fund-raising and public relations purposes.

The enactment of the Amateur Sports Act led to the inclusion of the following in the Objects and Purposes Section of the USOC Constitution:

> To encourage and provide assistance to amateur athletic programs and competition for handicapped individuals, including, where feasible, the expansion of opportunities for meaningful participation by handicapped individuals in programs of athletic competition for able-bodied individuals (Article II, 13, p. 2).

To achieve this objective, Group E membership and a Handicapped in Sports Committee were established by a USOC Constitution Amendment in 1980. Group E membership was then and is now available to national amateur sport organizations that serve the disabled population and sponsor national athletic competitions in two or more sports included on the program of the Olympic or Pan American Games.

The organization of the USOC also encompasses at least 20 standing committees including a Legislative Committee, an Athletes Advisory Committee, and a Handicapped in Sports Committee. The USOC is governed by a House of Delegates, primarily for constitutional matters; a smaller Executive Board, primarily for policy and budgetary matters; and an even smaller Administrative Committee, primarily for operational matters. Each Group E member organization is entitled to a vote at the House of Delegates, and one representative Group E member is a voting member of the Executive Board of the USOC.

The USOC does not receive appropriations from the United States Government; the money primarily comes from fund-raising efforts. Although NGBs are autonomous and receive no funding for operations, some money is available for Games Preparation and Developmental programs. Standing committees are supported within the operating budget of the USOC.

Handicapped in Sports Committee

The Handicapped in Sports Committee was designated as a Standing Committee of the USOC (Article, XVI, 1, p. 15). At the first meeting of the Handicapped in Sports Committee (now known as the Committee on Sports for the Disabled), Kathryn Sallade was elected the chairperson to serve as such for the rest of the quadrennium through December 1980. Also in attendance were two representatives from each of the initial five Group E members: K. Sallade and R. Caswell (American Athletic Association for the Deaf [AAAD]), A. Copeland and D. Beaver (United States Association for Blind Athletes [USABA]), R. Montague and D. deVarona (Special Olympics), B. Lipton and D. Richardson (National Wheelchair Athletic Association [NWAA]), and C. Huber and J. Lamarre (National Association of Sports for Cerebral Palsy [NASCP]). Six additional members were appointed by Robert J. Kane, 1978-80 quadrennium president of the USOC: D. Baker, W. Davenport, D. Fisher, H. Gorrell, R. Schwartz, and L. Walker. Bob Paul served as the staff liaison to the committee. Not only was this meeting the first time that members of these five organizations had met to discuss mutual problems, but the committee, by design, assumed the role of catalyst for coordinating the sport movement for disabled athletes (*Sports 'N Spokes*, 1979).

The president of the USOC, William Simon, appointed the second Handicapped in Sports Committee for the 1981-84 term. Two representatives from each of the Group E member organizations were appointed: D. Ammons and R. Caswell (AAAD), A. Copeland and D. Beaver (USABA), R. Montague and R. Shontz (Special Olympics), L. Shaver and A. Fleming (NWAA), and C. Huber and D. Wyeth (NASCP). Members at large included U. Boornazian, K. DePauw, B. Lipton, D. Markland, R. Schwartz, and L. Walker.

At the first meeting of this newly appointed committee on September 12, 1981, in New York, the following were specified as the future directions for the 1981-84 term:

1. Enlist more support from and involvement by the national governing bodies.
2. More agressively promote the concept of sport for the handicapped.
3. Coordinate competitive sport events for athletes with disabilities.
4. Influence international handicapped sport bodies and organizations to a greater degree.
5. Foster more and better research on sport for handicapped individuals.
6. Enhance the status of sport for the handicapped within the USOC.
7. Obtain a "fair share" of the USOC funds.

Committee on Sports for the Disabled

At the April 1983 meeting of the USOC House of Delegates, the name of the committee was officially changed to Committee on Sports for the Disabled (COSD), reflecting the wishes of the athletes themselves. Today membership on the COSD consists of two representatives, each from the Group E member organizations, and others appointed by the president of the USOC. By constitutional requirement, at least one of the two representatives from each Group E member must have a disability. In total, 20% of the members must be or must have been internationally competitive athletes within the last 10 years. From the membership of the COSD, the president of the USOC appoints a chair to serve for the quadrennium to report to the House of Delegates and to the Executive Board. The director of the USOC Sports Medicine Division, Dr. Kenneth S. Clarke, serves as the staff liaison to the COSD.

The COSD meets semiannually to conduct its business. The responsibilities include: (a) developing interest and participation throughout the United States in sport for handicapped athletes; (b) minimizing conflicts in the scheduling of competitions; (c) keeping amateur handicapped athletes informed of policy matters and reasonably reflecting the views of such athletes in recommendations to the USOC governing bodies; (d) considering matters related to international sport for handicapped athletes; (e) working with the USOC NGBs to assist amateur athletic support programs for handicapped individuals and, where feasible, to assist in the expansion of opportunities for meaningful participation with able-bodied individuals; (f) disseminating technical information on physical training, equipment design, and coaching and performance analysis, and seeking to improve documentation of such information through clearinghouses, information centers, and networks; (g) encouraging and supporting research, development, and dissemination of information in areas of sport medicine and sport safety pertaining to handicapped individuals in sport; (h) providing liaison service to the USOC to guarantee that Olympic training facilities and other facilities are fully accessible to handicapped athletes; (i) maintaining an active role in informing the public and the USOC NGBs about the needs and accomplishments of handicapped athletes; (j) working with the USOC Budget and Audit Committee to seek appropriate allocation of all funds available to the USOC for sport for handicapped individuals; and (k) discharging such other duties as assigned. In addition to the regularly scheduled meetings of the COSD, business is conducted through the use of ad hoc committees, task forces, individual assignments, and general communication throughout the year.

Issues of the Quadrennium

Among the major issues addressed during the 1981–84 term were the following:

1. Additional Member Organizations: Criteria, as specified in the Constitution, were applied to other organizations seeking membership on the COSD. The United States Amputee Athletic Association (USAAA) and the Na-

tional Handicapped Sports and Recreation Association (NHSRA) became members during the quadrennium.

2. Support for Disabled Sport: Grants, in-kind services, assistance from and inclusion within NGBs, representation on the Athletes Advisory Council, and inclusion of disabled athletes in the National Sports Festivals are examples of support requested during the quadrennium. Initially $250,000 was provided to the five Group E members to help defray expenses (in 1981, $50,000 was given to each of the five groups). By the end of the quadrennium, $600,000 had been allocated to the COSD including the planning grant for the 1984 International Games for the Disabled. Group E members are entitled to the benefits, privileges, and services provided for Group A members. For the first time in 1985, participation by athletes with disabilities will be included in the National Sports Festival.

3. Support for Games for the Disabled during the Olympic Year: Financial assistance was requested and granted ($100,000 each to the 7th World Wheelchair Games and the International Games for the Disabled). Use of the term *Olympics* in conjunction with sport for disabled athletes was denied, but permission was obtained to fly the International Olympic Committee flag throughout the Games.

4. Publicity and Public Recognition of Disabled Sport Organizations: Workshops for NGBs and sport medicine were conducted. A special feature in the *Journal of Physical Education, Recreation and Dance* (DePauw, 1984) was published; a sport medicine manual (Morris, in press) was developed. An in-depth workshop on sport for the disabled was held in conjunction with the American Alliance for Health, Physical Education, Recreation, and Dance's annual convention in Anaheim, CA in April 1984. For the first time in history a research section on sport and disabled athletes was included in the International Scientific Congress, held in conjunction with the Olympic Games each quadrennium (Sherrill, 1984). A clearinghouse on sport and recreation for the disabled was established at the USOC.

5. Coordination among Sport Organizations: Two subcommittees successfully coordinated efforts for the International Games for the Disabled and the Winter Games for the Disabled. Other subcommittees have coordinated efforts at the international level.

Chronology of Action

A Chronology of the main events and major issues at the 1981–84 term follows:

On September 21, 1981, the Committee on Sports for the Disabled

- recommended that the name of the Handicapped in Sports Committee be changed to Disabled in Sports Committee;
- supported requests by AAAD and USABA for use of the Olympic Training Center (OTC) at Colorado Springs;
- sought approval for the use of the term *Olympics* in connection with the 1984 International Games for the Disabled, endorsed the concept of a

coordinating committee for the 1984 International Games, and requested a grant of $80,000 to assist in planning the International Games;

- recommended that the USOC plan and conduct a 1–2 day workshop on sport medicine and handicapped athletes in sports; and
- recommended that a special allocation made available by the USOC for disabled sports be distributed equally among the five Group E members. Each group received $50,000 in 1981.

On March 20, 1982, the committee

- recommended the establishment and maintenance of a quadrennium calendar of national and international events;
- appointed a task force to explore alternatives for inclusion of disabled athletes in the National Sports Festival held annually between the Olympic years;
- received a request from USAAA for admission to Group E membership; and
- appointed a subcommittee on International Affairs to prepare criteria/rationale for use of *Olympics* for international events, to design a coordinated multiple venue international competition, and to develop an operating code for future international matters.

On April 17–18, 1982, the committee

- held the USOC Planning Workshop on Sports Medicine and the Athlete with a Disability. A summation included recommendations for (a) unification of the Sports Medicine Council with COSD for understanding athletes with disabilities, (b) identification and classification of common problems, and facilitation of coordinated effort, (c) development of a plan for educating coaches, trainers, and physicians in the application of sport medicine concepts, (d) development of an information retrieval system, and (e) organizational coordination for accommodating both summer and winter sports.

On September 25, 1982, the committee

- submitted a name change of the Committee on Sports for the Disabled through the Legislative Committee to the Executive Board and House of Delegates for approval;
- received notification that the USOC increased the level of support to $100,000 from the requested $80,000 for planning the 1984 International Games for the Disabled to be equally divided between the New York and Illinois [actually held in England] venues ($10,000 in 1982; $25,000 in 1983; $15,000 in 1984);
- recommended to the president of the USOC that the USAAA be accepted as a Group E member;
- recommended that the Lake Placid Training Center be made accessible to athletes with disabilities;
- recommended that the USOC Constitution be amended to include a member from each Group E member organization to the Athletic Advisory Council (this was not accomplished during the quadrennium);
- proposed that a seminar be conducted for the NGBs prior to the House of Delegates meeting;

- proposed and endorsed the development of a Sports Medicine Manual for Athletes with Disabilities as a result of the recommendation for the Sports Medicine Planning Workshop;
- received a request from the National Handicapped in Sport and Recreation Association (NHSRA) for membership; and
- established and funded a meeting of the Coordinating Committee for the Winter Games for the Disabled.

On December 4, 1982, the USOC's

- Executive Board approved the change of the name of the committee, and forwarded it to the House of Delegates; and
- Athletes Advisory Council passed a resolution saying that the council supported the endeavors and intent of the disabled athletes in spirit and encouraged the attendance of various disabled athletes as guests at council meetings.

On April 14, 1983, the committee

- received notification that the COSD's request for participation by athletes with disabilities in the 1983 National Sports Festival was rejected and resubmitted the request for the 1985 National Sports Festival;
- recommended that the NHSRA be accepted as a Group E member;
- supported the concept and agreed to be a participant in the Sports for the Disabled Workshop to be held in conjunction with the American Alliance for Health, Physical Education, Recreation and Dance (AAHPERD) convention;
- agreed to submit articles for a feature on Sport Opportunities for Athletes with Disabilities to the *Journal of Physical Education, Recreation and Dance*;
- supported the need for a national clearinghouse on sport and recreation for disabled people as identified by the American Academy of Orthopedic Surgeons and agreed to establish it; and
- requested that the USOC public relations prepare a film on sport for individuals with disabilities.

On April 15, 1983, the committee

- conducted a workshop for the NGBs and urged each to establish its own COSD committee.

On April 16, 1983, the committee

- received notice that the name change to the Committee on Sports for the Disabled had been approved by the House of Delegates; and
- received notice that the USAAA was approved as a Group E member by the House of Delegates.

On November 4, 1983, the committee

- received notification that the AAAD team would be able to train at the OTC during the summer of 1985;
- reiterated the recommendation that athletes with disabilities be included in the National Sports Festivals during the 1985–88 term and appointed a subcommittee to pursue it;

- received notification that the Sports Medicine Manual for Disabled Athletes had received funding by M&M Mars. A. Morris was appointed editor and AAHPERD agreed to publish it in 1985; and
- recommended that the COSD cosponsor a self-sustaining workshop on Sports Medicine and the Disabled Athlete with the USOC Sports Medicine Council Disabled Athlete Committee.

On March 28, 1984, the committee

- reaffirmed the resolution that the National Sports Festival include a demonstration of sport for disabled people;
- received notification of the availability of a drug testing program for Group E members;
- endorsed the pursuit of a special budget to support a film on sport for disabled athletes (funding sources were not found);
- approved a questionnaire to collect needed data about sport and recreation opportunities for the clearinghouse; and
- suggested goals for the 1985–88 term including (a) a more equitable share of support from the USOC, (b) more representation of the U.S. on International bodies for disabled athletes, (c) facilitation of research and its application through a subcommittee on research, (d) expansion of opportunities for disabled athletes in NGB programs, (e) inclusion of Group E organizations in the USOC's insurance programs, (f) athlete representation of Group E organizations on the USOC Athletes Advisory Council, and (g) formation of a coordinating committee for the Summer Games.

On April 7, 1984, the committee

- received notification that the House of Delegates had approved the NHSRA as a Group E member.

On April 13, 1984, the committee

- received notification that the 1985 National Sports Festival might include, on a demonstration basis, competition for athletes with disabilities with a maximum of 50 athletes.

On October 19, 1984, the committee

- received initial plans for a conference on Sports Medicine and the Athlete with a Disability, tentatively scheduled to be held in the fall of 1986;
- established a subcommittee on Research on Sports for the Disabled.
- recommended that the representative from the COSD to the Executive Board be an athlete with a disability;
- appointed a subcommittee to establish plans for participation at the 1985 National Sports Festival;
- recommended that Group E members receive their fair share of the funds received by the USOC from the LAOOC, and
- established a subcommittee to review the purposes, objectives, and structure of the COSD.

Effects of the Amateur Sports Act

During the relatively short duration of the COSD's existence, it has successfully addressed each of the responsibilities as identified by the USOC Constitution and Bylaws. Increased interest and participation in sport for athletes with disabilities have resulted from publications and presentations at professional conferences as well as from the leadership and advocacy of various organizations and individuals. Intraorganizational conflicts were minimized, and coordination was emphasized as exemplified by the Coordinating Committee for the Winter Games and the Committee for the 1984 International Games for the Disabled. The COSD has been active in issues of accessibility concerning facilities and services of the USOC and the Olympic Training Center. Athletes from the USAAA, USABA, and NASCP have utilized the facilities at the Olypmic Training Center; the United States Deaf team will train for 2 weeks during the summer of 1985 on the way to the World Games for the Deaf to be held in Los Angeles in 1985, and a national wheelchair basketball tournament was held at the Center. Of major significance is the USOC's willingness to endorse and share its logo and name in the promotion of Group E-sponsored events (Clarke, 1984). Some future COSD goals are demonstrations at the National Sports Festival, a representation on the Athletes Advisory Council, and a facilitation of research on sport for athletes with disabilities.

Not only is the influence of the Amateur Sports Act of 1978 apparent in the activities of the COSD but also in the commitment of the USOC to athletes with disabilities. The ultimate effect of the enactment of the Amateur Sports Act upon the sport for the disabled movement will be demonstrated by (a) increased awareness and acceptance of athletes with disabilities, (b) participation by athletes with disabilities in National Sport Festivals and in Olympic and Pan American Games, (c) establishment of developmental programs for aspiring young individuals with disabilities, and (d) increased sport and recreational opportunities for individuals with disabilities. This is an exciting and rapidly changing time in the sport movement for individuals with disabilities. The movement is a reality whose time has come.

References

Amateur Sports Act of 1978, 36 U.S.C. §§ 371–382b, 391–396 (1982).

Clarke, K.C. (1984). The Amateur Sports Act of 1978 and the athlete with disability. *Rehabilitation World, 8,* 19–20.

DePauw, K.P. (1984). Commitment and challenges: Sport opportunities for athletes with disabilities. *Journal of Physical Education, Recreation & Dance, 55,* 34–35.

Education Amendments of 1972, Title IX, 902–xxx 20 U.S.C. §§ 1681–1686, 29 U.S.C. §§ 203 and 213, and 42 U.S.C. §§ 2000c, 2000c–6, 2000c–9, 200h–2 (1982).

Education for all Handicapped Children Act of 1975, Pub. L. No. 94–142, 20 U.S.C. §§ 1232, 1400, 1401, 1405, 1406, 1411–1420, 1453 (1982).

Morris, A. (in press). *Sports medicine manual for athletes with disabilities*. Reston, VA: American Alliance for Health, Physical Education, Recreation, and Dance.

Report of President's Commission on Olympic Sports. (1977). Washington, DC: U.S. Government Printing Office.

Rehabilitation Act of 1973, 29 U.S.C. §§ 701–796i (1982).

Sherrill, C. (1984). Viewpoint: Sports and disabled athletes. *Adapted Physical Activity Quarterly,* **1**(3), 181–184.

U.S. Olympic Committee organizes handicapped in sports committee. (1979). *Sports 'N Spokes,* **5**, 15.

United States Olympic Committee. (1980). *United States Olympic Committee Constitution and By Laws*. Colorado Springs, CO: USOC.

5

International Perspectives: Physical Education and Sport for Participants With Handicapping Conditions

Julian U. Stein
GEORGE MASON UNIVERSITY
FAIRFAX, VIRGINIA, USA

Worldwide attention was focused on people with handicapping conditions during the 1981 UNESCO-initiated International Year for Disabled Persons (IYDP). Many nations continued this emphasis during 1982 with National Years for Disabled Persons (NYDP). Now the thrust continues through 1992 with the Decade for Disabled Persons.

The effect of these continuing efforts has been a guarantee of equal opportunities in all of life's activities to every handicapped person, regardless of type or severity of the individual's condition. Attention continues to be placed upon each individual's abilities and potential. Emphasis is on accentuating the positive and eliminating the negative. Enabling each handicapped individual to become as independent as possible and be a contributing citizen to every society in each nation of the world continues to develop the desired outcomes of these worldwide efforts. Assuring each individual a chance to become a productive member of society in which he or she lives and to attain a high-quality, challenging, and rewarding life is basic. Recognizing the worth and dignity of every person is fundamental. Exemplified are Helen Keller's immortal words—"It is not enough to give the handicapped life; they must be given lives worth living."

This social and cultural revolution reflects man's humanity to man at its best. It has increased worldwide interest in the roles and contributions of active participation in physical education, recreation, and sport activities by handicapped participants, regardless of the individuals' ages, the type or severity of their conditions, or their stations in life.

Early Milestones

Although events and activities documenting interest in and contributions of physical education, recreation, and sport participation by people with handicapping conditions have been provided in different parts of the world, their inclusions in the IYDP and related NYDP efforts focused worldwide attention on such opportunities for handicapped individuals. Some of the milestones in these areas included the following:

- The work of Sir Ludwig Guttmann (England), which identified important roles of sport in rehabilitating World War II veterans with spinal cord injuries.
- James Oliver's 1956 Packwood Study (England), which emphasized the values of physical activities and sport on the overall growth and development of mentally retarded boys (Oliver, 1958).
- The First International Conference of Ministers and Senior Officials Responsible for Physical Education and Sport (UNESCO, April 1976), which established that "the handicapped also have a right to participate in physical education and sport." This landmark meeting gave impetus to the development of an international charter on physical education and sport and the creation of an international development fund.
- The participation and cooperation of international sport bodies around the world (i.e., the International Council for Health, Physical Education, and Recreation (ICHPER); the International Council on Sport and Physical Education (ICSPE); the International Sports Organization for the Disabled (ISOD); and others too numerous to mention), which have led the way in producing local, national, regional, and international studies and publications; organizing symposia, conferences, and workshops; and conducting special athletic events.
- The enactment of laws, regulations, mandates, and executive orders promoting necessary standards and codes to attain least restrictive educational and community environments, individualization of programs, and greater participation in physical education, recreation, and sport programs for handicapped people.
- The United Nations's 1981 IYDP leading the way in providing improved conditions for people with handicapping conditions. As a result of the Universal Declaration of Human Rights, the Declaration of the Rights of the Child, the Declaration on the Rights of Disabled Persons, and the Nils-Ivar Sundberg Declaration, all aspects of handicapped people's lives have been greatly enhanced. It is the responsibility of all to assure that the education of handicapped individuals becomes an integral part of cultural development and that equal access to leisure activities becomes inseparable from social integration.

International Interchange

Organized, systematic international interchange and exchange relating to physical education, recreation, and sport for handicapped people have been slow in coming. A major recommendation from a Study Conference on Research and Demonstration Needs in Physical Education and Recreation for Handicapped Children (February 16–19, 1969) emphasized an urgent need for concerted activity to insure international cooperation in all aspects of physical education, recreation, and sport activities involving handicapped participants.

However, international interchange and exchange did not begin to attain systematic activity and organized effort until the latter part of the 1970s. These activities and efforts have increased into the 1980s. Indications suggest even greater growth in the remaining years of the 1980s, through the 1990s, and well into the 21st century. Many international, national, and subnational plans for celebrating the 1985 UNESCO-sponsored International Youth Year have given full recognition to activities for handicapped youth. Physical education, recreation, and sport for handicapped youth are being given special attention and consideration in these efforts.

The International Federation for Adapted Physical Activities had its roots in Canada. Initially, interested individuals came together from different universities throughout Canada to afford greater communication and exchange among themselves. In March 1977 these efforts resulted in the First International Symposium on Adapted Physical Activities in Quebec City. Response over this much-needed means for international exchange resulted in the Second International Symposium on Adapted Physical Activities in Brussels, Belgium, in November 1979, the Third International Symposium in New Orleans in November, 1981, the Fourth International Symposium in London in September 1983, and the Fifth International Symposium in Toronto, Canada in October 1985. The Sixth International Symposium has already been scheduled for Brisbane, Australia for June 1987.

The International Federation for Adapted Physical Activities is now a reality with a 10-member board of directors representing six countries—Australia, Belgium, Canada, Germany, the United Kingdom, and the United States. Activities are designed to promote ongoing exchanges among members throughout the world and through biannual symposia. Emphasis continues to be upon programmatic personnel preparation, research, and documentation concerns.

The Council of Europe has been a major coordinator throughout Europe. An integral concern of the Sport for All Information Center has been physical education and sport information and materials relating to handicapped participants. Two activities have been important in attaining information about the status of programs in different countries and in identifying mutual needs throughout Europe. These efforts include (a) Sports for the Handicapped, a technical study for the Third Conference of European Ministers Responsible for Sport, as a contribution to the IYDP; and (b) Seminar on Sport for the Mentally Handicapped, held in Brussels, May 27–30, 1980. Activities of this special interest area within the Council of Europe Sport for All Information Center continue to motivate individual and coordinated efforts in physical education and sport for handicapped people within and among European countries.

Stimulated by and organized through efforts of the International Council for Health, Physical Education, and Recreation (ICHPER), the Caribbean and Central American Commission on Physical Education for the Handicapped (CACEFI) has become a reality. Conferences started in 1980 in Santa Domingo, the Dominican Republic, and have been held annually since in St. Germain, Puerto Rico, Caracas, Venezuela, Bogota, Colombia, and Aruba. The sixth and seventh of these conferences are to be held in San Salvador in May 1985 (tentatively) and in the Dominican Republic in June 1986. The conferences, supported in part by the Organization of American States, are to expand and include all of Latin America starting with the 1985 conference.

A number of follow-up workshops and in-service activities in Guatemala, Venezuela, Colombia, Peru, and Puerto Rico have resulted from CACEFI annual conferences. Identification of resource personnel and exemplary programs and the creation of specialized documentation centers and a basis for a specialized charter on physical education for special populations are representative of ongoing CACEFI activities that have increased program productivity and brought personnel closer together throughout Latin America.

UNESCO sponsored two historic activities that resulted in a greater attention to and understanding of the status of physical education, recreation, and sport opportunities involving handicapped participants. Both of these activities were done in conjunction with ICHPER.

An international survey, The Development of Physical Education and Sport for the Physically and Mentally Handicapped Throughout the World, was conducted to collect data relative to the needs of UNESCO and its member states in developing physical education, recreation, and sport programs for handicapped people. Diverse responses were found within countries as well as between some developing and some developed UNESCO member states. Recommendations were reviewed, classified, and organized into one of the following categories: (a) program development, (b) program administration, (c) facilities and equipment, (d) instructional methods and techniques, (e) personnel preparation, (f) documentation, (g) research, and (h) international cooperation and coordination (Stein & Gepford, 1982).

The International Symposium on Physical Education and Sport Programs for the Physically and Mentally Handicapped, held at College Park, Maryland in November 1982, represented the first truly coordinated effort to attain worldwide interchange and cooperation in these areas. Communication within individual countries, among countries within the same geographic region, and worldwide was identified as the highest need among symposium participants. Communication, as the first step, would lead to greater cooperation and coordination within, between, and among nations of the world. Basic to such communication was the need for UNESCO to serve as a catalyst, stimulator, and support system to ensure quality and quantity of the needed and desired exchange. Among the most consistent specific recommendations that emanated from this symposium were to

- Develop and implement an effective dissemination system to serve a variety of purposes and functions.

- Institute programs and opportunities for the exchange of personnel within countries, between nations, and throughout the world on a systematic, planned, and continuous basis.
- Provide both in-service and preservice training activities as priorities of the highest magnitude.
- Actively involve handicapped individuals at all levels and in all aspects of physical education and sport programs. (The importance of this as a high priority was emphasized and reaffirmed continually throughout the symposium.)
- Develop concerted public relations and public information programs and activities as important necessities in fulfilling many of the action-oriented projects recommended by symposium participants.
- Integrate and mainstream participants in activity programs as a major thrust in all settings.
- Encourage UNESCO to consider an International Year in Physical Education and Sport for Persons with Handicapping Conditions (UNESCO, 1982).

Symposium participants from the Scandinavian countries—Denmark, Finland, Norway, and Sweden—on their return trip home from the UNESCO/ICHPER Symposium formed a permanent group to continue deliberations and coordinate activities within their region. Several meetings with three representatives from each of these countries have already been held; the meeting location is rotated among the capital cities of each of the four participating countries. Deliberations continue to deal with ways in which physical motor needs of handicapped people can best be met. Sharing resources, developing coordinated documentation centers and services, scheduling regional training and service activities, and addressing mutual problems are representative of topics being dealt with by this group.

The 1984 International Games for the Disabled, held in Nassau County, New York, was extremely successful and focused worldwide attention on the abilities of handicapped people in general and athletics involving participants with handicapping conditions in particular. Special demonstration wheelchair races brought even greater attention to athletic exploits, skills, and excellence of these populations that culminated in Los Angeles at the 1984 Olympic Games.

International qualifying rounds were held in conjunction with the 1984 International Games for the Disabled. Sixteen finalists were chosen for the Games from 27 women and 37 men. The chosen eight women and eight men, some of the finest wheelchair racers in the world, thrilled the sport world on August 11, 1984, with their outstanding performances in 800 m (women) and 1500 m (men) races. In full view of 92,000 howling spectators and an estimated one-and-a-half billion television viewers, these 16 athletes, representing seven countries, put on an astonishing display of athletic skill and excellence.

National and Regional Contributions

Numerous other activities in different countries continue to have implications for handicapped participants in other countries and nations throughout the world. Representative of these activities follows:

- In Canada the Sport Information Resource Centre (SIRC) maintains a data bank that has information about instructional materials, publications, periodical articles, audio-visual materials, and some research related to physical education and sport for handicapped people. This centre has published special bibliographies and information sheets on general and specific topics in areas related to special populations; materials are collected from sources all over the world. This computerized data base is accessible through various commercial resource networks all over the world. Presently, the SIRC data base has been recommended to UNESCO as the official worldwide data base for physical education and sport.
- The ICHPER maintains a data bank of professional personnel in these disciplines throughout the world. Through this data bank, special attention is given to personnel serving handicapped people through physical education, recreation, and sport activities.
- In the United States a comprehensive study was conducted of programs, activities, personnel, and other resources within each of the 50 states, commonwealths, and protectorates. This study resulted in a detailed report, Physical Education and Recreation for Impaired, Disabled, and Handicapped Individuals—Past/Present/Future (1976), and computerized resource listings that included information about (a) programs and activities of sufficient quality to warrant visitors interested in starting or enriching their programs and activities for handicapped people, and (b) competencies of personnel who could be contacted for specific purposes in program development, personnel preparation (preservice and in-service activities), and research. This same pattern is now being explored and will be developed on an international basis by the ICHPER.
- Through Partners of the Americas, individuals and teams from the United States have participated in exchange activities with countries in Latin America and the Caribbean region. In one of the first of these efforts in 1976 a wheelchair basketball team from the Washington, DC area and selected consultants toured Brazil, conducted clinics, and put on exhibition wheelchair basketball games. As a follow-up in 1977, teams and individuals from Brazil traveled to the United States to observe programs, meet with consultants, play exhibition games, and benefit from program opportunities in the United States. These exchanges resulted in closer and better relationships between these countries and among individuals, teams, and communities involved and provided opportunities for ongoing international exchanges.
- The Pan American Wheelchair Games and All European Wheelchair Championships have provided opportunities for competition, scientific seminars, coaching clinics, and other means of exchange among individuals and teams involved in such activities throughout America and Europe. As a result, individuals and teams participate in exchanges stimulated by contacts made through activities associated with these games. This pattern has been explored by representatives of other sport groups such as those concerned with blind, deaf, and cerebral palsied participants. The Special Olympics have also contributed to the same ends through its international, national, regional, and local games along with periodic workshops and other training opportunities for individuals working in these programs.

- Teams of handicapped athletes from Israel, European countries, the United States, and Canada have toured other countries, taking part in exhibition games, conducting clinics, giving demonstrations, and exchanging information and materials with interested and involved coaches, teachers, leaders, administrators, researchers, therapists, and physicians. Such activities have had direct and immediate benefits for and among participants and also have had indirect and subtle effects by developing in the athletes more sensitivity and awareness of each other as individuals and of each others' cultures and folkways.

- In England, for over 30 years, the Stoke Mandeville Games have provided opportunities for handicapped athletes—especially those with spinal cord injuries who must participate in wheelchairs—to compete against each other in international competition. Beyond the immediate benefit of international competition, these annual games—held every year except during Olympic years—have afforded individuals involved in these programs the opportunity to take part in scientific sessions as well as clinics designed to provide the latest theory, research, and practice. From humble beginnings evolved the ISOD and the International Stoke Mandeville Games Federation (ISMGF), initial international governance bodies for these populations, from which national level equivalents evolved.

  A number of other international governance bodies have arisen in recent years to coordinate and promote competition among athletes with specific handicapping conditions (i.e., Cerebral Palsy—International Sport and Recreation Association, and International Blind Sport Association). Discussions and deliberations have been going on for some months to develop similar international organizations for individuals classified as les autres and as amputees. A special and high-level conference is to be held in Warsaw, Poland during April 1985, to explore the future of various international governance bodies and the interrelationships among such organizations.

  The International Coordinating Committee (ICC) has served as the coordinating body for these different international bodies. The ICC had much responsibility at decision- and policy-making levels and for the logistics of the 1984 International Games for the Disabled. In addition, the ICC has been the recognized representative of sport for handicapped athletes with the International Olympic Committee. This relationship resulted in the two wheelchair demonstration events during the 1984 Olympic Games in Los Angeles. Preliminary agreements have already been reached for events with handicapped athletes during the 1988 Olympic Games in Seoul, Korea. The ICC is also supposed to coordinate the 1988 International Games for the Disabled, also scheduled for Seoul.

  Activities of these governance organizations have furthered causes such as greater uniformity and consistency in playing and administering sports, more scientific and higher quality teaching and coaching methods and techniques, and greater international coordination among involved individuals and organizations. These efforts have also led to national affiliations with many of these international organizations in countries throughout the world.

- In Canada during September 1978, 50 outstanding wheelchair athletes from Belgium, Holland, and Canada met in an innovative and exciting competition—the Super Challenge International. Traditional wheelchair competition was organized to allow athletes of both sexes and with different levels of physical handicapping conditions to compete against each other equitably. Both men and women chose five events from 10 events typically found in wheelchair sport competition including track and field events, archery, weightlifting, and slalom. The top four finishers in the 1978 Super Challenge international represented four different medical classifications and both sexes. This viable and sound approach has many implications for furthering competitive opportunities among handicapped athletes and between able-bodied and handicapped athletes.

Representative Programs Around the World

Consistent findings in both the UNESCO/ICHPER International Survey and the UNESCO/ICHPER International Symposium included greater differences within countries than between nations in programs and activities involving persons with handicapping conditions in general in their physical education recreation and sport opportunities for these populations in particular. These consistencies were noted from input received from both developed and developing nations. Through visits, participation in programs, and the review of materials from a number of countries in various parts of the world, numerous outstanding programs and exemplary approaches have been observed. Many of these observations revealed innovative applications of theory into practice, especially as related to integration or mainstreaming of handicapped people into ongoing community programs. In addition, an appropriate combination of theory and practice was noted in all types of activities including recreation and sport as well as in educational, housing, and vocational settings. A key ingredient in each of these applications was the individual participation and what was best and most appropriate for the individual in terms of his or her needs, abilities, disabilities, and personal interests. Other dominant characteristics in many of these programs included continuity and articulation between successive steps and progressive stages in program placement and the active involvement of handicapped individuals' families during the time period from rehabilitation through reassimilation into family and community life.

Frambu Helsesenter (Norway) provides treatment and information to handicapped children *and* their parents throughout Norway. Two-week courses for parents and their handicapped children are also offered along with health camps during the summer months for these populations. Frambu concentrates on treating the handicapped individual within the family unit. The Frambu idea is to make both the family and society better able to cope with problems related to different handicapping conditions. When information and help are provided early, many secondary handicapping conditions that develop later can be diminished or even avoided—this makes it easier for the family to cope and for the handicapped individual to become a part of, not apart from, the family, community, and society.

Beitostolen Sporthelsesenter (Norway) uses participation in vigorous physical and recreational activities as the first steps in rehabilitation. Program participants are involved daily in a variety of intensive and individualized physical, recreational, and sport activities for the 4 weeks spent at Beitostolen. These individuals who represent the full gamut of physical, mental, and emotional handicapping conditions gain from physiological, psychological, and emotional contributions of physical activity in rehabilitation. They also gain new or rejuvenate old interests and skills basic to continued participation through local sport clubs upon return to their homes. Many disabled individuals have increased their abilities to participate in normal activities at work and in recreation. Beitostolen approaches emphasize activating handicapped people who are opposed to passivity and isolation; these so easily and often become fates of this population.

This Norwegian center continues to provide information and materials about its programs, activities, and efforts through printed and graphic means. In addition, direct services are made available to individuals from countries throughout the world who travel to Norway to participate in health sport activities. Upon returning to their home countries many of these individuals continue to carry the Beitostolen programs to their native lands. Through efforts of the Norwegian government, the Sons of Norway in the United States (especially the affiliates in Minnesota), and the staff and participants of a Beitostolen companion center, Vinland (Loretto, Minnesota), the same types of opportunities and services are provided in the United States. These same Norwegian groups were instrumental in initiating the 1976 Ski for Light in the United States patterned after the Ridderrenn, which was started in Norway in 1964. Both Norwegian and United States events include cross-country skiing—recreation, instruction, competition, and fellowship—for blind and physically disabled individuals. Through these efforts the Paulk and its American counterpart (the Arroya), sled-like devices enabling double-leg amputees to ski, were developed. Many other examples abound that reinforce the Norwegian commitment to normalization principles in practice:

- Opportunities are afforded special education students in ordinary schools to be integrated with regular education students whenever possible and segregated where necessary; these placements vary from activity to activity for each student. For example, fully integrated swimming classes and recreational activities are provided to school-operated houses in towns that provide real environments for individuals to learn and develop independent living skills.

- A coordinated continuum of vocational opportunities includes sheltered workshops, occupational preparation programs, and competitive employment in both sheltered and regular settings.

- Community living facilities are organized in ways that enable each individual to live as independently as possible. Community homes are often found in pairs with a staff member and four to six adults living in one home and four to six adults living alone in an adjoining home. Coordination with more sheltered and more independent living arrangements is characteristic of this system.

- Residential facilities interact on a regular basis with agencies and people in the community in which each facility is located. In this way these residents feel like and are considered a part of communities in which they live.
- The National Sport Organization for the Disabled in Norway, as in many other nations of the world, is an integral part of the National Sport Organization. Such organizations thus receive support and financial assistance for their programs and activities in the same ways as all other sport organizations and clubs in their countries, and at local as well as national levels.

Similar programs and activities as described can be found in places in the United States. However, basic differences between Norway and the United States are the pervasiveness of these patterns throughout the country and the wholehearted involvement and acceptance by the general population.

Jyvaskyla (Finland) provides an outstanding example and prototype of the continuum from special programs in segregated facilities to fully integrated physical, recreational, and sport opportunities. In addition, it shows how diverse laws—the Public Health Law of 1972 and the Sport Law of 1980—and activities sponsored and supported by different agencies can work together by complementing and supplementing one another. Dominant factors in this process are the interests and needs of each participant as an individual. For this well developed and coordinated system

- physical activities are provided for rehabilitation purposes at the local health center;
- recreational and sport activities are introduced to enhance further physiological, psychological, and emotional aspects of rehabilitation;
- leisure counseling and leisure education activities are included in programs and services of the health center so that participants are aware of and encouraged to participate in activities sponsored by local sport clubs;
- recreational and sport activities sponsored by local sport clubs are participated in for the same reasons and with the same motivations as by individuals without handicapping conditions;
- instruction for and opportunities at advanced levels with the potential of leading to elite participation are also available through local sport clubs and also can provide entry to activities sponsored by special sport groups; and
- additional opportunities sponsored by other community groups such as the Office of Culture and Adult Education and the School Office broaden the spectrum of activities and further extend the total involvement, cooperation, and coordination of all community agencies in Jyvaskla.

Beit Halochem in Israel is a sport, rehabilitation, and social center for Israel's disabled war veterans and their families. Except for therapeutic and rehabilitation services, all of the facilities and installations are open to wives and children as well as to the disabled veteran. The family unit is justifiably recognized as a major factor in the overall rehabilitation process of veterans.

The special services, variety of programs, and modern elaborate facilities combine to make up a unique center. The comfortable specially designed facilities have turned Beit Halochem into a focus of lively activities, which in turn helps to set up a new social framework. This constitutes first-class rehabilitation elements and helps Israel's war-disabled to overcome their own personal struggles in reentering and reintegrating into the working productive society—in short, in regaining first-class citizenship.

ILAN Sport Center for the Physically Disabled is located in Ramat-Gan, a suburb of Tel Aviv, Israel. This facility was founded more than 25 years ago. Basic principles and philosophies of ILAN are similar to those of Beit Halochem, although the organizational and administrative patterns are quite different.

ILAN provides opportunities for physically disabled people of all ages, but does not include their families. Basic to the success of ILAN's efforts is the fact that sport activities have proven to be an essential rehabilitation channel in stimulating disabled people to turn from states of helplessness toward productive and meaningful lives. Over 2,000 disabled athletes, mainly children and teenagers, are involved in daily physical activities, including 14 branches of wheelchair sports.

Facilities include indoor and outdoor basketball courts, sports halls, indoor and outdoor swimming pools, a special table tennis hall, a weight-training area, a 100 m oval track, and tennis courts. While rehabilitation is the body and soul of ILAN programs, wide-ranging everyday athletic activity is an integral part of the venture.

Kol U'dmama (Israel) is a performing dance group consisting of hearing and deaf individuals. The group represents creative dance at its best. Special techniques make it impossible to distinguish between hearing and deaf dancers. Procedures include making sound beats offstage by striking a wooden pole against the floor, increasing the volume on the record player, and developing routines that involve a great deal of touching among all of the dancers. Kol U'dmama represents an integration in principle and practice at its best.

One of the oldest and most outstanding wheelchair dance troupes in the world was established in the Philippines during the late 1940s, shortly after the conclusion of World War II. This group performs virtually all Philippine folk and cultural dances while in full regalia. Members of this troupe continue to perform and amaze audiences in various parts of the world with their skill and grace.

Lady MacLehose Pokfulam PHAB Centre in Hong Kong provides facilities and programs so that physically handicapped and able-bodied people can participate together—hence PHAB (Physically Handicapped Able-Bodied). Facilities include a main activity hall for basketball, wheelchair basketball, badminton, volleyball, table tennis, folk dance, and holding meetings, seminars, and exhibitions; a specially designed, fully accessible swimming pool for instructional and recreational swimming; an outdoor basketball court; an archery range; and an area for outdoor barbecues and picnics. Dormitory spaces (25 spacious rooms) and a dining hall can accommodate up to 100 residents.

Virtually all recreation and sport facilities in Hong Kong are fully accessible for handicapped participants. Both handicapped individuals and groups of handicapped people are encouraged to use all of Hong Kong's facilities. Examples of such facilities include all of the swimming pools, each exemplary in its own design; the Community Sports Centre for recreational activities and sport training; the Sai Kung Outdoor Recreation Centre; and the Lady MacLehose Holiday Camp.

The Jubilee Sport Centre, an independent organization devoted to raising the standard of performance in sport in Hong Kong and stimulating participation in sport and recreation generally, is used extensively by agencies supporting and sponsoring sport competition for participants with handicapping conditions. Uses by these agencies are the same as for able-bodied groups and include both training and instructional camps, seminars for coaches and other leaders, and sites for some actual competitions.

Recently a fully integrated basic course in skin and scuba diving was successfully completed. Seven individuals with several different physical handicaps and seven able-bodied individuals took this course together, working as partners in all aspects of instruction and practice. The follow-up steps include plans for partners to move together to open water diving as teams. Outward Bound programs and activities in Hong Kong have also been successfully integrated.

These few representative examples of the many outstanding facilities and programs in Hong Kong reflect philosophies and principles emanating from the highest governmental levels:

> Sports and recreation—essential to a balanced life—are of particular importance to the disabled, and so the government provides assistance to voluntary agencies which organize suitable events. The emphasis is on integrating the able-bodied and the disabled through participation in leisure activities. (*Rehabilitation in Hong Kong*)

The goal in Hong Kong is to fully integrate handicapped individuals into the community. An official Hong Kong government white paper, Integrating the Disabled Into the Community: A United Effort, which has been in effect since October 1977, gives guidance to assist in fulfilling this goal in all life areas— counseling, housing, residential care, transportation, education, work, accessibility, sport, and recreation (*Rehabilitation in Hong Kong n.d.*).

Five years of workshops in the Caribbean and Central American Region have stimulated a number of follow-up in-service activities, brought about the creation of some special and unique programs, and resulted in the identification of outstanding personnel and program resources. Some examples of these ongoing activities in Latin America include:

- The development of a specially adapted physical education diagnostic center in Maracaibo, Venezuela in which medical, special education, and physical education personnel work together closely and cooperatively. This center was initiated through the leadership of Carlos Vera Guardia, the president of CACEFI and a Maracaibo resident, and Tom Vodola, the innovative founder and director of Project ACTIVE (All Children Totally Involved Exercising).
- The inclusion of information and materials about physical education, recreation, sport, and related activity areas in a special rehabilitation documentation center in Bogota, Colombia. Leadership for this effort in the coordinated documentation, and for the development of a special Physical Education and Sport Preparation Programme in the National Rehabilitation Centre has been provided by Valerie May Townsend, the Head of Public and International Relations, Fundation Pro-Rehabilitacion del Minnsvalido (Carrera 23 No. 94-A-35, Bogota, Colombia).

• The outstanding physical education, recreation, and sport programs with dedicated and highly competent leadership, identified in Guatemala for participants who are mentally retarded, blind, and deaf. Performances of severely and profoundly mentally retarded people of all ages were felt to be among the best that have been observed for these populations in any nation any place in the world.

In Conclusion

These examples undoubtedly show the importance of unselfish and cooperative relationships among individuals, organizations, and governments within, between, and among countries to further the knowledge and status of physical education, recreation, and sport programs and activities involving handicapped participants. Crucial factors contributing to the success of these processes include (a) positive and accepting attitudes; (b) social consciousness and responsiveness to the needs of those less fortunate than the masses; (c) the commitment of professional personnel from different disciplines in meeting the interests and needs of handicapped people through active participation in vigorous physical, recreational, and sport programs; and (d) the acceptance by the general population of implementing mainstreaming.

When the people of any nation or political subdivision want something to happen, it can be done and will happen. As attitudinal barriers come tumbling down, all facilities become accessible and every program is designed to accomodate all who desire to participate. Handicapped individuals are then truly integral parts of the mainstream of society in every community. An important cornerstone of this process is the increased sharing through wholehearted international exchange and interchange.

References

American Association for Health, Physical Education, and Recreation. (n.d.). *Physical Education and Recreation for Handicapped Children: Proceedings of a Study Conference on Research and Demonstration Needs.* Washington, DC: AAHPER.

American Association for Health, Physical Education, and Recreation. (1976). *Physical Education and Recreation for Impaired, Disabled, and Handicapped Individuals—Past, Present, Future.* Washington, DC: AAHPER.

Oliver, J.N. (1958). The Effect of Physical Conditioning Exercises and Activities on the Mental Characteristics of Educationally Subnormal Boys. *British Journal of Educational Psychology,* **28**, 155-165.

Rehabilitation in Hong Kong. (n.d.). Hong Kong: Department of Rehabilitation.

Stein, J., & Gepford, G. (1982). *International Survey on Development of Physical Education and Sport for the Physically and Mentally Handicapped.* Washington, DC: International Council for Health, Physical Education, and Recreation. UNESCO Contract No. 516291 with ICHPER.

United Nations Educational, Scientific, and Cultural Organization. (1976). First International Conference of Ministers and Senior Officials Responsible for Physical Education and Sport. Paris, France: UNESCO.

United Nations Educational, Scientific, and Cultural Organization. (1982). International Symposium on Physical Education and Sport Programs for the Physically and Mentally Handicapped. Final Report. Paris, France: UNESCO. UNESCO Contract No. 518.015 with the United States National Commission for UNESCO.

6

World Games for the Deaf

Donalda Kay Ammons
GALLAUDET COLLEGE
WASHINGTON, DC, USA

The oldest of the international organizations on sport for disabled people is the Comite International des Sports des Sourds (CISS). (The English translation of this is International Committee on Silent Sports, but the commonly used abbreviation (CISS) is derived from the French name.) Immediately after the first World Games for the Deaf (WGD) in 1924 in Paris, E. Ruben Alcais of France and Antoine Dresse of Belgium founded the CISS. The date was August 16, 1924. Alcais became the first president of the CISS, serving from 1924 to 1953. Other presidents included D. Ryden from 1953 to 1955, J.P. Nielson from 1955 to 1961, Pierre Beinhard from 1961 to 1971, and Jerald Jordan from 1981 to the present.

The current president, Jerald Jordan, is director of Records Management at Gallaudet College in Washington, DC, the largest liberal arts institution for deaf people in the world. He has been deaf since the age of 7 years when he had spinal meningitis. Most of the leadership of CISS is deaf.

Summer and Winter World Games

Although best known for its Summer World Games begun in 1924, CISS has conducted Winter World Games every 4 years since 1949 and Pan American Games periodically since 1958. The sites of these Games appear in Table 1. The Summer World Games include competition in eight individual sports and five team sports (see Table 2).

To send athletes to the World Games for the Deaf, a nation must be affiliated with the CISS. The number of CISS-affiliated nations has grown steadily from seven in 1924 to 44 nations today. Each CISS member-nation sends two delegates to all CISS meetings. Table 3 names the countries that did and did

Table 1. Dates and sites of World Summer and Winter Games and Pan American Games for the deaf

Year	Site	Country winning most
World Summer Games for the Deaf		
1924	Paris, France	France
1928	Amsterdam, Netherlands	Germany
1931	Nuremberg, West Germany	Germany
1935	London, England	Great Britain
1939	Stockholm, Sweden	Germany
10-year hiatus due to World War II		
1949	Copenhagen, Denmark	Denmark/Sweden
1953	Brussels, Belgium	Germany
1957	Milan, Italy	Italy
1961	Helsinki, Finland	Soviet Union
1965	Washington, DC, United States	United States
1969	Belgrade, Yugoslavia	Soviet Union
1973	Malmo, Sweden	United States
1977	Bucharest, Romania	United States
1981	Cologne, West Germany	United States
1985	Los Angeles, CA, U.S.	
World Winter Games for the Deaf		
1949	Seefield, Austria	
1953	Oslo, Norway	
1955	Oberamergau, West Germany	
1959	Montana-Vermala, Switzerland	
1963	Are, Sweden	
1967	Berchtesgaden, West Germany	
1971	Abelboden, Switzerland	
1975	Lake Placid, NY, U.S.	
1979	Meribel, France	
1983	Madonna Di Campiglio, Italy	
Pan American Games for the Deaf		
1958	Buenos Aires, Argentina	
1961	Montevideo, Uruguay	
1983	Santiago, Chile	
1967	Rio De Janeiro, Brazil	
1971	Buenos Aires, Argentina	
1975	Maracaibo, Venezuela	

Table 2. Summer World Games sports

Individual	Team
Cycling (men)	Soccer (men)
Wrestling: Greco Roman and Freestyle (men)	Water Polo (men)
	Handball (men)
Swimming (men and women)	Volleyball (men and women)
Track & Field (men and women)	Basketball (men and women)
Tennis (men and women)	
Table Tennis (men and women)	
Badminton (men and women)	
Shooting (men and women)	

The Winter World Games include competition in Alpine and Nordic skiing and in speed skating.

not participate in the 1981 Summer World Games in Cologne, West Germany. Since 1961, the United States and the Soviet Union have dominated the number of medals won in the World Summer Games as indicated in Table 4. Prior to 1961, Germany, France, Italy, Great Britain, Finland, and Sweden were the leading medalists. The Winter World Games are dominated by Norway, Switzerland, Finland, and the Soviet Union.

In July 1985, the XV World Summer Games for the Deaf were in Los Angeles. Approximately 2,000 athletes from 30 nations competed in 13 different sports. The U.S. team alone included over 250 athletes, coaches, and officials.

Among the top deaf athletes in the world are U.S. swimmers Elisabeth Lutz (world records in the 50 m, 100 m, 200 m, 400 m, and 800 m freestyle) and Jeffrey Float (world records in the 200 m, 400 m, 800 m, and 1500 m freestyle, 200 m back, and 100 m butterfly). Timo Karvoven of Finland holds the most world track and field records (5) among the men, and Rita Windbrake of the Federal Republic of Germany holds the most world track and field records (5) among the women. G. Calissano of Italy holds the most world records (7) in shooting.

Conditions of competition in the WGD are closely related to the Olympic Games. In 1951, the International Olympic Committee officially recognized the CISS as the only federation responsible for the administration of all sports involving the deaf. In turn, CISS athletes and affiliated organizations maintain amateur status and subscribe to the principles of the IOC code. With deep pride, the CISS is the only federation representing disabled athletes that is recognized by the IOC. As of 1984, the CISS remained autonomous of any other sport organization for disabled athletes. So far, it has not become involved in the International Coordinating Council for Sports Organizations for the Disabled, which was founded in 1981.

The hearing population, in general, knows little about the WGD and the activities of the many sport clubs for deaf athletes throughout the world. Only two articles on international competition have appeared in the *Journal of Health, Physical Education, and Recreation* (Ammons, 1984; Pannella, 1974). The journal in which most information on sport for deaf people can be found is *The Deaf American* (previously *The Silent Worker*).

Eligibility Standards for World Games

All athletes must submit an audiogram to CISS not more than 1 year prior to participation in the World Games. To be eligible for participation in the Games, an athlete must have a hearing loss of 55 decibels (dB) or greater in the better ear (three frequency pure tone average at 500, 1000, and 2000 Hertz [Hz]). These results are reported with respect to the International Standards Organization 1964 standard reference values. According to Davis and Silverman (1978), a 55–70 dB loss in the better ear is categorized as a marked or moderate disability; a 70–90 dB loss in the better ear is considered a severe disability; and any loss over 90 dB is an extreme handicap because amplification does not help in hearing the speech of others. For purposes of competition, however, CISS does not classify athletes according to their degree of hearing loss. All people with a hearing loss of 55 dB or greater in the better ear compete against one another.

American Athletic Association of the Deaf (AAAD)

The AAAD is the parent body of sports for the deaf in the United States (Ammons, 1984). It is an organization of volunteer officers that provides and promotes competitive sport opportunities for individuals with hearing impairments. Founded in 1945 in Akron, Ohio, the AAAD is the oldest of the sport organizations for disabled individuals in the United States. Its first president, Art Kruger, served in this capacity from 1945 to 1947, then became chairman of the USA Team Committee of World Games for the Deaf in 1966 until 1982. The current president is Lyle Mortensen. AAAD began as a national basketball tournament for deaf associations initiated by Art Kruger, expanded in 1947 to sponsor national softball tournaments, and today holds regional and national tournaments in basketball and softball.

Currently the AAAD comprises approximately 160 member clubs nationally and approximately 20,000 individual members. On the organizational level, the jurisdiction is divided into eight regions:

1. The Eastern Athletic Association of the Deaf consists of New York, Delaware, New Jersey, and Pennsylvania, with the exception of the environs of Buffalo, New York, and Erie, Pennsylvania.
2. The Central Athletic Association of the Deaf consists of Ohio, Kentucky, Illinois, Indiana, Michigan, Wisconsin, the Province of Ontario, and the environs of Buffalo, New York, and Pittsburgh and Erie, Pennsylvania.
3. The Midwest Athletic Association of the Deaf consists of Missouri, Iowa, North Dakota, South Dakota, Minnesota, Kansas, Colorado, Wyoming, and Nebraska.
4. The Farwest Athletic Association of the Deaf consists of Arizona, Southern California, Nevada, New Mexico, and Hawaii.
5. The Southwest Athletic Association of the Deaf consists of Louisiana, Mississippi, Arkansas, Texas, Oklahoma, and the environs of Memphis, Tennessee.

6. The Southeastern Athletic Association of the Deaf consists of Maryland, the District of Columbia, Virginia, West Virginia, Tennessee, North Carolina, South Carolina, Georgia, Alabama, and Florida.
7. The Northwest Athletic Association of the Deaf consists of Northern California, Washington, Utah, Idaho, Montana, Oregon, British Columbia, and Alaska.
8. The New England Athletic Association of the Deaf consists of Maine, Vermont, New Hampshire, Massachusetts, Connecticut, Rhode Island, and the environs of Montreal, Canada.

The Administrative Board of the AAAD consists of a president, a vice president, a secretary-treasurer, a publicity director, a softball commissioner, and the chairman of the World Games Committee. The president of each region, along with the administrative officers constitute the Executive Committee. The annual meetings are held at the host site of the national basketball and softball tournaments.

The objectives of the AAAD are to foster and regulate athletic competition among member clubs to develop uniform rules governing interclub competition, and to provide adequate competition for those members primarily interested in interclub athletics. Thus the AAAD acts to improve interclub relationships and provide special activities of interest to members and their families. Additionally, AAAD sponsors a Hall of Fame to honor deaf (as well as hearing) people who have contributed exceptional service to the deaf in the world of sport as players, leaders, or coaches. Annually it awards a plaque to the Outstanding Deaf Athlete of the Year.

The AAAD also coordinates international participation of U.S. deaf athletes in the World Games for the Deaf. As such, the AAAD is affiliated with the United States Olympic Committee as a Group E member—under the Committee on Sports for the Disabled. The United States Committee of World Games for the Deaf is responsible for promoting and maintaining interest in participation in and representation of the U.S. in the CISS World Summer and Winter Games and Pan American Games for the Deaf. This committee is a standing committee of AAAD, Inc., and operates under the rules and regulations of the AAAD. The committee is headed by a chairman, elected for a 4-year term by the delegates at the annual meeting of the AAAD following the quadrennial World Summer Games. The chairman appoints four capable members to assist him or her in the following capacities: Vice-Chairman, Treasurer, Team Director, and Secretary-Public Relations Director. A good number of the U.S. representatives to the Games are developed and trained through the regional and national tournaments sanctioned by the AAAD and run by its affiliates.

The primary objective of the AAAD/World Games for the Deaf Committee is to develop and upgrade amateur sport nationwide, providing our hearing-impaired with the opportunity to compete in national and international meets, including the World Games for the Deaf, which are held every 4 years in an Olympic format. Also we strive to improve and maintain the standards of deaf athletes to the point where they can gain and hold respect in competition with hearing teams.

The Sports Development Camp's concept for deaf athletes was first implemented in 1983, offering intensive training in seven Olympic sports at three different sites in the country. In addition, the camps also concentrate on uniting coaches of hearing-impaired athletes to upgrade their coaching knowledge, philosophy, and technique. These camps hopefully have been preparing athletes for the 1985 World Games in Los Angeles. The people who qualified in the 1984 tryouts were invited to a 3-week intensive training camp held at the U.S. Olympic Training Center at Colorado Springs in preparation for the 1985 World Games.

U.S. Involvement in World Games

Participation of the United States in international competition began with the IVth World Games in 1935 in London. Mr. Robey S. Burns, head coach of the Illinois School for the Deaf, took two American competitors to London. U.S. participation has grown steadily since then. At the 1981 Games in Cologne, West Germany, the U.S. made its most impressive showing—over 172 American athletes brought home a record 110 medals, including a record 45 gold medals. Tables 3 and 4 indicates the number of U.S. athletes who

Table 3. Statistical synopsis of the XIV World Games for the Deaf (1981)

Nations	Gold	Silver	Bronze	Total
United States	45	29	35	109
Soviet Union	21	20	14	55
West Germany	3	9	17	29
Italy	6	9	4	19
Bulgaria	3	6	6	15
Iran	7	5	2	14
Japan	7	4	2	13
France	1	5	5	11
Australia	3	3	3	9
Canada	0	4	4	8
Yugoslavia	5	0	2	7
Poland	1	2	4	7
Hungary	1	3	2	6
Denmark	1	1	4	6
Great Britain	0	1	5	6
Austria	3	2	0	5
Finland	3	0	0	3
East Germany	1	2	0	3
New Zealand	1	2	0	3
Sweden	1	1	1	3
Belgium	0	1	2	3
India	0	2	1	3
Switzerland	0	2	0	2
Norway	0	1	1	2
Holland	1	0	0	1
Spain	0	0	1	1

Cont.

Table 3. (Cont.)

Nations				
Israel	0	0	0	0
Venezuela	0	0	0	0
Ireland	0	0	0	0
Mexico	0	0	0	0
Bangladesh	0	0	0	0
Greece	0	0	0	0

Thirty-two nations participated with 1,258 athletes. 172 athletes bore the USA insignia.
The 10 CISS member nations that did not participate in the XIV World Games were Brazil, Chile, Colombia, Costa Rica, Czechoslovakia, Portugal, Romania, South Africa, Turkey, Uruguay.

Table 4. Number of U.S. deaf athletes competing and winning each quadrennium

Year	Athletes	Medals	Gold	Silver	Bronze
	Record of U.S. Participation in Winter Games				
1967	14	2	2	0	0
1971	13	3	2	1	0
1975	14	3	0	1	2
1979	11	0	0	0	0
1983	11	0	0	0	0
	63	8	4	2	2
	Record of U.S. Participation in Summer Games				
1935	2	4	1	2	1
1939	1	1	0	1	0
1949	2	1	0	1	0
1953	8	9	2	0	7
1957	40	37	17	9	11
1961	92	67	37	16	14
1965	147	91	26	37	28
1969	120	110	46	30	34
1973	143	125	58	35	32
1977	133	152	71	50	31
1981	165	171	91	42	38
	853	768	349	223	196

NOTE: The American Athletic Association for the Deaf did not officially sponsor the American athletes at the Games prior to 1957. There was a hiatus between 1939 and 1949 due to World War II.

competed in the World Games each quadrennium and the number of medals won. The U.S. World Games for the Deaf Committee states that

its efforts can produce not only victories in the field of athletic competition but victories for our deaf athletes. It is a proud moment in the life of our American deaf athletes when, while wearing the uniform of the United States, they commit strength and spirit in international competition. An even prouder moment comes to those outstanding American deaf athletes who face our nation's flag on the victory stand even though—in the perpetual silence that surrounds them—they cannot hear the "Star Spangled Banner." (Hammer, 1984, p. 14)

References

Ammons, D. (1984). American Athletic Association for [of] the Deaf. *Journal of Physical Education, Recreation, and Dance, 55*, 36–37.

Davis, H., & Silverman, R. (1978). *Hearing and deafness.* New York: Holt, Rinehart, & Winston.

Hammer, K. (Ed.). (1984). *XV World Games for the deaf United States team: 1985 media guide.* Garden City, Hofstra University and U.S. Committee of the World Games for the Deaf.

Pannella, L. (1974). XII World Games for the Deaf. *Journal of Health, Physical Education, and Recreation, 45*, 12–14.

7

The Special Olympics Sport Program: An International Sport Program for Mentally Retarded Athletes

Thomas B. Songster
SPECIAL OLYMPICS, INC.
WASHINGTON, DC, USA

In the summer of 1963, Eunice Kennedy Shriver established at her home a day-camp for mentally retarded individuals in order to test their abilities in a variety of sports and physical activities. The Kennedy Foundation then began to fund other summer day-camps for mentally retarded people across the country. During the next five summers, hundreds of community and private organizations established similar camps. Mrs. Shriver soon realized that there should be an event in which mentally retarded individuals could demonstrate their athletic abilities to the public—an event large enough to draw attention to the needs of mentally retarded people for greater opportunities in sport training and competition.

In July of 1968, the Kennedy Foundation, with the help of the Chicago Park District, planned and financed the First International Special Olympics Games. These historic games were held at Chicago's Soldier Field, where more than 1,000 mentally retarded athletes from 26 states and Canada participated in track and field and swimming competitions. Soon after, Special Olympics, Inc. was established as a nonprofit charitable organization and was given official approval by the U.S. Olympic Committee to be one of only two organizations in the U.S. entitled to use the name "Olympics."

At present, Special Olympics is the world's largest program of sport training and competition for mentally retarded individuals. The program encompasses more than one million athletes from the U.S. and 60 countries, and hundreds of thousands of dedicated volunteers and coaches worldwide. The official Special Olympics sports now include aquatics, athletics (i.e., track and field), basketball, bowling, gymnastics, floor and poly hockey, figure and speed skating, alpine and cross country skiing, soccer, softball, and volleyball. Competition in these sports is offered at local, area, chapter, national, and international events. Also offered at these events are clinics in Official Special Olympics Demonstration sports, including: canoeing, cycling, equestrian sports, racquet sports, roller skating and weight lifting.

In addition, Special Olympics, Inc. established a Developmental Sports Skills program to train mentally retarded individuals with low motor-abilities in sensorimotor and basic motor skills. The goal of the program is to reach more severe and profound mentally retarded people and introduce them to the benefits of physical fitness and sport activities.

The Special Olympics Philosophy

The mission of Special Olympics is to provide year-round training and competition in a variety of Olympic-type sports for all mentally retarded children and adults. Through its sport programs, Special Olympics provides mentally retarded individuals with continuing opportunities to develop physical fitness, demonstrate courage, experience joy, and share their skills and friendships with family members, other Special Olympians and their communities. Program activities are conducted by expert clinicians and sport professionals who train the athletes in 8- or 10- week training sessions in preparation for Special Olympics Games and competition events. This training also provides many athletes with the confidence and skills they need to participate in sport programs for the nonhandicapped.

Mentally retarded individuals 8 years of age or older are eligible to participate in the Special Olympics program. Generally, participants have IQ scores of 70 or less. Athletes who are members of regular interscholastic or intramural teams are not eligible to take part in the Special Olympics programs. Graduating Special Olympians from the Special Olympics program into regular sport programs is a principal objective.

In Special Olympics competition the athletes participate in events that present the athletes in an atmosphere of Olympic quality and human dignity. Every competitor receives an award (a medal or a ribbon) which accurately reflects his/her performances. This policy helps each athlete to realistically assess his or her performance and take pride in that achievement. What makes Special Olympics competition so important for Special Olympics athletes is that they do get the chance to participate and to understand that, win or lose, they have done their best. This is the true meaning of sport and the true spirit of the Special Olympics program.

Establishing Equal Ability Groups

To ensure fairness in competition, the Special Olympics program places athletes in equal ability groups based on age, gender, and previous sport performances.

Also, the program uses the official sport rules of national sport-governing organizations to ensure consistency between its own program and regular sport programs in the U.S. Competition based on equal ability groups helps to accomplish several goals: it promotes the true spirit of Special Olympics by providing sport training and competition for all mentally retarded people; it provides fair and equitable conditions for competition; it protects the physical well-being of the athletes; and it promotes uniformity so that no competitor can obtain an unfair advantage over another.

Physically handicapped Special Olympians are placed in competition divisions in a similar manner: athletes compete against other athletes with approximately the same best scores or times. For example, athletes in wheelchairs compete in the appropriate division of the softball throw, but not in a separate wheelchair division. An athlete with crutches competes in the appropriate division of the 100 m dash according to his or her age, gender, ability level, and previous times, not according to his or her handicap.

Through these rules, the athletes are organized into fair and equal ability groups, which, in turn, allow greater opportunities for the athlete's success. With success comes confidence, and with confidence comes the sense of self-worth and accomplishment. Furthermore, as Special Olympians gain poise and confidence, the people around them begin to focus on their abilities and not their handicaps.

International Games Development

The First International Special Olympics Games were held in July 1968, and successive International Games were held every 2 years until 1972. In 1975, the Fourth International Special Olympics Games were held at Central Michigan University, with 3,200 athletes from 11 countries taking part. The 1975 International Games became the first of the quadrennial International Summer Special Olympics Games.

The 6th International Summer Special Olympics Games, which took place in July 1983, at Louisiana State University in Baton Rouge, comprised the largest Special Olympics International Games to date, as 4,393 mentally retarded athletes from the U.S. and 52 countries competed in 13 official Special Olympics sports. The current need for more international development is reflected in the fact that there were four-and-a-half times as many U.S. athletes as foreign athletes at the Games. Approximately one million mentally retarded individuals are involved in the United States Special Olympics program. About 250,000 mentally retarded individuals participate in national Special Olympics programs in more than 50 other countries.

In addition, approximately 1,000 coaches and 4,000 relatives of the athletes attended the Games in 1983. Officials estimated that the opening ceremonies attracted more than 65,000 spectators to LSU's Tiger Stadium. The closing ceremonies drew nearly as many fans. The Games were covered by 300 media people representing newspapers, magazines, television, and radio stations around the world, and ABC's Wide World of Sports devoted an entire 90-minute program to the Games.

Table 1. 1983 International Summer Special Olympics Games

Event	Sex	Athlete	Best marks		Affiliation
Aquatics					
1 m Dive	(M)	Scott Campbell	57.6	points	USA-MI
	(F)	Michelle Sprague	48.7	points	USA-TX
25 m Backstroke	(M)	Don Walker	17.0	sec	Canada
	(F)	Cindy Murphy	19.4	sec	USA-CO
25 m Butterfly	(M)	Haakon Hougen	18.0	sec	Norway
	(F)	Ruth Burdick	26.5	sec	USA-KS
25 m Butterfly	(M)	Christopher Byrne	15.2	sec	USA-NJ
	(F)	Anne Clinton	21.4	sec	USA-IL
25 m Freestyle	(M)	Alberto Perez	14.0	sec	Puerto Rico
	(F)	Nicole Deveault	17.4	sec	Canada
50 m Freestyle	(M)	Atle Viste	31.0	sec	Norway
	(F)	Tracy McDougall	39.4	sec	United Kingdom
100 m Relay Freestyle			1:04.4	sec	USA-AR
Athletics					
50 m Dash	(M)	James Hagood	5.93	sec	USA-AL
	(F)	Denise Taylor	6.85	sec	USA-AL
200 m Dash	(M)	Juan Noble	24.70	sec	Puerto Rico
	(F)	Paulette Tibbs	28.30	sec	USA-LA
400 m Run	(M)	Jai Rodriguez	53.03	sec	Puerto Rico
	(F)	Paulette Reid	1:07.84	sec	Jamaica
400 m Relay	(M)		51.66	sec	USA-AL
	(F)		57.47	sec	USA-LA
Mile Run	(M)	Jose Gonzales	4:43.92	sec	Puerto Rico
	(F)	Loretta Clairborne	5:42.17	sec	USA-PA
High Jump	(M)	Angel Vazquez	1.72	m	Puerto Rico
	(F)	Claudia Huygens	1.27	m	Belgium
Softball Throw	(M)	Enele Muliaga	69.58	m	American Samoa
	(F)	Cheryl O'Neil	46.40	m	USA-MA
Gymnastics					
Tumbling	(M)	Dewayne Gass	9.6	points	USA-KY
	(F)	Lisa Stambaugh	9.5	points	USA-KY
	(F)	Loris Shoulas	9.5	points	District of Columbia
	(F)	Cheryl Lynn Arnal	9.5	points	USA-ND
	(F)	Sheryl Hudacky	9.5	points	USA-PA
Balance Beam	(F)	Marlene Yorgey	8.9	points	USA-PA
Free Exercise	(M)	Tommy Smith	9.9	points	USA-AL
	(F)	Holly Blair	9.9	points	USA-TN

One measure of the success of the Special Olympics program is the list of best marks from the 1983 Summer Games (see Table 1). Consider that exceptional, nonhandicapped athletes can run the 50 m dash in 5.8 seconds and that a 5-minute mile is much better than average for most people. The abilities of mentally retarded athletes and the effectiveness of the Special Olympics program is exemplified by comparing these nonhandicapped standards to the marks posted by Special Olympians at the 1983 Summer Games.

Growth of Winter Sports

In February 1977, the First International Winter Special Olympics Games were held at Steamboat Springs, Colorado, with over 500 athletes competing in winter sport events. At the 1981 International Winter Special Olympics Games, a total of 621 athletes participated in competition. Only three foreign countries were represented at these games: Canada, Belgium, and Taiwan. While the number of foreign athletes was far below the number of U.S. athletes, a steady increase in Winter Sports competition by Special Olympics programs around the world was noticeable.

At the 1985 International Winter Special Olympics Games, more than 800 athletes from 11 nations participated. In the U.S. alone, the number of athletes participating in chapter or regional winter sport competitions has increased from about 2,500 in 1977-78 to over 9,500 in 1984-85. As in 1981, competition events at the 1985 International Winter Games included men's and women's figure skating; speed skating (75 m, 300 m, and 800 m, races); alpine skiing (slalom, giant slalom, and downhill races); and cross country skiing (100 m, 1 and 2 km races). Because of the increasing popularity of the International Winter Games, more and more mentally retarded people around the world are joining winter sport programs.

Review of Research on Special Olympics

Numerous studies of Special Olympics have been conducted over the past 15 years. Most of the research involved reactions to and opinions of the program and concentrated on the impact of the program on the athletes, their parents, and their communities (Barnes, 1983; Huettig, 1982; King, 1980; Smits, 1981; Wright, 1977). The studies have been relatively limited in scope for several reasons: (a) the Special Olympics program is still relatively new, having been started in 1968; (b) Special Olympics is based on human principles and spiritual values as opposed to attendance or track records; and (c) worldwide studies of the program are logistically impractical.

In the past, Special Olympics, Inc. and the Kennedy Foundation have commissioned a number of research projects on the Special Olympics program. In 1971 Larry Rarick (1978) assessed the impact of Special Olympics on participants, schools, and community programs by studying the programs in two metropolitan areas. Bell, Kozar, and Martin (1977) followed Rarick's lead by conducting a more up-to-date study on the impact of Special Olympics on 224 selected participants, their parents, and the citizens of their communities. This study was conducted over a 3-year period from headquarters at Texas Tech University. In 1979 Bryant Cratty investigated the psychological and social-psychological effects of coed participation among individuals in Special Olympics.

At present, a number of specific issues should be considered for study, including (a) measuring specific psychological and/or physiological changes in mentally retarded individuals who participate in the Special Olympics program; (b) the changes that occur in individuals who enter the program at the earliest possible age, as opposed to those who start at a later age; and (c) tracking mentally retarded individuals who have not or do not participate or have discontinued participation in the program and determining the reasons for same. Special Olympics, Inc. would welcome these types of studies and others by the research community.

Dr. David Auxter (1984), of Slippery Rock University in Pennsylvania, has raised a multitude of questions in a paper he prepared on the possibilities for research on the Special Olympics program. We are grateful to Dr. Auxter for his work and for letting us include the following abridged list of his questions to this review:

1. What are the effects of different training systems for parents to assist with the development of Special Olympics sport skills and positive social behavior of mentally retarded people?
2. What are the best methods to facilitate the coordination of public and private agencies to maximize benefits for mentally retarded people through Special Olympics?
3. What are the most effective training systems for professionals or volunteers in human services to develop Special Olympics sport skills for mentally retarded people?
4. What are the best procedures for training volunteers to generalize acquired social traits through Special Olympics participation in sport skills of mentally retarded people?
5. Which are the better technologies that can be applied to train nonprofessional or professional volunteers to facilitate the acquisition of Special Olympics sport skills?
6. What are the effects of training volunteers to apply behavioral principles or the social learning theory to the acquisition of Special Olympics sport skills and team strategies for mentally retarded people?
7. What are the effects of generalization of learned concepts through participation in Special Olympics sport skills to domestic, vocational, or recreational environments of mentally retarded people?
8. What are the effective methods of training school administrators to raise the social consciousness of others through the normalization principle of environmental design of the mentally retarded through Special Olympics?

Anyone who is interested in conducting further research on Special Olympics should contact the National Office of Special Olympics in Washington, DC.

Conclusion

In summary, the Special Olympics program is meeting the needs of many mentally retarded individuals and is well prepared to offer quality sport training and competition to many more special people who have not yet had the chance to experience the joy and sense of achievement that can be had through participation in Special Olympics.

In the coming years, there will be new challenges for the program. For example, we must attempt to reach out to more mentally retarded people. One method for doing this is to persuade school administrators and school systems to incorporate Special Olympics in their curricula. A second challenge is to create more competition, especially at the local and area levels, by arranging year-round league play in a variety of team sports. A third challenge is to draw more families, high school and college students, and citizens of all communities into the ranks of volunteers and supporters. Lastly, the greatest challenge of all is to make Special Olympics a clear and open channel to the mainstream of society and not leave it as an end in itself. The athletes who participate in Special Olympics must be encouraged to enter regular school and community sport programs and to live as independently as possible.

References

Auxter, D. (1984). *Recommendations concerning research needed on Special Olympics*. Unpublished manuscript, Slippery Rock University, Pennsylvania.

Barnes, L. (1983). *Special Olympics—Case studies of adult special olympians*. Unpublished master's thesis, Texas Woman's University, Denton.

Bell, N.J., Kozar, W., & Martin, A.W. (1977). *The impact of Special Olympics on participants, parents, and the community* (Research study funded by Special Olympics, Inc.) . Lubbock, TX: Texas Tech University.

Cratty, B.J. (1979). *Coed participation: Psychological and social-psychological feelings and effects among participants in the Special Olympics program* (Research study funded by Special Olympics, Inc.). Los Angeles: University of California at Los Angeles.

Huettig, C. (1982). *Motives of Special Olympics volunteers*. Unpublished doctoral dissertation, Texas Woman's University, Denton.

King, E.W. (1980). *Attitudes of Special Olympians toward coed competition*. Unpublished doctoral dissertation, Oklahoma State University, Stillwater.

Rarick, G.L. (1978). Adult reactions to the Special Olympics. In F.L. Smoll & R.E. Smith (Eds.), *Psychological perspectives in youth sports* (pp. 229–247). New York: Halstead Press.

Smits, P. (1981). *A partnership of service: A study of the relationship between American higher education and Special Olympics*. Unpublished doctoral dissertation, State University of New York at Buffalo.

Wright, J. (1977). *Changes in self-concept and cardiovascular endurance of mentally retarded youth in a Special Olympics swimming program*. Unpublished master's thesis, Texas Woman's University, Denton.

8

Facilitation of Integrated Recreation

Peter W. Axelson
BENEFICIAL DESIGNS, INC.
SANTA CRUZ, CALIFORNIA, USA

Every human being possesses the desire to live, work, and play in a manner that allows physical, intellectual, and spiritual self-expression. One half million people with spinal cord injuries and millions of other individuals with disabilities must meet their basic needs in an alternative way. In 1975, while a cadet at the U.S. Air Force Academy, a mountain climbing accident left me with a spinal cord injury, requiring me to use a wheelchair for mobility. This paper presents my personal perspectives on sport, recreation, and rehabilitation from the perspective of an engineer, designer, and person who lives with a disability.

While the continual evolution and redefinition of the term *rehabilitation* is of positive consequence to people with disabilities, the rehabilitation process has in general failed to recognize the importance of developing recreational skills which integrate the individual back into society. Instead, many rehabilitation programs tend to emphasize the development of independent living and vocational skills that enable people with disabilities to return to work. Just as each individual, prior to disability, had a balance between vocation, recreation, and daily living activities, the person with a disability must continue life with a balance of activities.

During the rehabilitation process, many individuals go through an initial period of shock and denial during which they are not ready to participate in the vocational and recreational aspects of a rehabilitation program. These individuals are often released from the rehabilitation center before the coping stage of dealing with their disability is reached. Psychosocial and recreational learning opportunities must therefore be available inside and outside of the formal rehabilitation process.

Recreation is the refreshment of body, mind, and spirit after work. It may be play, amusement, or relaxation. Whatever form it takes, recreation should offer many options, allowing individuals to select activities that are personally meaningful and satisfying. Unfortunately, recreation is often included in the rehabilitation process as a form of entertainment. Movies, games, and activities are generally brought into the rehabilitation center. In contrast to this practice, people with disabilities should be moved out of the center and into the community as much as possible. They need opportunities for interaction in integrated social environments to facilitate their development of recreational skills for future use. Because the financial cost of rehabilitation is high, however, the individual's program is often rushed with little or no attention to recreational programming. This occurs even though it is known that recreation enhances the physical, social, and spiritual needs of the individual's rehabilitation process (Beaver, Jackson, McCann, Messner, & Ryan, 1978).

Recreation programs for people with special needs do exist. Courage Center in Golden Valley, Minnesota, provides recreation, sports, camping, educational programs, and residential services to people with physical disabilities and speech, hearing, and vision disorders (Heer, 1984). The Colorado Outdoor Education Center for the Handicapped in Breckenridge offers year-round wilderness experiences (McKinney, 1982). Vinland National Center, near Minneapolis, an education/training center for people with disabilities, offers training and experience in such activities as alpine and cross country sled skiing, canoeing, kayaking, distance wheeling, and aerobics (Gwinner, 1982). *Sports 'N Spokes* magazine describes the success of physically disabled people in numerous organized sporting activities, often initiated by individuals with disabilities (Axelson & McCornack, 1983; Rappoport, 1981; Taylor, 1983).

All too often, however, the recreation activity or sport environment is modified to meet the perceived needs of the individual with detrimental consequences. Frequently segregated activities (i.e., for wheelchair uses only) abound. When activities are oriented around the concept of a disability, they tend to be defined by the boundaries of the person's current abilities. The missing link is that people are often unable to recreate in an interactive manner with family and friends within a society that is based upon normal function and ability.

Sport Alternative for People with Disabilities

Five basic categories of sport activities are available to people with disabilities: (a) segregated competitive (e.g., wheelchair basketball), (b) segregated noncompetitive (e.g., wheelchair square dancing), (c) integrated participation/segregated competition (e.g., marathon running/road racing), (d) integrated competition (e.g., sailboat racing), and (e) integrated noncompetitive (e.g., cycling). It is only natural that many people with disabilities desire to exert and express the maximum potential of their abilities by pursuing sport and recreational activities adapted to their personal abilities. The individual and team sports that have been developed specifically to utilize the abilities of people in wheelchairs have done a great service in raising the conscience of organizations as prestigious as the United States Olympic Committee, which recently initiated a Committee on Sports for the Disabled (DePauw, 1984). Adapted and segregated activities also provide the opportunity for people with similar abilities and limitations to group and interact together. However, all individuals with disabilities desire to recreate, at least part of the time, in a social manner with family and friends who do not have physical disabilities.

The physical, intellectual, and spiritual abilities of each person vary, as does the degree to which any one person desires to exert a given percentage of his or her physical potential while recreating. Many individuals have the desire to experience risk or at least the illusion of risk as well (Riggins, 1983). Therefore a combination of adaptive methodologies, equipment modifications, and new devices are needed to enable people with varying abilities to recreate.

Sporting activities adapted and limited to groups of people with similar abilities tend to be dominated by individuals who desire to exert the best of their own abilities in a competitive nature. Furthermore, an indication shows that athletes who compete in segregated types of sporting activities are similar in emotional disposition to their able-bodied counterparts (Henshen, Horvat, & French, 1984). Some sport-oriented people with disabilities, however, prefer to engage in recreational activities that are not competitive in nature and spend their leisure time in integrated activities that allow recreation with family and friends.

For the individual with a disability, the search for recreational alternatives that allow recreation with family and friends can be a frustrating and painstaking process in a challenging and recreative way. If the needs and desires of the individual are known, clear choices for recreation exist between the following types of activities:

- Integrated versus segregated activities
- Equipment versus minimal equipment activities
- Active versus passive activities
- Dependent versus independent activities
- Competitive versus noncompetitive activities
- Individual versus group activities
- Modified versus unmodified rules

Other distinctions can be made, but the point is that choices are available. More than one reason exists as to why a sport or recreational activity may or may not be satisfying to a particular individual. The same point needs to be made to the directors of adapted and therapeutic recreational programs. Understanding the needs and desires of program participants with limited abilities is important in determining appropriate recreational alternatives and activities. Table 1 presents some choices for possible recreational activities appropriate for individuals with lower limb paralysis.

The most common way of adapting a sport to an individual is to change the rules. By specifically modifying the rules of an activity, the varying needs of people with physical disabilities are considered, permitting them to recreate with more equal ability in a given sport (Rehabilitation Research Institute, 1981). For example, modifying the rules to allow for a second bounce during a game of tennis or racquetball has allowed people who use a wheelchair to demonstrate abilities equal to that of able-bodied players. The use of 5-second

Table 1. Choices for recreational activities appropriate for individuals with lower limb paralysis

Recreational Activities	Segregated	Integrated	Passive	Active	Independent	Group	Competitive	Integrated
Archery		X	X		X	X	X	X
Billiards		X	X		X	X	X	X
Flying		X	X	X	X	X	X	X
Hand Cycling	X	X		X	X	X	X	
Horseback Riding	X	X		X	X	X	X	X
Ice Picking	X			X	X	X	X	
Kayaking	X	X	X	X	X	X	X	X
Road Racing	X	X		X	X	X	X	X
Sailing	X	X	X	X	X	X	X	X
Snow Skiing		X		X	X	X	X	
Tennis	X	X		X	X	X	X	X
Wheelchair basketball	X			X		X	X	

violation in the key rather than 3 seconds, the modification of the dribble, and a point system for equalizing the ability of competing teams have contributed to wheelchair basketball's recognition as the most popular competitive sport for people with spinal cord injuries.

Games and activities can also be modified by asking participants without disabilities to assume a role equaling that of the participants with limited abilities. This is often called *reverse mainstreaming* (i.e., it permits integration of athletes with and without physical disabilities).

Techniques, Approaches, and Alternative Solutions

Experienced therapeutic recreation and adapted physical education specialists often develop techniques for incorporating individuals with varying needs into activities that would traditionally be defined as normal. Rafting, rock climbing, swimming, and skiing are all examples of activities that may or may not require utilization of adaptive techniques. For example, an individual with a visual impairment may snow ski with no specialized adaptive equipment by utilizing a highly refined protocol for communicating with a trained guide or ski-buddy.

The development of adaptive modifications for people with varying disabilities has great potential for participating in activities that are based upon equipment. The development of new systems and devices, which allow people to move within environments otherwise inaccessible, provides the opportunity of access for those with varying physical abilities as well. The use of horses (Hay, 1982), adapted water skis (Wilkinson, 1982), all-terrain vehicles (Slagle,

1982), hand-bicycles, sit-sleds, and aircraft (Axelson, 1984; Axelson & McCornack, 1983) provides access to integrated recreation.

Often the adaptation or modification of the control or seating interface of a recreational device or system will facilitate an individual's ability to utilize the device. For example, when a person with a spinal cord injury tries to utilize a horse, a saddle must be developed to appropriately interface the individual with special seating needs to the animal.

The adaptation of throttle, brake, and clutch mechanisms in automobiles, aircraft, and other vehicles can facilitate control by an individual with no function in his or her lower extremities. Often the functional abilities of an individual can be improved to permit use of an existing control system. The use of a hand splint by an individual with limited functional grip can enhance the use of video game controller or a radio controlled sailboat or glider.

When developing control modifications, it is important to design them in such a way that the device or system can be used by individuals without special needs in its traditional manner. As illustrated in Figure 1, the addition of leg

Figure 1. Peter Axelson prepares his preflight checklist in the Pterodactyl Ascender II ultralight aircraft equipped with leg support straps, side car for carrying wheelchair, seating modifications, and hand controlled ground steering and brakes. Photo courtesy of Toni James, Beneficial Designs, Inc., Santa Cruz, CA.

support straps, specialized seating to provide optimum skin protection and positioning for control, and hand controls for utilization of ground steering and brake control facilitate the use of an ultralight aircraft by people without use of their lower extremities and allows all controls to function in a traditional manner.

Where an add-on device is not appropriate, it may be necessary to replace the inaccessible control interface with a modified one. The permanent modification of the controls on a camera, tripod, or stereo system are common examples.

When considering the possibility of designing completely new devices and systems for interacting with otherwise inaccessible environments, many recreational opportunities open up. Several products have evolved to allow individuals with mobility impairments to recreate in an able-bodied manner. The development of the ARROYA sit-skiing system allows individuals with mobility impairments to snow ski with family and friends (Axelson, 1984; Taylor, 1983). While the capabilities and limitations of this type of equipment are different from that of traditional snow skis, the individual, as shown in Figure 2, is moving within a snow environment with capabilities comparable to those of traditional stand-up advanced-intermediate skiers. It is important to maintain compatibility with the chairlifts at a ski area (as shown in Figure 3) when existing resources must be utilized.

In a similar fashion the development of a hand powered, two-wheeled bicycle, as viewed in Figure 4, enables individuals with mobility impairments to bicycle with family and friends.

Figure 2. A sit-skier leans into a right-hand turn during the downhill competition at the 1983 National Handicapped Ski Championships at Squaw Valley, California. Photo courtesy of Toni James, Beneficial Designs, Inc., Santa Cruz, CA.

Figure 3. Peter Axelson, skier, and Punky Jensen, director of sit-skiing program at Dodge Ridge Ski Area, California, ride the chairlift at Squaw Valley, California, and inspect the race course prior to the giant slalom. Photo courtesy of Colleen Monahan, Beneficial Designs, Inc., Santa Cruz, CA.

Figure 4. Peter Axelson pedals the hand bike, a hand-powered two-wheeled bicycle, in the Santa Cruz mountains. Photo courtesy of Colleen Monahan, Beneficial Designs, Inc., Santa Cruz, CA.

Plan for Developing Integrated Recreation Solutions

Three primary avenues are available for expanding opportunities for individuals with limited abilities in a social recreational environment:

1. Programming methodologies, often packaged in the form of printed and video-taped materials, can be made available to individuals desiring to improve access to their programs or to initiate programs directed toward the needs of people with limited mobilities.
2. Recreational equipment which already exists can be adapted or modified.
3. New recreational equipment can be designed, manufactured, and marketed.

To utilize these three avenues to solve a problem, an information resource base needs to be developed and made accessible to individuals desiring to meet the needs of people with varying abilities. Service and sport organizations and associations are in a position to make such information available.

Interdisciplinary sport teams, composed of therapists, educators, and consumers, should be developed and funded to promote the concept of bringing individuals with disabilities into the recreational community to promote various concepts of integrated recreation. People with an interest in adapting and modifying equipment, like university students in engineering, should be encouraged to seek internships within adapted physical education and therapeutic recreation programs.

Often the inclusion of people with disabilities is difficult because of the inexperience of staff within a particular recreation program. The development and utilization of a planning guide for initiating a recreation program or for implementing accessibility within an existing program would enhance the services of any community.

Sports which in themselves allow participation by people with a wide range of abilities need to be encouraged. Priorities need to be implemented within insurance companies, government agencies, and service organizations to fund equipment and training for recreation as a part of normal services. Funding and/or manufacturing incentives are needed to stimulate research and development to (a) investigate and document recreation programming methodologies that include people with varying abilities, (b) develop or make available equipment modifications as options to existing recreational equipment, (c) design and manufacture adaptive equipment that facilitates integrated recreational activity within existing sport and recreational activities, and (d) examine the psychosocial effects of sport and recreational activities upon the development of independent living and vocational skills for people with disabilities.

Conclusion

All individuals with disabilities desire, at least part of the time, to recreate in a social manner with family and friends who do not have physical disabilities. Increased attention should be given to techniques, approaches, and solutions that will facilitate meaningful and satisfying integrated recreation.

Although some adaptive equipment and systems are now available, new products and designs are needed to expand recreational options. Ways must be found to increase the commitment of manufacturers, consumers, and others to develop new products and adapt existing equipment. It is positive to see that creative designs are costing less and meeting the needs of more people.

References

Axelson, P. (1984a). Sit-skiing Part I. *Sports 'N Spokes*, **9**(4), 16-17.

Axelson, P. (1984b). Sit-skiing Part II. *Sport 'N Spokes*, **9**(6), 34-40.

Axelson, P., & McCornack, J. (1983). Mixin' it up. *Sports 'N Spokes*, **9**(4), 16-17.

Beaver, D., Jackson, R., McCann, B., Messner, D., & Ryan, A. (1978). Sport and recreation for the handicapped. *The Physician and Sports Medicine*, **6**(43), 44-47.

DePauw, K. (1984). Commitment and challenges: Sport opportunities for athletes with disabilities. *Journal of Physical Education, Recreation, and Dance*, **55**(2), 34-35.

Gwinner, L. (1982). Vinland experience. *Sports 'N Spokes*, **8**(3), 13-16.

Hay, C. (1982). Wilderness travel on horseback. *Sports 'N Spokes*, **7**(6), 6-8.

Heer, M. (1984). A new generation of athletes learn the ropes. *Sports 'N Spokes*, **9**(5), 34-36.

Henschen, K., Horvat, M., & French, R. (1984). A visual comparison of psychological profiles between able-bodied and wheelchair athletes. *Adapted Physical Activity Quarterly*, **1**(2), 118-124.

McKinney, N. (1982). The wilderness experience. *Sports 'N Spokes*, **7**(5), 10-12.

Rappoport, A. (1981). Skiing by the seat of your pants. *Sports 'N Spokes*, **7**(4), 8-13.

Rehabilitation Research Institute. (1981) Sports for disabled individuals. *Rehabilitation Briefings*, **4**, 1-4.

Riggins, R. (1983). A risk continuum: Strategies for risk programming. *Parks & Recreation*, **17**(1), 82-83.

Slagle, D.K. (1982). ATVs, three-wheelers, and other alternate modes of transportation. *Sports 'N Spokes*, **7**(6), 12-19.

Taylor, P. (1983). Pete Axelson: Building a better ski sled is only part of the story. *Sports 'N Spokes*, **8**(6), 28-30.

Wilkinson, K. (1982). Skiing on water. *Sports 'N Spokes*, **8**(2), 17.

PART II

Sports Classification for Equalizing Competition

9

Controversies in Medical Classification of Wheelchair Athletes

Michael Weiss
SANTA CLARA VALLEY MEDICAL CENTER
SAN JOSE, CALIFORNIA, USA

Kathleen A. Curtis
SANTA CLARA VALLEY MEDICAL CENTER
SAN JOSE, CALIFORNIA, USA

Since their inception in 1946, competitive wheelchair sports have evolved from participatory activities to serious competitions. The history of wheelchair sports has been reviewed by Rosen (1973) and others. Medical classification was introduced to allow fair competition based on athletic ability rather than physical disability. Many people involved in wheelchair sports, however, feel that the classification systems are unfair, ineffective, and in need of change. This paper reviews the classification systems of the National Wheelchair Athletic Association (NWAA), National Wheelchair Basketball Association (NWBA), and the International Stoke Mandeville Games Federation (ISMGF). These systems are similar, and all attempt to integrate wheelchair athletes with a variety of disabilities. Six major areas of controversy are considered:

1. anatomical versus functional approaches,
2. influencing factors,
3. split classification,
4. very severe or minimal disability,
5. equipment, and
6. open competition.

Classification

When wheelchair sports were introduced no classification system existed. It soon became evident, however, that open competition often favored the less disabled. More severely disabled athletes were either noncompetitive in individual sports or, worse, were practically excluded from participation in team sports.

Classification of wheelchair athletes is intended to "enable competitors with even the most severe disability to compete in a fair manner with other competitors with similar degrees of disability" (ISMGF, 1982). The idea is to allow athletic prowess, rather than sheer physical advantage, to determine the victor. The concept is analogous to weight classes in wrestling or boxing.

The three classification systems to be discussed are outlined in Table 1. They are all based on levels of complete spinal cord injury. For cases that are not clearly delineated on physical examination, functional characteristics are used to place an athlete in an appropriate class.

Controversy and Change

Anatomical versus Functional Approaches

All three systems are anatomically based. Classification is determined by manual muscle testing of upper and lower extremities and trunk balance. In contrast, functional classification requires cooperation on the part of the athlete and a subjective assessment of effort and performance by the classifier. A trend has been to utilize functional assessment more in classification. Dr. Horst Strohkendl of West Germany, perhaps the strongest proponent of functional assessment, has developed a new functional classification system for wheelchair basketball which was used in international competition for the first time in July 1984 (Strohkendl, 1983a).

Functional classification may not be an improvement over anatomical classification for several reasons. Training does affect function. A functional classification can penalize the best athletes and may improperly classify new athletes who have not achieved their functional potential. An example of this is sitting balance in wheelchair basketball. Good athletes may use tricks of wheelchair design (like slinging a backrest) or improved timing and coordination of hand movement to improve balance. New athletes may have deconditioned trunk muscles with poor balance even though innervation is present. Also, occasionally an athlete will try to fool the classifier to achieve a competitive advantage. Functional evaluation deals with classification problems by supplementing the initial classification with an individual, anatomically based examination. Anatomical evaluation deals with problem classifications by adding a functional evaluation and observation of the athlete in competition. For the more difficult cases, the distinction between anatomical and functional classification becomes blurred.

Table 1. NWBA, NWAA, ISMGF (except basketball) classifications presented by spinal cord anatomical site, muscle strength, and balance

	NWBA	NWAA	ISMGF (except basketball)
C-5	IA	Triceps 0-3	IA
C-6	IB	Triceps 4-5	IB
C-7		Wrist flexion/extension present	
C-8	IC	Finger flexion/extension 4-5 No useful hand intrinsics No useful abdominals No lower intercostals	IC
T-1	I Motor loss at T7 or above Sitting balance poor		II
T-2			
T-3			
T-4			
T-5			
T-6		Upper abdominals good. No useful lower abdominals. No useful lower trunk extensors.	
T-7	II Abdominal and spinal extensor muscle strength 3-5		
T-8			
T-9	III	Poor to fair sitting balance	III
T-10			
T-11	IV Sitting balance fair to good	Good abdominals and spinal extensors. Some hip flexors/ adductors.	IV
T-12			
L-1	Hip flexors ≤ 4 Hip adductors ≤ 3 Quadriceps ≤ 2 Includes bilateral	Fair to good balance Quad strength < 3 Includes bilateral hip disarticulation	Good balance 1-20 points traumatic 1-15 points postpolio Amputees not included
L-2			

Cont.

Table 1 (Cont.)

	NWBA	NWAA	ISMGF (except basketball)
L-3	hip disarticulations III Trunk control, pelvic control Sitting balance	V amputees	V
L-4	Good to normal Quads 3-5	Normal balance Quad strength ≥ 3 < 40 points Most amputees AK & BK In V/VI	Normal balance 21-40 points traumatic 16-35 points polio Amputees not included
L-5	All other amputees	VI (Swimming only) ≥ 40 points	VI (Swimming only) 41-60 points traumatic 36-50 points polio
S-1			Not eligible > 61 points traumatic > 51 points polio

Note. Points: 5 points each by muscle test grade given for hip flexors, extensors, adductors, abductors, knee flexors-extensors, ankle plantar flexors, dorsiflexors.

Influencing Factors

The second group is a set of factors which Dr. Caibre McCann calls the "influencing factors" in classification (McCann, 1979). These are spasticity, sensation, orthoses, deformities, and surgical procedures.

Spasticity is generally thought to be a disadvantage in wheelchair sports; yet it is carefully discounted by the ISMGF, NWBA, and NWAA classification sytems, except to allow strapping for reasons of safety (NWBA, 1983). The ISMGF guide does state that some competitors may use spasticity to their advantage (e.g., extension of trunk). Strohkendl (1983b) has shown that body position caused by spastic limbs may impede swimmers. Strapping to the chair for spasticity is thought to be an advantage by some competitors, and complaints have led to a liberalization of the strapping rules for all competitors, spastic or not.

Sensation, especially position sense, in contrast, is regarded as a great advantage. The ISMGF, NWAA, and NWBA recommend use of sensory level as an aid to borderline anatomical classification. Athletes disabled with polio or muscle diseases are often able to utilize bracing for functions like walking because of their intact sensation, whereas spinal cord injured athletes cannot. The advantage in competition, however, depends on the event. It is of great advantage in basketball and table tennis, probable advantage in slalom, possible advantage in swimming and field events, and minimal advantage in track, archery, and riflery. This has not, however, been documented.

Deformities and surgical procedures may also make classification difficult. Fixed contractures and fusions are considered functionally in all classifications except the NWBA. An example of this is spinal fusion, where trunk muscle function may be present but functional mobility may be quite limited. This also needs assessment.

Split Classification

In an athlete whose pattern of impairment does not fit a classification, split classification may be a fair alternative. Examples are incomplete quadriplegia, spotty paralysis of polio, proximal weakness in neuromuscular disease, and ataxia in multiple sclerosis, in which athletes may be classified differently for each event. Obviously this is not practical in basketball. Such classification invariably draws protests because of its subjectivity, and, if improperly utilized, it will shut out disabled athletes from fair competition in their appropriate classes.

Very Severe or Minimal Disability

The next group involves the two ends of the spectrum of disability—very severe and minimal disability. At each end some athletes are excluded from competition. This is especially true for quadriplegics in team sports This problem has fostered several changes and also has led to the development of new team sports like "Murderball," designed for quadriplegics (Goodin, 1983; Mikkelson & Goodin, 1981). The other end of the spectrum is the temporarily or minimally disabled athlete. For instance, should athletes with impairments such as torn knee cartilage, chondromalacia patella or forefoot amputation be allowed to compete? The ISMGF rules against participation by minimally disabled athletes.

It also has excluded participation by athletes with nonspinal cord related disabilities, like amputees (although recently they have been allowed in wheelchair basketball). NWAA and NWBA rules require permanent physical disability that precludes able-bodied competition. Minimal required disability is vague and is variably enforced. Often peer pressure is the main determinant.

Equipment

Anyone familiar with wheelchairs has seen significant changes in design and construction derived largely from competitive wheelchair sports. These chairs are expensive, yet provide a real competitive advantage in track, slalom, and wheelchair basketball (LaMere & Labanowich, 1984). Chair modifications for improved power, efficiency, stability, and maneuverability are seen at most athletic meets. Some designs may predispose athletes to contractures and decubiti if used as day-to-day wheelchairs. Some wheelchairs have been judged to give an unfair advantage to athletes, such as using a handcrank instead of a pushrim for track events (Murray, 1982; Theis, 1982). Serious competitors probe the limits and look for ways to capitalize on their strengths and compensate for their weaknesses. Equipment that minimizes the extent of a functional deficit in some events, such as track, is believed by some experts to eliminate the need for an extensive classification system (McCann, 1981).

Open Competition

A recent phenomenon has been the incorporation of wheelchair track events into able-bodied track meets and road races such as a number of marathons in the U.S., the European Track Tour, and the exhibition events at the Olympic Games in Los Angeles. These are open competitions, without classification. The disabled wheelchair racers who compete are serious athletes with years of hard training behind them. Classification is unnecessary for these elite athletes.

Evaluation of Classification

Despite controversy and changes, no systematic evaluation of the medical classification approach had been conducted prior to this study. How well does medical classification achieve its goal of fairly grouping wheelchair athletes to allow fair competition in track, field, swimming, and other NWAA events?

This question was approached by selecting a random sample ($n = 105$, 10% of the NWAA membership) to obtain information on the distribution of the various causes of disability and medical classifications among the wheelchair athletes who belonged to the organization in 1984. This comprised the normative sample against which comparisons were made. The winners of track, field, and swimming events at the National Games in 1973 and 1983 were identified by classification and cause of disability (condition). The distribution of disabilities in the three groups was compared statistically, using a Chi-square test. These findings are presented in Table 2.

Table 2. Percentage of first place winners in NWAA track, field, and swimming events by condition in 1973 and 1983 compared with NWAA sample

Condition	1984 NWAA Sample $n = 105$	1973 $n = 27$	1983 $n = 73$
Spinal cord injury			
Motor complete	50	41*	40**
Motor incomplete	9	4*	19** ≠
Postpolio	10	30*	18** ≠
Spina Bifida	13	7*	1
Amputation	8	7	11**
Cerebral Palsy	3	7	7
Osteogenesis imperfecta	2	4	4
Brain injury	4	—	—
Muscle disease	1	—	—

*χ^2 (3) = 14.6, p<.01, significantly different from NWAA sample
**χ^2 (3) = 7.4, p<.05, significantly different from NWAA sample
≠χ^2 (2) = 13.2, p<.001, significantly different from event winners, 1973 to 1983

If the classification system is working (i.e., athletic ability and not physical disability determines the victors), then there should not be a significant difference in the causes of disability seen among the winners of events from the causes of disability in the general membership of the NWAA. This is not the case. In 1973 athletes with spinal cord injuries (45%) and spina bifida (7%) were significantly underrepresented, and athletes with post-polio (30%) were overrepresented among the winners, compared to their respective percentages in the 1984 sample. In 1983, motor incomplete spinal cord injury (19%) and amputation (11%) joined post-polio as significantly overrepresented causes of disability among the first place finishers.

Does this prove that the medical classification system of the NWAA is unfair? No, it merely suggests that it is not working as intended and may not have been for a long time. Further study is necessary to support this assertion. It is also not clear whether this problem is a fault of the classification system or its enforcement, because post-polio and incomplete spinal cord injury present variable motor patterns and thus are more difficult to classify.

It should be emphasized that this question is approachable by statistical analysis. Any changes that are made in the systems should be tested to see if they achieve the desired effect. Improved data collection in competitive wheelchair athletics is needed to help ensure that changes are rational and effective. Otherwise, they are likely only to introduce more controversy.

Conclusion

Competitive wheelchair sports have evolved since their introduction 40 years ago. Medical classification of wheelchair athletes attempts to provide a system whereby the disabled can compete fairly based on athletic ability. Whether any of the classification systems have achieved this goal is controversial. Despite changes, both past and impending, little systematic study that evaluates the efficacy of medical classification has been completed. This is surely necessary if the changes are to be rational and effective.

References

Goodin, G. (1983). Quad rugby: The Canadian sport of murderball. *Sports 'N Spokes,* **9**(4), 26-27.

International Stoke Mandeville Games Federation. (1982). *Guide for doctors.* Aylesbury, England: Author.

LaMere, T.J., & Labanowich, S. (1984). The history of sport wheelchairs—part III. *Sports 'N Spokes,* **10**(2), 12-16.

McCann, B.C. (1979). Problems and future trends in classifying disabled athletes. In R. Steadward (Ed.), *Proceedings of First International Conference on Sport and Training of the Physically Disabled Athlete* (pp. 25-35). Edmonton, Canada: University of Alberta.

McCann, B.C. (1980). Medical classification—Art, science or instinct. *Sports 'N Spokes,* **5**(5), 12-14.

McCann, B.C. (1981). Does the track athlete need medical classification. *Sports 'N Spokes,* **7**, 22-24.

Mikkelson, B., & Goodin, S. (1981). Murderball, a team sport for male and/or female quads. (Available from B. Mikkelson, 118 Mercury Dr., East Grand Forks, MN 56721)

Murray, G. (1982) Cranks: Guest editorial. *Sports 'N Spokes,* **8**(2), 4.

National Wheelchair Basketball Association. (1983). *Physical classification handbook.* Lexington, KY: Author.

Rosen, N.B. (1973). The role of sports in rehabilitation of the handicapped. *Maryland State Medical Journal,* **22**(2), 30; **22**(3), **11**; **22**(6), **78**; **22**(11), **35.**

Strohkendl, H. (1983a). Classification system for wheelchair basketball. *Report to the ISMGF Basketball Subcommittee.* (Available from Dr. Stan Labanowich, 110 Seaton Bldg., University of Kentucky, Lexington, KY 40506).

Strohkendl, H. (1983b). Technical aspects of swimming for children with various levels of myelodysplasia. In American Academy of Orthopaedic Surgeons (Ed.), *Proceedings of the Winter Park Seminar: Sports and Recreational Programs for the Child and Young Adult with Physical Disability* (pp. 7-8). Chicago: American Academy of Orthopaedic Surgeons.

Theis, J. (1982). Racing crank chairs: Guest editorial. *Sports 'N Spokes,* **8**(3), 5.

10

The New Classification System for Wheelchair Basketball

Horst Strohkendl
UNIVERSITY OF COLOGNE
COLOGNE, WEST GERMANY

An efficient and effective classification system is a prerequisite to the establishment of fair and equitable competition within the International Stoke Mandeville Games Federation (ISMGF). The classification system must give each physically disabled individual an equal opportunity to compete on a national and international level. No reasonable arguments exist to exclude any individual from competition because of the nature, cause, or severity of the disability.

Fairness in wheelchair basketball depends on team balance, which is based on a point system. Each player is assigned a sport classification based upon functional ability and other factors, which has a numerical value of 1, 2, or 3 under U.S. rules or 1, 2, 3, or 4 under world (ISMGF) rules. Under U.S. rules players on the floor cannot total more than 12 points, whereas under world rules players cannot total more than 14 points. Only five players make a team.

This paper presents the new wheelchair basketball classification system that was used for the first time in international competition in July 1984 at the VIIth World Games in Aylesbury, England. Whereas in the past points were assigned on the basis of level of spinal cord lesion only, this new classification includes three parts: medical, functional, and game observation.

This new system, which stresses a functional rather than a medical approach to classification, now serves as the official protocol for all international basketball competition under the aegis of the ISMGF. The system has also been adopted, with minor changes (three classifications instead of four), by the National Wheelchair Basketball Association (NWBA), the U.S. governing body.

Rationale for a New Classification System

The skills, talents, and level of training of a player should not affect his or her sport classification. The classification system should be based instead on the functional limitations caused by the physical disability. The disability understandably affects the player's capability for performing the different skills of wheelchair basketball such as pushing (wheeling) the chair, catching and throwing the ball, shooting, and dribbling.

If we observe premier players with different functional limitations, then we readily recognize that the level of trunk function directly affects performance capability in regard to the different skills involved. Therefore, the level of sitting balance and trunk movement of the athletes become the fundamental elements used in the definition of classes and in the development of a testing procedure fair to all.

The definition of classes is considerably easier to achieve than the development of a precise classification procedure. As many classes as possible are needed for fairness; yet we possess only a limited number of precise objectives to reduce the classes to a reasonable number. The limiting factor in the classification system is the quality of the classification procedure. Therefore we resort to the definition of four classes because we believe that the procedure is most applicable to that number. This new method seeks to integrate medical, biomechanical (kinesiological), and specific technical information derived from both research and past experience.

The classification system should be as simple as possible. On the one hand, it is believed that each player and official should have an insight into its principles and methods. On the other hand, it is felt that one is obliged to tolerate the functional differences within each class; these differences are inevitable if we are to spread these four classes over the wide range of functional difference.

Description of Classes Under the New Procedure

The new procedure combines information about the level of spinal cord lesion with pass and fail ratings of three functional tests that measure trunk mobility and sitting balance. Table 1 summarizes the procedure.

Table 1. ISMGF Basketball classifications based on Strohkendl procedure

| Class | Level of Lesion | Functional Tests | | |
		Horizontal plane (Sitting upright)	Sagittal plane (Bending forward and backward)	Frontal plane (Bending sideward)
I	T-8 and above	−	−	−
II	T-9 to L-2	+	−	−
III	L-3 to L-5	+	+	−
IV	S-1 to S-2	+	+	+

Note. + denotes pass/positive rating; − denotes fail/negative rating.
T-9, L-3, and S-1 refer to first nonfunctional segment.

A detailed description of each of the four classes follows:

Class I: Class I athletes have no functional sitting balance when in a wheel-chair without support of a back. The trunk cannot be moved in any plane without the help of at least one arm. The functional potential is represented by paraplegics with complete lesions originating at thoracic level 8 (T-8) and above.

Class II: Class II athletes have fair to good sitting balance. They are able to rotate their trunks to the right and left when sitting upright without the support of the chair back. They cannot move their trunks for-ward maximally. They need at least one arm holding onto the wheelchair to perform downward, upward, and sideward trunk bending. The functional potential is represented by paraplegics with complete lesions originating from thoracic level 9 (T-9) to lumbar level 2 (L-2).

Class III: Class III athletes have an optimal sitting balance and optimal trunk movements in the horizontal and sagital planes without the help of one arm holding any part of the wheelchair. The functional poten-tial is represented by paraplegics with complete lesions originating from lumbar level 3 (L-3) to lumbar level 5 (L-5).

Class IV: Class IV athletes have an optimal sitting balance and optimal trunk movements in all planes. A significant limitation in movement to one side of the frontal plane (i.e., sideward bending) must be tol-erated. The functional limitations is represented by paraplegics with complete lesions originating from sacral 1 (S-1) to sacral 2 (S-2).

Classification Procedure: An Overview

The classification procedure has three parts that increase the probability of arriving at a fair determination, especially in the case of athletes who are on the borderline of the class. The three parts include the following:

1. The medical part, which provides an approximate determination of the level of trunk function while seated in a wheelchair. This procedure entails evalua-tion of the following:
   (a) the motor innervation of arm and shoulder muscles, abdominal and back muscles, hip and leg muscles and the level of lesion,
   (b) the level of sensation,
   (c) any additional impairments such as amputation, fusion, spasticity, and contracture, and
   (d) the wearing of orthotic devices.
2. The functional part, which entails testing of the athlete's level of trunk move-ment and sitting balance while seated in the wheelchair.
3. The observation during the game when the testing does not lead to a clear decision.

The official ISMGF Classification Form appears on page 104.

ISMGF Classification Form for Wheelchair Basketball Player

Medical examination

Diagnosis:

Spinal cord injury
- complete
- incomplete
- motor level
- sensation
- spasticity
- contractures

Poliomyelitis

Amputation
- hip disarticulated
- lesser trochanter
- bilateral above knee
- unilateral above knee
- bilateral above knee/lower knee

Dysmelie

Cerebral palsy

Other

Muscles (left / right)

Muscle	left	right
Trapezius	☐	☐
Deltoideus	☐	☐
Biceps	☐	☐
Triceps	☐	☐
Wrist muscles	☐	☐
Hand muscles	☐	☐
Abdominals	☐	☐
Extensors thoracic	☐	☐
Extensor lumbar	☐	☐
Hip flexors	☐	☐
Adductors	☐	☐
Knee extensors	☐	☐
Foot extensors	☐	☐
Abductors	☐	☐
Hip extensors	☐	☐
Knee flexors	☐	☐
Foot flexors	☐	☐

Joints (fusion) (left / right)

Joint	left	right
Shoulder	☐	☐
Elbow	☐	☐
Wrist	☐	☐
Spine thoracic	☐	☐
Spine lumbar	☐	☐
Hip	☐	☐
Knee	☐	☐
Ankle	☐	☐

Functional test — Observation during game

Functional test		Observation during game
Raising the arm negative	l. ☐ r. ☐	Class I ☐
Wheeling a chair negative	l. ☐ r. ☐	Class I ☐
Picking up a ball negative	l. ☐ r. ☐	Class I ☐
Test I negative	☐	Class I ☐
Test I positive	☐	Class II ☐
Test II positive	☐	Class III ☐
Test III positive	☐	Class IV ☐
Running and jumping negative	☐	Class IV ☐

Name: _____

Address: _____

Date: _____

Place: _____

1. Examiner: _____

2. Examiner: _____

Class: I / II / III / IV

Points: 1 / 2 / 3 / 4

Medical Examination

Most people are already familiar with this procedure because it has been used more-or-less in the same way since the 1940s. Therefore this discussion is limited only to considerations that will help differentiate between classes. Guidelines for classifying amputees appear in Table 2.

Table 2. Medical examination guidelines for classifying amputees

1. Bilateral amputees with stump length shorter than the lesser trochanter are Class II.
2. Bilateral amputees with stump length greater than the lesser trochanter are Class III or Class IV. (It depends on the remaining trunk functions).
3. Bilateral amputees with one stump length shorter than the lesser trochanter and one above the knee are Class III or Class IV. (It depends on the remaining trunk functions).
4. Unilateral amputees are Class IV.

Primary Differences Between Classes I and II

Class I is reserved for athletes who have a complete spinal cord lesion originating at T-8 or above and who have an additional impairment in at least one arm. Athletes who have good arms and full trunk sensation (e.g., those with polio) cannot be classified as Class I. Athletes who have a significant loss of function of one or both arms with paresis at the hand, elbow, or shoulder joint, or a fusion of the corresponding joints, are to be classified as Class I (regardless of whether sensation is present or not) or Class II. For final judgment see Functional Tests and Observation during the game.

Primary Differences Between Classes II and III

The primary difference between Class II and III athletes is the lack of hip joint control. A Class II athlete has no innervation of adductor, abductor, or extensor muscles. There is no functional advantage, for instance, in wearing orthotic devices or in fusions of the hip joint, which have a positive effect on the remaining trunk functions when sitting in a wheelchair. Class II athletes may have, maximally, innervation of the hip flexors. Functional trunk and hip muscles with additional spastic tendencies must be taken into account. Athletes with this type of incomplete lesion may be classified fairly only when observed during a game. A final judgment cannot be made on medical reasons alone.

Primary Differences Between Classes III and IV

The primary difference between Class III and IV athletes is the lack of control of the abduction of at least one leg (or thigh). A Class III athlete has no innervation of the abductors and extensors of the hip joint or the knee flexor muscles. They have maximally the innervation of the hip flexors, adductors, knee extensors, and foot extensors. The wearing of orthotic devices can give a functional advantage and make an athlete Class IV. Class IV athletes can move at least one thigh to the side, meaning that they can enlarge the base for the trunk to the side.

Primary Differences Between Class IV and Nondisabled People

A Class IV athlete has a significant, permanent physical impairment. The minimal medical signs are single forefoot amputation or peroneous paresis or a complete fusion of one ankle joint or other comparable impairments.

Functional Examination

Use of functional abilities to help classify athletes is a new procedure in wheelchair basketball. Therefore the three tests devised for this purpose are presented in this section of the paper.

Test 1—Assessment of sitting stability and rotation of the trunk

Instructions: Sit as straight as possible in your chair. Bounce and catch the ball with both hands at the same time while changing the side of the chair after each try. Rotate your trunk as far as possible to each side without losing your balance or leaning back in the chair.

Performance expectations

Level of lesion	Performance	Resulting basketball classification
T-7 and above	Fail	I
T-8 to L-1	Pass	II
L-2 to L-5	Pass	III
S-1 to S-2	Pass	IV

Illustrative pass and fail performance

Pass: Performance of person with paraplegia caused by T-11 lesion shows no loss of balance.

Fail: Performance of person with paraplegia caused by T-5 lesion tends to fall to one side or lean too far back in the chair.

Test 2—Assessment of forward/backward bending of trunk

Instructions: Assume a forward bending position (trunk touching thighs) with hands behind neck. Now raise your trunk to a normal sitting position without removing your hands from behind your neck.

Performance expectations

Level of lesion	Performance	Resulting basketball classification
T-7 and above	Fail	I
T-8 to L-1	Fail	II
L-2 to L-5	Pass	III
S-1 to S-2	Pass	IV

Illustrative pass and fail performance

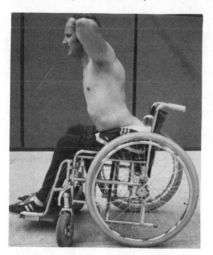 

Pass: Sit-up by person with paraplegia caused by L-4 lesion with work done by trunk muscles, not the arms and shoulders.

Fail: Inability to perform sit-up without arm and shoulder action by person with paraplegia caused by L-1 lesion.

Test 3—Assessment of sideward bending of trunk (i.e., lateral flexion)

Instructions: A ball is lying to the side of your wheelchair. Pick up the ball with both hands simultaneously using a sideward bend. Bring the ball over your head and place it on the floor to the other side of your wheelchair. Do this without bending your body forward. Repeat the test to the opposite side.

Performance expectations

Level of lesion	Performance	Resulting basketball classification
T-7 and above	Fail	I
T-8 to L-1	Fail	II
L-2 to L-5	Fail	III
S-1 to S-2	Pass	IV

Illustrative pass and fail performance

Phase 1 Movement   Phase 2 Movement

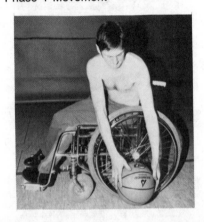   

Pass: Person with S1 to S2 lesion performs side bend and overhead lift of ball with little difficulty. If the hip abductors and knee flexors are not completely paralyzed, some movements of the legs are available to help with balance.

Test 3 cont.

Fail: Person with paraplegia caused by L4 lesion loses his balance and leans the trunk and/or arms on the wheel. Forward, but not sideward, raising of ball is possible.

Guidelines for Differentiating Between Classes

Following are guidelines for differentiating between classifications by means of the functional test.

Primary Differences Between Class I and II

1. Test 1 is applied.
2. Physically disabled athletes with a loss of arm functions.
   Functional disabilities:
   Inability to lift a basketball from the ground with one hand and without any support, or
   Significant differences in arm function when pushing or steering a wheelchair: pushing with one arm is weak, or not simultaneous, or done by lifting one shoulder, or one arm cannot be extended at the elbow joint, or
   The inability to raise one arm over the head.

If one of the corresponding tasks (lifting the basketball, wheeling a chair, raising the arm) is negative on both arms, then the athlete is a Class I (see Test 1, p. 106).

If one of the corresponding tasks is negative only on one arm, then the athlete is a Class I if the remaining trunk functions are comparable with Class I and II; the athlete is Class II if the remaining trunk functions are comparable with Classes III and IV.

Final judgments are made by observation during the game.

Primary Differences Betweeen Classes II and III

Test 2 is applied. The athlete is sitting in a wheelchair and wearing all orthotic devices that he or she is using during the game (see Test 2, p. 107).

Primary Differences Between Class III and IV

Test 3 is applied. The athlete is sitting in a wheelchair and wearing all orthotic devices that he or she is using during a game.

Primary Differences Between Class IV and Nondisabled People

A Class IV athlete cannot jump or run like an able-bodied person. Jumping and running are dangerous or disadvantageous for the health of the athlete (see Test 3, pp. 108-109).

Observation During the Game

The observation form below is used. This is the final phase of the classification procedure.

Observation Form for Classification in Wheelchair Basketball

Team A:

Player Number	Wheeling	Dribbling	Ball control	Rebound	Class
3	1 2 3 4	1 2 3 4	1 2 3 4	1 2 3 4	_____
4	1 2 3 4	1 2 3 4	1 2 3 4	1 2 3 4	_____
6	1 2 3 4	1 2 3 4	1 2 3 4	1 2 3 4	_____
7	1 2 3 4	1 2 3 4	1 2 3 4	1 2 3 4	_____
8	1 2 3 4	1 2 3 4	1 2 3 4	1 2 3 4	_____
9	1 2 3 4	1 2 3 4	1 2 3 4	1 2 3 4	_____
10	1 2 3 4	1 2 3 4	1 2 3 4	1 2 3 4	_____
11	1 2 3 4	1 2 3 4	1 2 3 4	1 2 3 4	_____
12	1 2 3 4	1 2 3 4	1 2 3 4	1 2 3 4	_____
13	1 2 3 4	1 2 3 4	1 2 3 4	1 2 3 4	_____
14	1 2 3 4	1 2 3 4	1 2 3 4	1 2 3 4	_____
15	1 2 3 4	1 2 3 4	1 2 3 4	1 2 3 4	_____

Criteria: Sitting balance; trunk movements; leg movements; arm movements; height of cushion; height of seat; height of seat back; incline of seat; compensation techniques; leaving or entering a wheelchair.

Observer: _____   Place: _____

Date: _____

Primary Differences Between Classes I and II

Class I athletes use a wheelchair with a high back. They lose their balance when lifting both arms at the same time over their heads. They need both arms when lifting their trunks from their thighs. They are unable to turn their heads far behind and sit without support during a high-ball situation.

Class II athletes use a wheelchair with a lower back, need only one arm when supporting the movements of their trunks, and possess fair balance when lifting both hands over their heads or executing a high ball. They show deliberate dorsal flexion of the trunk.

Athletes with arm impairments are Class I if they show significant functional limitations when pushing and steering the wheelchair in any direction or catching a normal pass by preferring to use only one hand.

Primary Differences Between Classes II and III

Class II athletes cannot raise their trunks from their laps without the support of one arm. They are not able to start with only one hand and bounce the ball simultaneously or wheel their chair and bounce the ball at high speed. They lose their balance easily in rebound situations. Class III athletes show deliberate trunk movements in the sagital plane at least. They can pick up the ball with both hands from in front of the footplates, dribble with one hand without restriction, and steer by crossing the free arm to grasp the opposite wheel.

Primary Differences Between Classes III and IV

Class III athletes have functional limitations in trunk movements in the frontal plane. They use one hand to hold the handrim when leaning to the opposite side. Class IV athletes use their legs, moving their feet and their thighs to the side. They use both arms in rebound situations even if they are leaning sideward.

Primary Differences Between Class IV and Nondisabled People

Class IV athletes have no fair chance to compete with nondisabled people because they are unable to run fast and jump with both legs.

Recommended Credentialing Procedure for Examiners

The ISMGF Basketball Subcommittee will encourage physicians, physical educators, physiotherapists, and interested players to attend educational clinics to become certified for classifying wheelchair basketball players. A recommended team for classification is a medical person and a physical educator (see the classification form on page 104).

Differences Between U.S. and World Systems

Class I is the same for both ISMGF and NWBA competition. Table 3 shows the major differences between the other classifications:

Table 3. Differences in classifications

Class	ISMGF	NWBA
Class II	T-8 to L-1	T-8 to L-2
Class III	L-2 to L-5	L-3 and all other disabilities
Class IV	S-1 to S-2	No Class IV

The level of lesion is defined by the first functional segment above the lesion in most U.S. literature on ISMGF classifications whereas Strohkendl in Table 1 defines level of lesion as first nonfunctional segment.

11

Classification and Other Issues in Sports for Blind, Cerebral Palsied, Les Autres, and Amputee Athletes

Claudine Sherrill
TEXAS WOMAN'S UNIVERSITY
DENTON, TEXAS, USA

Carol Adams-Mushett
NATIONAL ASSOCIATION OF SPORTS FOR CEREBRAL PALSY
NEW YORK, NEW YORK, USA

Jeffrey A. Jones
UNITED CEREBRAL PALSY ASSOCIATION OF DETROIT
DETROIT, MICHIGAN, USA

More important than any other principle governing sport for disabled athletes is ability/disability classification to assure equitable competition. Three international sport organizations, each with its own classification system, cooperated in the conduct of the 1984 International Games for the Disabled. The International Sports Organization for the Disabled (ISOD), founded in 1964, initially governed sports for all physical disabilities except spinal cord injury (Lindstrom, 1984). Both disability-specific and integrated competitive events were held. In general, however, disability-specific competition dominated the Games. In swimming, for instance, separate events were run for males and females representing 27 disability-specific classifications as follows: amputees, 9 classes; blind, 3 classes; cerebral palsied, 8 classes (one of which has 2 subclasses); and les autres, 6 classes (i.e., a total of 54 competitions for each race). From an organizational standpoint, many people believed that this number of events was unwieldy. Others pointed out that many races, particularly in swimming, had three or fewer competitors. Many questions arose. Should such races be canceled or held as originally planned? In the future could some events be integrated (i.e., open to all disabilities of a particular ability level)? Integrated competition was made available to amputee and les autres athletes in air pistol, air rifle, archery, basketball, volleyball, and weight lifting; these were conducted by ISOD rules.

Several issues surrounding classification emerged during the 2 weeks of competition. Should classifications be medical or functional? Disability-specific or integrated? Sport-specific (i.e., a classification for each sport) or general (one classification for several sports)? Should sports be adapted to be accessible to all athletes, or should individuals be required to possess minimal functional abilities to qualify as international competitors? Should the status of elite athlete be attainable by all athletes, regardless of the level of disability, or should it be reserved for people whose sport performances most closely resemble able-bodied elitism?

The intent of this paper is to describe the athletes eligible to compete under the International Blind Sports Association (IBSA), the Cerebral Palsy-International Sports and Recreation Association (CP-ISRA), and the ISOD, respectively, to present the classification system(s) used by each governing body, and to state the rationale of each. Classification and eligibility issues of mutual concern are discussed, and philosophies are contrasted. Differences between international and U.S. practices are stated also.

On the issue of functional versus medical classification, the CP-ISRA and the ISOD are in agreement. Both favor functional classifications based on appraisal of strength, range of motion, motor coordination, and balance, rather than determining the site of the lesion and etiology of the condition. This is in marked contrast with the medical classification system used by the International Stoke Mandeville Games Federation (ISMGF).

Classification of Blind Athletes

Functional classification also is favored by the IBSA, but the function assessed is the amount of usable vision rather than the movement capability. The functional classification system used is presented in Table 1.

Blind athletes are reclassified annually by a certified optometrist or ophthalmologist. Until 1982, the United States Association for Blind Athletes

Table 1. Sport classifications for blind people

B-1. Encompasses a range in sightlessness from no light perception at all in either eye up to ability to perceive light, but inability to recognize objects or contours in any directions and at any distance.

B-2. Ability to recognize objects or contours up to a visual acuity of 2/60 and/or a limitation of field vision of 5 degrees.

B-3. 2/60 to 6/60 (20/200) vision and/or field of vision between 5 and 60 degrees.

(USABA), which was formed in 1976, used a slightly different system (A, B, C) from that adopted by the IBSA in 1981. In both the IBSA, and the USABA, athletes only compete against people with the same visual classifications except in goal ball, wrestling, and power lifting. In goal ball, visual ability is equalized by all players wearing blindfolds. Although IBSA rules make no allowance for the time of onset of blindness (congenital vs. adventitious), many people believe that this factor makes a difference and should be subjected to research. Table 2 presents an analysis of 49 of the 59 U.S. blind athletes who competed in the 1984 International Games for the Disabled.

Table 2. Amount of usable vision of male and female blind U.S. athletes competing in the 1984 International Games for the Disabled

Vision status	Males	Females	Total
B-1			
Congenital	4	1	5
Adventitious	11	1	12
Total	15	2	17
B-2			
Congenital	3	3	6
Adventitious	4	1	5
Total	7	4	11
B-3			
Congenital	10	9	19
Adventitious	2	0	2
Total	12	9	21

Note. This table includes 34 of the 36 males and 15 of the 24 females who competed.

Cerebral Palsied Athletes

Cerebral palsy (CP) is a group of neuromuscular conditions, not a disease. It is caused by damage to an area or areas of the brain which control and coordinate muscle tone, reflexes, and action. This brain damage can vary widely; therefore, the degree of muscular involvement in CP can range from severe spasticity to slight speech impairment. CP is not hereditary, contagious, or progressive (Jones, 1984).

Much of the rationale for the disability-specific classification system in cerebral palsy sport pertains to the prevalence of associated dysfunctions that occur in conjunction with upper motor neuron lesions. Unlike spinal cord injured athletes and competitors whose disabilities only affect the strength, balance, and range of motion of their lower extremities, people with cerebral palsy typically have to cope with abnormal reflex activity and muscle tone, perceptual-motor problems, visual dysfunction, learning disabilities, and other "soft signs" of neurological damage such as attentional deficiencies, hyperkinesis, and impulsivity (Bleck & Nagel, 1982; Sherrill, 1981; Thompson, Rubin, & Bilenker, 1983). Although these problems are not discussed in current

CP-ISRA and National Association of Sports for Cerebral Palsy (NASCP) manuals, official classifiers are trained to observe and take them into consideration when making classification judgments.

It has been estimated that 88% of the general CP population has three or more disabilties (Thompson et al., 1983, p. 87). While much has been published on the general CP population in regard to associated dysfunctions, little is known about CP athletes as a specific subpopulation. The major difference between the general CP population and the CP athlete subpopulation seems to be cognitive functioning. Current texts state that 30–70% of the general CP population have mental retardation (Bleck & Nagel, 1982, p. 72; Levine, Carey, Crocker, & Gross, 1983, p. 792; Thompson et al., 1983, p. 88). In marked contrast to this, CP sport experts indicate that only 10–15% of NASCP athletes have mental retardation (Sherrill & Adams-Mushett, 1984). The performance qualifying standards for national and international CP competition are such that few people with both cerebral palsy and mental retardation can demonstrate the times and distance required for inclusion in sport events. The 1983 *NASCP Manual* (p. 11) specifically states that CP sports are for athletes who are not eligible for the Special Olympics (i.e., people with cerebral palsy who demonstrate average or better intellectual functioning). Current assessment theory emphasizes the difficulties in accurately determining the IQs of several disabled cerebral palsied individuals, however, and much work is needed in this area. Many people with cerebral palsy, previously considered mentally retarded because of communication and other disorders, are now believed to have IQs within the average range.

Newer texts (Thompson et al., 1983) are beginning to stress learning disabilities rather than mental retardation as characteristic of much of the general CP population. Illustrative of this trend is the following:

> Subtle deficiencies in central processing manifest themselves as *an uneven profile* or *scatter* on psychologic testing and as learning dysfunction in the school-age child. In cerebral palsy, scatter is simply a marker of disordered neurologic functioning. In our experience, children who ''scatter'' seldom do as well as would be predicted by the summary scale . . . The prevalence of learning dysfunction in cerebral palsy is unknown but appears high. (Thompson et al., 1983, pp. 88–89)

In order to contrast the percentage of associated dysfunctions reported for the general CP population with what seems to characterize the CP athlete subpopulation, Sherrill (1984) requested five CP sport experts to estimate the percentages of each dysfunction for Class 1–4 and 5–8 athletes. The results of this survey appear in Table 3. To emphasize the difference between CP athletes and the CP general population, these findings are compared with those reported in medical texts.

Concerning visual problems, CP experts estimate that 25% of their athletes are affected. Bleck and Nagel (1982) give no statistics but state that

> Many . . . are far sighted (hyperopia); nearsightedness (myopia) is seen mostly in prematures. Inwardly crossed eyes (esotropia) are six times more common than turned-out eyes (exotropia). Failure of the upward gaze is characteristic of athetosis due to Rh incompatibility. (p. 17)

Table 3. Mean percentages of associated dysfunctions in cerebral palsied athletes based on estimates by five CP sport experts

Associated dysfunctions	Class 1–4	Class 5–8	Total
Visual problems	30	20	25
Perceptual disorders	75	50	63
Hearing problems	15	8	12
Learning disabilities	55	40	48
Reflex problems	85	50	68
Seizures	40	20	30
Mental retardation	15	10	13

Thompson et al. (1983, p. 90) state that strabismus (crossed eyes) affects approximately 50% of the CP population and is the most common visual disturbance associated with cerebral palsy. Of CP persons with hemiplegia (lateral paralysis), 25% have been diagnosed as having homonymous hemianopsia (i.e., blindness in one half of the field of vision, specifically blindness of the nasal half of one eye and the temporal half of the other eye). This is usually associated with a sensory deficit on the affected side.

With regard to perceptual-motor disorders, CP experts estimate that approximately 60% of their athletes are affected. Problems with spatial relationships (seeing things in a distorted manner) particularly affect staying in lanes during track events, positioning in soccer, and activities requiring targets. Molnar and Taft (1977) stated that 25–50% of the pediatric CP population have perceptual deficits. Little research, however, has been conducted on perceptual deficits in CP (Abercrombie, 1964); one reason for this is the difficulty in assessing whether the obvious problems are of an input, processing, or output nature.

CP sport experts estimate that about 12% of their athletes have hearing problems. Bleck and Nagel (1982) indicate that only 2% of people with spasticity have hearing problems but that hearing loss is common in people with athetosis, particularly that caused by rubella or Rh factor incompatibility. Thompson et al. (1983, p. 89) estimate that 6–16% of the CP population is deaf, with kernicteric athetoid children having the greatest incidence (about 60%).

Approximately 30% of CP athletes are believed to have seizures. This is consistent with Thompson et al. (1983, p. 91), who state that 25–35% of children with CP have seizures. In marked contrast, Bleck and Nagel (1982, p. 71) indicate that convulsive disorders occur in 86% and 12% of people with spasticity and athetosis, respectively. Molnar and Taft (1977) estimate that 25–50% have epilepsy.

Abnormal reflex activity and muscle tone, however, are the greatest problems affecting CP athletes. Almost all (85%) Class 1–4 athletes must cope with these, and 50% of Class 5–8 athletes are affected. The reflex problems of cerebral palsy are well documented (Bobath, 1980; Fiorentino, 1981; Kottke, Stillwell, & Lehmann, 1982), although percentages are seldom stated for adults. Bleck (1975) indicated that 94% of a nonambulatory CP sample retained primitive reflexes into adulthood. Muscle tone abnormalities are hypertonus (i.e., spasticity) and fluctuating hyper- and hypotonus (i.e., athetosis). Asked which type of cerebral palsy dominated or influenced their sport abilities most, 200 national level CP athletes indicated the following: spasticity, 61%; athetosis, 17%; other, 10%; and not applicable, 12% (Sherrill, Rainbolt, & Adams-Mushett, 1984).

Clearly the associated dysfunctions that characterize cerebral palsy athletes form a strong rationale for disability-specific rather than integrated classifications. Dr. Cairbre McCann, Chairperson of the Medical Committee of the ISMGF and also a member of the advisory committee of the NASCP, the U.S. governing body, summarized the justification for disability-specific classification as follows:

> Speaking as a physician who has witnessed the tremendous difficulties in attempting to match in sports competition cerebral palsied persons and paraplegics or quadriplegics in wheelchairs, it has been evident to me for a long time that in no way can fair competition exist in most cases in which we have attempted to fit the cerebral palsied competitor in the existing classification system [ISMGF] . . . The key element in this testing procedure [ISMGF] is the assessment of strength. Since persons with cerebral palsy may have very adequate strength but poor ability to coordinate or put this strength to use in athletic competition, the result has usually been in the past that the cerebral palsied person found himself [herself] placed in a totally unsuitable and unfair competition so that he [she] usually has been outclassed. (McCann, 1976, p. 19)

Classification of Cerebral Palsied Athletes

With reference to the medical versus functional classification issue, CP experts favor the functional approach. Not only is this classification system disability-specific but it is also sport-specific with each athlete assigned a classification for track, field, and swimming separately. Most athletes end up with the same classification for these three events, but approximately 15% have split classifications (e.g., Class 3 in track but Class 4 in field). When this occurs and one classification must be used for all athletes, as in research, the track classification is believed to be the most indicative of overall functional ability. Horseback riding entails a slightly different classification system with placements more similar to swimming than to track or field. The *NASCP Manual* stresses the following:

> An important point to conceptualize about the classification process is that two athletes may have the same *functional ability*, but the quality of their *performance* may differ due to better technique and conditioning. Also, it is conceivable that an athlete may improve his/her functional ability because of vigorous participation in sport and therefore necessitate a possible change in classification. (NASCP, 1983, p. 14)

The sport ability classifications used for track and field by the CP-ISRA, as well as the NASCP, are presented in summary form in Table 4.

In summary, about half of all cerebral palsied athletes compete in wheelchairs (i.e., are functionally nonambulatory), and about half are ambulatory. An

Table 4. Sport classifications for persons with cerebral palsy

Class 1. Uses motorized wheelchair because almost no functional use of upper extremities. Severe involvement in all four limbs, limited trunk control, has only 25% range of motion. Unable to grasp softball.

Class 2. Propels chair with feet and/or very slowly with arms. Severe to moderate involvement in all four limbs. Uneven functional profile necessitating subclassification as 2 Upper (2U) or 2 Lower (2L), with adjective denoting limbs having greater functional ability. Has approximately 40% range of motion. Severe control problems in accuracy tasks, generally more athetosis than spasticity.

Class 3. Propels chair with short, choppy arm pushes but generates fairly good speed. Moderate involvement in three or four limbs and trunk. Has approximately 60% range of motion. Can take a few steps with assistive devices but not functionally ambulatory.

Class 4. Propels chair with forceful, continuous arm pushes, demonstrating excellent functional ability for wheelchair sports. Involvement of lower limbs only. Good strength in trunk and upper extremities. Has approximately 70% range of motion. Minimal control problems.

Class 5. Ambulates without wheelchair but typically uses assistive devices (crutches, canes, walkers). Moderate to severe spasticity of either (a) arm and leg on same side (hemiplegia) or (b) both lower limbs (paraplegia). Has approximately 80% range of motion.

Class 6. Ambulates without assistive devices, but has obvious balance and coordination difficulties. Has more control problems and less range of motion in upper extremities than Classes 4 and 5. Moderate to severe involvement of three or four limbs, with approximately 70% range of motion in dominant arm.

Class 7. Ambulates well but with slight limp. Moderate to mild spasticity in (a) arm and leg on same side or (b) all four limbs with 90% of normal range of motion for quadriplegia and 90–100% of normal range of motion for dominant arm for hemiplegia.

Class 8. Runs and jumps freely without noticeable limp. Demonstrates good balance and symmetric form in performance but has obvious (although minimal) coordination problems. Has normal range of motion.

analysis of 200 adult athletes in the Fourth National Cerebral Palsy Games in the United States revealed that 47% were in Classes 1–4 and 53% were in Classes 5–8 (Sherrill et al., 1984).

Classification Procedure

To assure valid, up-to-date classifications, athletes are required to go through the classification process immediately prior to each meet. The CP-ISRA procedure is similar to that described in the NASCP Manual as follows:

The first procedure is to compare the functional profile of the athlete with the functional profile described for each of the eight classes. This is done through observation and a series of questions about the athlete's daily living skills. From this initial assessment, a classifier will be able to determine an overall classification group.

The next procedure is to conduct a series of eight tests which measure upper extremity and torso function and an additional four tests for ambulant athletes to assess lower extremity function and stability. The tests measure speed, accuracy, and range of motion rather than strength, as coordination and motion are the deterring effects of cerebral palsy rather than strength.

Each test has an affixed set of points. Each class has a range of points. The addition of the points, along with the classifier's functional assessment, determine the classification for each athlete in track, field, and swimming. (NASCP, 1983, p. 13)

For assignment of swimming classifications, the NASCP National Advisory Committee recently agreed that the observational process should take place in a swimming pool. McCann, a member of this Advisory Committee and a physician with many years of experience in ISMGF classification, discussed the merits of certifiers' observing athletes during actual competition to reduce faking and optimize classification validity. Faking has been a problem with spinal cord injured athletes (McCann, 1980), and McCann emphasized that steps should be taken to prevent similar problems with CP athletes. Several athletes have noted that such faking and/or incorrect classification was occurring at the 1984 International Games for the Disabled. Class 2 to 4 athletes cannot (by classification standards) be functional walkers, even with assistive devices. Yet several Class 2 to 4 athletes were observed functionally walking, and some were so bold as to leave their chairs and ambulate up to the awards stand to receive medals. Clearly many problems must still be resolved in the classification of CP athletes. Many of these problems relate, at least in part, to the qualifications of the classifiers.

Certification of Official CP Sport Classifiers

Classification procedures are implemented by certified classifiers who have extensive backgrounds in neurology, biomechanics, exercise physiology, and CP sports as well as special, intensive training in the classification process itself. At present these testing procedures are implemented primarily by physicians and physical therapists as is the practice in ISMGF with spinal cord injured athletes. A topic open to debate is whether classification primarily should be the domain of medicine or open to anyone who meets specified standards. Some experts favor physicians and physical therapists whereas others believe continued adherence to a medical model implementation procedure is incongruent with the concept of functional classification. Doctoral level adapted physical education and therapeutic recreation specialists, with graduate training in neurophysiology, perceptual motor function, biomechanics, exercise physiology, and CP sports, may well be as competent as physicians and physical therapists in functional classification matters. All experts agree, however, that the training and certification process for official classifiers should be very stringent and that certification should be updated at least every 2 years. The cadre of official national and international classifiers should be limited to 10 to 15 individuals of excellence.

Les Autres Athletes

Les autres, the French term for "the others," is used in sport literature to denote other locomotor disabilities. Competition for les autres is governed by the ISOD, which also governs competition for amputees. Twenty of the 52 countries competing at the 1984 International Games for the Disabled brought les autres athletes. Countries winning the most les autres medals were Great Britain (55), Spain (38), and the United States (26). The conditions of the 15 les autres members of the USA team were as follows:

Muscular dystrophy—4	Arthrogryposis—1
Multiple sclerosis—2	Osteogenesis imperfecta—3
Friedreich's ataxia—2	Short stature—1
Organic brain syndrome—1	Ehlers-Danlos syndrome—1

Brief descriptions of these conditions and others listed in the *ISOD Handbook* (1983) include

1. Dwarfism. (Dwarfs are better known in the United States as *little people* because of the efforts of their self-advocacy organization.) Dwarfism is medically defined as short stature (i.e., physical growth which is more than three standard deviations from the mean for the age group). Although many causes of dwarfism have been established (Bleck & Nagel, 1982), the *chondrodystrophies* (defects of endochondral ossification resulting from failure of the skeleton to respond to the normal hormonal growth stimuli) appear most common. Among terms used to specify dwarfism are the skeletal dysplasias, achrondroplasia, and the Morquio syndrome.

2. Congential disorders of bones and connective tissue like osteogenesis imperfecta and Ehlers-Danlos syndrome. *Osteogenesis imperfecta* (OI) is an inherited condition in which bones are abnormally soft and brittle and therefore are easily breakable. These breaks peak between 2 and 15 years, after which the incidence of fractures is reduced. Characteristics include short stature and small limbs that are bowed in various distortions resulting from repetitive fractures. Joints are hyperextensible with a predisposition for dislocation. Most athletes with OI are in wheelchairs. *Ehlers-Danlos syndrome* is an inherited condition characterized by hyperextensibility of joints with a predisposition for dislocation at the shoulder girdle, shoulder, elbow, hip, and knee joints. Other features are loose and/or hyperextensible skin, slow wound healing with inadequate scar tissue, and fragility of blood vessel walls. Smith (1976, p. 284) states that these people should be cautioned to avoid traumatic situations.

3. Arthrogryposis multiplex congenita (AMC). AMC is a nonprogressive congenital contracture syndrome usually characterized by internal rotation at the shoulder joints, elbow extension, pronated forearms, radial flexion of wrists, flexion and outward rotation at the hip joint, and abnormal

positions of knees and feet. Most athletes with AMC are in wheelchairs and have a very limited range of motion.

4. Limb deficiencies, including *dysmelia* (absence of arms or legs) and *phocomelia* (absence of the middle segment of a limb, but with intact proximal and distal portions). In the latter, hands or feet are attached directly to shoulders or hips respectively. It is sometimes unclear, from casual observation, whether limb deficiencies should be considered as les autres or as congenital amputations. The *ISOD Handbook* (1983, III-6-1) states that in swimming, for instance, congenital amputations leaving hands or feet intact, in most cases, belong to the amputee classes. The limb deficiency category of les autres was designed for conditions not classifiable within the amputee system.

5. Anisomelia. Anisomelia, referring to a condition of asymmetry between limbs, characterizes many individuals who have recovered from poliomyelitis and diseases or injuries that paralyze only one side of the body. The eligibility requirement is at least 7 cm asymmetry for most sports and 10 cm for swimming. In contrast to this ISOD rule, athletes with postpolio disability in the U.S. compete with spinal cord injured rather than with les autres athletes.

6. Ankylosis, arthrodesis, or arthritis of major joints. *Ankylosis* is a stiffening or restriction of the normal range of motion of a joint by tissue changes within or without the joint cavity (Brashear & Raney, 1978, p. 170). It results from chronic arthritis, infection, or trauma, including severe burns around a joint. Among the more common types is *ankylosing spondylitis* (Bechterew disease or chronic arthritis of the sacroiliac joints and lumbar spine). *Arthrodesis* (i.e., fusion) is the surgical fixation of a joint used to stabilize a paralyzed or excessively hypotonic limb like a flail (dangle) foot or any joint in which muscle paralysis causes subluxation, dislocation, or complete lack of limb control (Drennan, 1983, pp. 92–128).

7. Conditions characterized by muscle weakness that are caused by peripheral nerve (axon) damage like the Barre-Guillain and Charcot-Marie-Tooth syndromes. Barre-Guillain syndrome, a transient condition of muscle weakness, is similar in symptomology to polio (Brashear & Raney, 1978, p. 222). Recovery is usually complete but may require many months of bracing and therapy; some individuals are left with residual muscle and respiratory weakness (Kottke et al., 1982, p. 686). In contrast, people do not recover from Charcot-Marie-Tooth syndrome, which usually occurs between ages 5–10 years and progresses very, very slowly (Brashear & Raney, 1978, pp. 222–223). Clinically, Charcot syndrome begins with the involvement of the peroneal (lateral lower leg) muscles and moves slowly upward. Steppage gait (increased flexion of the hip and knee during swing-phase) compensates for the drop foot caused by peroneal weakness. Eventually upper extremity weakness interferes with throwing and catching activities and fine motor control is diminished. Motor performance and physical capacity vary widely among people with Charcot-Marie-Tooth syndrome; six specific types have been identified (Drennan, 1983, pp. 171–177).

8. Muscular dystrophies (MDs). MDs are genetically determined conditions in which muscular weakness is attributed to changes in muscle fibers. Muscle cells degenerate and are replaced by fat and fibrous tissue. The most common types are Duchenne, Facio-Scapular-Humeral, and Limb Girdle.

9. Multiple sclerosis (MS). MS is a condition of a progressive muscle weakness with many associated problems (vision, speech, bladder) caused by disintegration of the myelin covers of nerve fibers throughout the body. MS is characterized by periods of relative incapacitation followed by periods of remission.

10. Friedreich's ataxia. Friedreich's ataxia is an inherited condition in which the sensory nerves of the limbs and trunk progressively degenerate (Bleck & Nagel, 1982, pp. 309-312). The most common of the spinocerebellar degenerations, Friedreich's ataxia first occurs between ages 5-15 years. The primary characteristics are ataxia (poor balance), clumsiness, and a lack of agility; but many associated defects (slurred speech, diminished fine motor control, discoordination and tremor of the upper extremities, vision abnormalities, and skeletal deformities) may develop and affect sport performance. Degeneration may be slow or rapid with many people becoming wheelchair users by their late teens; others may manifest only one or two clinical signs and remain minimally affected throughout their lives.

These brief descriptions serve to emphasize that some les autres athletes, like cerebral palsied, are affected by associated dysfunctions. Tremendous individual differences characterize the les autres disabilities as well as the athletes themselves.

Classification of Les Autres Athletes

Like the CP-ISRA and the NASCP, the ISOD supports functional rather than medical classifications. The *ISOD Handbook* (1983) specifies the following system for use in determining functional performance in relation to lower-limb strength, upper-limb strength, range of motion, amputation, anisomelia (inequality between two paired limbs), and back/torso deformities.

In addition to this general classification approach, the ISOD (like the CP-ISRA) presents functional profiles against which athletes are compared. A difference between the ISOD and the CP-ISRA is the extent to which the two organizations believe in sport-specific versus sport-general classifications. The CP-ISRA assigns three general classifications for athletes: (a) track, which is used also for slalom, soccer, bowling, bicycling, and tricycling; (b) field, which is used also for archery, riflery, table tennis, and weight lifting; and (c) swimming, which is generalized to horseback riding. In contrast, the ISOD offers functional profile descriptions for each of its 16 sports: air pistol, air rifle, archery, field, lawn bowling, swimming, table tennis, track, volleyball sitting, volleyball standing, weight lifting, Alpine and Nordic skiing, biathlon (10 k track and air rifle), nordic sledge, downhill sledge, sledge racing, and

Table 5. ISOD classification system for les autres athletes

1. *Partial or total paralysis of lower limbs:*
   At least a decrease in muscle strength of 10 points in the lower extremities when testing on the 0–5 scale grade system (not counting Grade 1 and 2). A normal person obtains 40 points in each lower limb. The following muscle functions shall be tested in lower limbs:

		Maximum
Hip	Flexion	5
Hip	Extension	5
Hip	Abduction	5
Hip	Adduction	5
Knee	Flexion	5
Knee	Extension	5
Ankle	Dorsiflexion	5
Ankle	Plantarflexion	5

Total sum each lower limb = 40

2. *Partial or total paralysis of upper limbs:*
   At least a decrease in muscle strength of 20 points in the upper extremities when testing on the 0–5 scale grade system (not counting Grade 1 and 2). A normal person obtains 60 points in each upper limb. The following muscle functions in the arm and hand shall be tested:

		Maximum
Shoulder	Flexion	5
Shoulder	Extension	5
Shoulder	Abduction	5
Shoulder	Adduction	5
Elbow	Flexion	5
Elbow	Extension	5
Wrist	Dorsiflexion	5
Wrist	Volarflexion	5
Finger	Flexion (finger 2–5) at the metacarpo-phalangeal joints	5
Finger	Extension (finger 2–5) at the metacarpo-phalangeal joints	5
Thumb	Opposition	5
Thumb	Extension	5

Total sum each upper limb = 60

3. *Joint mobility:*
   At least a permanent restricted movement of 30 degrees in shoulder, elbow, wrist, hip, knee, or ankle joint.

Cont.

Table 5. (Cont.)

4. *Amputation:*
   Minimum 4 fingers amputated. NOTE: In amputee based classification, minimum amputation is through wrist joint.

5. *Anisomelia:*
   At least 7 cm.

6. *Back and torso:*
   Severely reduced mobility or disfiguration of a permanent nature as in idiopathic scoliosis, dwarfism, or ankylosis of the spine.

Table 6. Track and field classifications for les autres athletes

L–1. Wheelchair bound. Reduced functions of muscle strength, and/or spasticity in throwing arm. Poor sitting balance.

L–2. Wheelchair bound with normal function in throwing arm and poor to moderate sitting balance. Or, reduced function in throwing arm, but good sitting balance.

L–3. Wheelchair bound with normal arm function and good sitting balance.

L–4. Ambulant with or without crutches and braces; or problems with the balance together with reduced function in throwing arm. Throw can be done from a standstill or moving position.

L–5. Ambulant with normal function in throwing arm. Reduced function in lower extremities or balance problem. Throw can be done from a standstill or moving position.

L–6. Ambulant with normal upper extremity function in throwing arm and minimal trunk or lower extremity disability. A participant in this class must be able to demonstrate a locomotor disability which clearly gives him/her a disadvantage in throwing events compared to able-bodied sportsmen and -women (Koch, 1984, p. 20).

---

sledge hockey. The sport ability classifications used for track and field by the ISOD are presented in summary form in Table 6.

Differences Between CP and ISOD Views

The NASCP in the United States, which at this time governs les autres competition, recently voted not to use the ISOD les autres classifications. The NASCP, which has offered national competition for les autres athletes since 1979, will continue to use the CP classification system for les autres athletes.

Although included in the same meets, CP and les autres competitive events are conducted separately in the U.S. Plans are now underway to develop a separate sport organization for les autres athletes that will be represented on the U.S. Olympic Committee. In the U.S., athletes with amputations also have a separate organization and compete only against other amputees except in wheelchair basketball and marathons. These U.S. practices highlight a major philosophical conflict between the ISOD and other national and international sport organizations: the issue of disability-integrated versus disability-specific sport. The ISOD strongly supports disability-integrated sport as evidenced by the following statements from its handbook:

4.3.1 *General*

The system is a functional classification system applicable to locomotor disabilities regardless of diagnoses. Athletes belonging to the categories of amputees, cerebral palsied and spinal cord affected (para-tetra-polio) are allowed to participate in certain events in the Les Autres classification. Therefore the classification code is uniquely defined for each sport.

4.1.2 In some sports it is from a functional viewpoint quite possible for athletes with different diagnoses to compete in the same class without major advantages or disadvantages for any of the athletes, i.e., shooting events, bench-press weightlifting, etc. In such cases combined classes in some events may be constructed. In such combined classes, classification will be described under the specific sports rules respectively.

A major proponent of integrated classification, Hans Lindstrom, Secretary-General of the ISOD, explains his stand in the next chapter. Two experts, Birgitta Blomgwist of West Germany and Dave Williamson of England, have extensively studied integrated classifications specifically in relation to swimming (Blomgwist, 1983; Williamson, 1984). Blomgwist approached the problem through biomechanical analysis whereas Williamson analyzed the success of each ability group and class in computer-simulated races based upon a proposed integration system. On a medal count in the computer-simulated races, Williamson reported that amputees dominated the tallies, les autres and spinal cord injured were about equal, and cerebral palsied athletes came in last. The integrated classification system is supported in the U.S. mainly by Julian Stein, Director of Programs for the Handicapped, American Alliance for Health, Physical Education, Recreation, and Dance, 1966–1981 (Stein, 1985) and Stan Labanowich, Executive-Director of the National Wheelchair Basketball Association (Labanowich, Karman, Veal, & Wiley, 1984).

Another major difference between CP and ISOD sport philosophy pertains to opportunity and elitism issues. The CP-ISRA and the NASCP believe that each of their major sports should be made available to all athletes regardless of the severity level of the disability. Thus classifications exist for individuals so disabled that their functional ability is limited to controlling a motorized chair, swimming with a personal flotation device, and projecting light objects (5 oz) at targets. These are the Class 1 and 2 athletes in the CP-ISRA and the NASCP. These organizations strongly believe that Class 1 and 2 athletes, as they progress to national and international competition, have the same right as the less severely disabled to be considered *elite*. As long as a person represents the best in his or her sport classification, opportunities for inclusion in international competition should be made available. In contrast, the *ISOD Handbook* (1983) states

4.1.1 ISOD classifies amputees and les autres . . . an athlete may be eligible for a certain sport in a certain class, but at the same time belong to another class in another sport, *or even be not eligible at all for some sport* [italics by authors].

Hans Lindstrom, Secretary-General of the ISOD, emphasizes that disabled people who require flotation devices to swim and other adaptations that grossly change the nature of a sport should not be allowed to compete. He recommends, in this regard, that a disabled person "choose a sport which best suits his functional ability" (Lindstrom, 1984, p. 16). This stance seems to disregard the fact that some people have such limited functional abilities that no sport, without considerable adaptation, meets their needs. Thus the U.S., by choosing to use CP rather than les autres classifications to govern les autres competition, affirms the right of any person to become an athlete, to compete against opponents of similar abilities, and to progress (if willing to work hard enough) to elite status.

Amputee Athletes

Amputee sports are governed by the ISOD. In the U.S., summer sports are ruled by the U.S. Amputee Athletic Association, founded in 1981, and winter sports are conducted under the auspices of the National Handicapped Sports and Recreation Association, founded in 1967. Many U.S. amputees compete in wheelchair basketball under the National Wheelchair Athletic Association (NWAA), which uses the integrated classification system described by Horst Strohkendl earlier in this volume. Others compete in the open category of such NWAA events as track, field, swimming, table tennis, archery, and riflery.

Classification of Amputee Athletes

Amputations may be congenital or acquired but this factor is irrelevant to the classification system. Limb deficiencies, described under les autres, should not be confused with amputations. Since May 1982, the U.S. Amputee Athletic Association has used the same classification system as the ISOD.

Combinations of amputations not specified in this code are placed in the class closest to the actual disability. Thus an AK + BK would be assigned to Class A-1 (wheelchair) in track, either A-1 or A-3 (standing) in field and table tennis depending upon his or her choice, and either A-1 or A-3 in swimming depending upon the length of the stumps.

Regulations concerning prostheses, orthoses, and assistive devices are important. In air pistol, air rifle, and swimming, for instance, prostheses and orthoses are not permitted. In archery the draw may be made with a prosthesis or orthosis, and a releasing aid may be used by Classes A-6, A-8, and A-9. These classes may also receive help with loading arrows into the bow. In field events the wearing of a prosthesis is optional. In volleyball lower-limb prostheses and orthoses are permitted, but upper-limb aids are not. In lawn

Table 7. Sport classifications for people with amputations

Nine General Classifications for Amputees

Class A-1 = Double AK	Class A-7 = Double BE
Class A-2 = Single AK	Class A-8 = Single BE
Class A-3 = Double BK	Class A-9 = Combined lower plus upper
Class A-4 = Single BK	limb amputations
Class A-5 = Double AE	
Class A-6 = Single AE	

Five Track Classifications for Amputees

A-1/A-3 (AK + BK – Double lower limb amputee) combined *wheelchair class* (A-1 – A-2 – A-3) and (AK + BK)

A-4 *ambulatory class*, which also includes A-9 competitors with lower limb disability corresponding to A-4

A-5/A-7 combined = A-5/A-7
A-6/A-8 combined = A-6/A-8

Seven Field Classifications for Amputees

A-1/AK + BK wheelchair (A-1)	A-4
A-2	A-5/A-7 combined
A-3/AK + BK	A-6/A-8 combined
	A-9

Note. Competitors with above knee plus below knee amputation have the right to choose to compete in either A-1 wheelchair or A-3 standing. Changing of class during a meet is not permitted.

Abbreviations used are as follows: *AK*, above or through the knee joint; *BK*, below knee, but through or above talotibial joint; *AE*, above or through elbow joint; *BE*, below elbow but through or above wrist joint.

bowling Classes A-5 and/or A-7 may use prosthesis or orthosis if they wish. In table tennis, however, these are not allowed. Individuals who are unable to perform a regulation serve because of their disabilities are allowed to bounce the ball on the table and then smash it across the net. Lower-limb amputees have the option in many sports of using a wheelchair or standing/walking/running/jumping. Some sports are organized primarily by sitting versus standing rules. Sitting volleyball encompasses Classes A-1 to A-9, whereas only athletes in A-2–A-4 and A-6–A-9 are eligible for standing volleyball. Volleyball is an integrated classification sport with les autres as well as amputee athletes permitted to compete. To equalize abilities, a point system is used similar to that in wheelchair basketball (see chapter by Horst Strohkendl).

In track and field fewer classifications are used than for the other sports. In all track events except Class A-4 (and A-9 where applicable) the wearing of a prosthesis is optional. A-4 competitors are required to use a prosthesis since hopping is not permitted. Crutches and sticks are prohibited in all events. High and long jump competition is available to all classes except A-1 and A-3. Additionally the triple jump is conducted for males in Classes A-5–A-9. Classes A-2 and A-4 may use a running, hopping, or standing start for high and long jumps. Prostheses are optional in all events; no mention of crutches is made in the ISOD rules.

Summary

This paper has described athletes eligible to compete under the rules of the IBSA, the CP-ISRA, and the ISOD respectively and has presented the classification system(s) used by each organization. Only summer sports were discussed, with emphasis upon philosophies and practices demonstrated at the 1984 International Games for the Disabled in New York. The issues concerning classification, eligibility, and rules adaptation are complex. Scientific research is needed to provide objective bases for decision-making.

References

Abercrombie, M. (1964). *Perceptual and visuomotor disorders in cerebral palsy.* London: Heinemann.

Bleck, E.E. (1975). Locomotor progress in cerebral palsy. *Developmental Medicine and Child Neurology, 17,* 18–24.

Bleck, E.E., & Nagel, D. (Eds.). (1982). *Physically handicapped children: A medical atlas for teachers* (2nd ed.). New York: Grune & Stratton.

Blomgwist, B. (1983). *Proposal for integrated swimming classifications.* West Germany. (Available from Dr. Julian Stein, Physical Education Department, George Mason University, Fairfax, VA 22030).

Bobath, K. (1980). *A neurophysiological basis for the treatment of cerebral palsy.* London: Heinemann.

Brashear, H.R., & Raney, R.B. (1978). *Shands' handbook of orthopaedic surgery* (9th ed.). St. Louis: The C.V. Mosby Co.

Drennan, J. (1983). *Orthopaedic management of neuromuscular disorders.* Philadelphia: J.B. Lippincott.

Fiorentino, M. (1981). *A basis for sensorimotor development—Normal and abnormal.* Springfield, IL: Charles C. Thomas.

International Sports Organization for the Disabled (1983). *ISOD handbook.* Farsta, Sweden: Author.

Jones, J. (Ed.). (1984). *Training guide to cerebral palsy sports* (2nd ed.). New York: United Cerebral Palsy Associations, Inc.

Koch, F. (1984). Disability classification for competition. In International Games for the Disabled (Ed.), *Official program for 1984* (p. 20). Nassau County, NY: Author.

Kottke, F., Stillwell, G.K., & Lehmann, J. (1982). *Krusen's handbook of physical medicine and rehabilitation.* Philadelphia: W.B. Saunders.

Labanowich, S., Karman, P., Veal, L., & Wiley, B.D. (1984). The principles and foundations for organization of wheelchair sports. *Sports 'N Spokes, 9*(6), 25–32.

Levine, M., Carey, W., Crocker, A., & Gross, R. (1983). *Developmental behavioral pediatrics.* Philadelphia: W.B. Saunders.

Lindstrom, H. (1984). Sports for disabled alive and well. *Rehabilitation World, 8,* 12–16.

McCann, C. (1976). Sports activities for the cerebral palsied. *Sports 'N Spokes, 2,* 19–20.

McCann, C. (1980). Comments on classification in Charlotte. *Sports 'N Spokes, 6,* 19.

Molnar, G., & Taft, L. (1977). Pediatric rehabilitation. Part I. Cerebral palsy and spinal cord injuries. *Current Problems in Pediatrics, 7,* 28.

National Association of Sports for Cerebral Palsy. (1983). *NASCP-USA classification and rules manual* (2nd ed.). New York: Author.

Sherrill, C. (1981). *Adapted physical education and recreation: A multidisciplinary approach* (2nd. ed.). Dubuque, IA: Wm C. Brown.

Sherrill, C. (1984). *Associated dysfunctions of cerebral palsied athletes.* Unpublished manuscript, Texas Woman's University, Denton.

Sherrill, C., & Adams-Mushett, C. (1984). Fourth national cerebral palsy games: Sports by ability . . . not disability. *Palaestra, 1,* 24–27, 49–51.

Sherrill, C., Rainbolt, W., & Adams-Mushett, C. (1984). *Characteristics of CP athletes competing in national meets.* Unpublished manuscript, Texas Woman's University, Denton.

Smith, D. (1976). *Recognizable patterns of human malformation* (2nd ed.). Philadephia: W.B. Saunders.

Stein, J. (1985). *Analyses of performance results related to classification of athletes in the 1984 International Games for the Disabled.* Unpublished manuscript, Physical Education Department, George Mason University, Fairfax, VA.

Thompson, G., Rubin, I., & Bilenker, R. (Eds.). (1983). *Comprehensive management of cerebral palsy.* New York: Grune & Stratton.

Williamson, D.C. (1984). *Swimming: An inquiry on the participation levels and comparative performances of competitors with particular focus on integrated competition.* Unpublished manuscript, Physical Education Division, Trent Polytechnic, Clifton, Nottingham, England NG11 8NS.

12

Sports Classification for Locomotor Disabilities: Integrated Versus Diagnostic Systems

Hans Lindström
SECRETARY GENERAL, ISOD
FARSTA, SWEDEN

Two different systems for classification of locomotor disabilities exist in the world: the diagnosis-oriented system and the integrated system.

1. The *diagnosis-oriented system* classifies one single type of disability either functionally (cerebral palsy [CP] sports) or medically (spinal cord injured sports) according to locomotive power/ability. The classification varies in different sports depending on what physical requirements are needed to perform in the sport. Only people with a specific type of disability (diagnosis) compete against each other in this classification system. The Stoke Mandeville Games for spinal cord injured athletes and the CP World Games are conducted according to this system. Some International Sports Organization for the Disabled (ISOD) sports with exclusive classification for amputees are also diagnosis-oriented (i.e., swimming, track, and field).
2. The *integrated system* classifies disabled athletes in one single sport functionally according to locomotive power/ability. The classification varies in the sports similarly to the diagnosis system. Any person fitting into the definition of locomotive disabilities is eligible. Winter sports for locomotor disabilities have an integrated classification. Because of the number of possible diagnoses, the classification system for les autres must be formulated as an integrated classification system. The ISOD has integrated classification shooting events, table tennis, volleyball, and weightlifting since it is believed that the physical requirements for these sports are independent

of whether the type of disability is amputee or les autres. The International Stoke Mandeville Games Federation (ISMGF) has integrated classification in wheelchair basketball. In a letter of agreement, in July 1982, the Cerebral Palsy-International Sports and Recreation Association (CP-ISRA), the ISMGF, and the ISOD agreed to accept the concept of the two different systems (Lindström, 1983).

Historical Background

The international development of sport for disabled people has unquestionably been led by the ISMGF under the formidable leadership of Sir Ludwig Guttmann and Joan Scruton, who also propelled the development of the ISOD for practically all of its years. Although definitely creating the basic ideals for all disabled sport, the ISMGF line of development was, from the beginning, naturally bound by the original concept, which concentrated on one single disability group—the spinal cord paralyzed. What could be more natural by the long-experienced international leadership but to expect other disability groups to undergo the same type of development?

This is also what happened in about half of the nations promoting disabled sport. But evolution took another path in the remaining half of the nations; They developed classification systems that integrated all types of locomotor disabilities into one classification for each sport. Some countries developed a coefficient system for national and bilateral use. Other countries developed a system of functional description of locomotor disabilities, normally a little different from sport to sport, depending on which functions the sport in question requires.

In 1984 it is clearly evident that two different systems for classification of locomotor disabilities exist in the world. Acceptance of this fact is essential for further development in competitive sports for locomotor disabilities on the international level.

Overall Classification Philosophy

Classification in sport has existed since the beginning of organized sport competition. To rule out differences in muscle mass between genders, men and women compete in different classes in sports where muscle mass is important. The male power sports (i.e., weightlifting, boxing, and wrestling) have a classification for exactly the same reasons. It is recognized that smaller and lighter men with lesser muscle mass have a wish and a right to compete on equal terms in these sports. In combative sports the safety factor is perhaps an additional reason for the classification. Large differences in muscle mass in combat situations create injury risks.

In view of these facts, it is perhaps more surprising than logical that sports for able-bodied people have not also developed classifications because of variations in physical qualities like, for instance, stature. A tall stature is definitely important for basketball scorers and high jumpers.

Another logical reason for classification in competitive sports is variation in the ability to move. Therefore disabled athletes with locomotor disabilities are classified according to such variation. The motive for this is recognition of the disabled athlete's wish and right to compete in sports on equal terms. This recognition is so far mainly limited to the disabled sport movement, but will in due time embrace the sport movement in total. Classification in competitive sports has identical motives for able-bodied and disabled athletes. It should be regarded as one single system.

Fairness in Classification

Classification in competitive sports is the means to fairness for individual athletes. Fairness in competitive sports singularly means that every participant in an event shall have equal possibilities to become the winner—the one who will receive the award and applause. It does not mean that all competitors in the event necessarily must be near to equal in performance. The degree of performance is proportional to the amount of training and talent. Fair classification for locomotor disabilities must therefore be based on equal possibilities in relation to functional (not performance) abilities. Among the international organizations that have developed classification systems according to the functional abilities principle are the CP-ISRA and the ISOD.

In constructing a classification system, it is totally impossible to obtain ultimate justice and still keep the competitive element. Total equality in weightlifting and the contact combat sports would require one class for about every kg of bodyweight, which would give us roughly about 50 classes. The individuals on the lower scale of each existing bodyweight class of about 10 kg will be at a disadvantage to the heavier competitors. This disadvantage can only be compensated through more training, better talent, and stronger willpower.

It is also impossible to create a totally fair classification system based on medical conditions. Length of amputated stumps and levels of traumatic injuries on the spinal cord together with functioning remaining muscle groups and functional profiles of cerebral palsied athletes will require an upper and a lower limit to define the classes, giving an advantage to the upper-limit fortunate people, just as in able-bodied sport classifications. Putting the type of disabilities together into one single classification system for each sport, based on locomotive power/ability, would not be fairer than the system for each disability. Nor would it be more unfair.

Disabled sports have a tendency to exaggerate the value of fairness. I call this the *justice syndrome* (Lindström, 1984). It probably originates from pity. The idea is that every disabled person should have a medal. After all, they are trying so hard. The idea assumes that justice must be built into the classification system and that every disabled person should have an opportunity to compete in practically any given sport. In extenso this would lead to one class for each disabled sportsman, since practically no disability is totally identical in two different people. The justice syndrome is the reason why swimming events exist in the International Games for the Disabled, in which the use of floating devices and the allowance of the coach swimming beside the "competitor" is permitted. Just as a person with a short stature would not choose high jumping or basketball for his sport, so a disabled person should not choose a sport that does not suit his or her functional ability.

At the 1980 Olympic Games for the Disabled in Arnhem, Holland, locomotor disabilities were divided into 18 different classes in shot put. According to current rules, now 26 classes exist for shot put for locomotor disabilities. Men and women together will require 52 gold medals in shot put during the 1984 International Games for the Disabled, not counting 6 medals for the blind. The 26 shot put classes reduce the value of a gold medal from a competitive point of view, just as an increase from 10 to 26 weight classes in able-bodied weightlifting would do to that sport. In approximately 15–20 of the 52 possible competitions in shot put at the 1984 International Games for the Disabled, there will not be enough entries to hold the competition.

No classification system in competitive sports, for able-bodied or disabled athletes, will ever be totally fair to every individual; those being near the upper limit of the class definition will always have an advantage over those near the lower limit. Although the amount of fairness increases with the number of intervals between upper and lower limits defining a class, the idea of competitive sport is gradually lost as the number of classes increases.

Labanowich, Karman, Veal, and Wiley (1984) have proposed the idea that only people who use wheelchairs should be eligible to compete in sports for disabled athletes. This is the wheelchair syndrome approach to fairness (Lindström, 1984). Its advocates insist that only people with disabilities in the lower extremities should be eligible for sports for disabled athletes. All others are referred to as sports for able-bodied athletes. Apart from disqualifying the deaf, the blind, and the mentally handicapped, this view also effectively blocks competitive sports for most people with locomotor disabilities. Although the use of a wheelchair often rules out variations of ability in disabled persons with handicapping conditions in the lower limbs, there are many interesting sports that some lower limb disabilities can and should do from a standing position, like for instance skiing and shooting events. Skiing is an activity which is very suitable for lower limb amputees because of its gliding movements in relation to the ground, whereas running for this group contains a rather unnatural movement with high stress on stumps and/or hip joints. So for track races, the wheelchair would be an alternative for lower limb amputees.

The Labanowich paper further does not recognize that many types of locomotor disabilities will not be able to handle a wheelchair (hemiplegics, little people, and quite a few more of particularly the les Autres group) although their disability is such that competition with able bodied would be very unequal.

Advantages of Integrated Classification

It is in the interest of the international organizations for disabled sports to jointly organize world level competition from time to time. Such major events focus media attention and serve to change attitudes in the community to the benefit of disabled people. On such occasions care must be taken to organize competition so that it is comprehensible to spectators. Integrated classifications tend to increase comprehensiveness, particularly for people who know little about sports for the disabled.

The integrated classification is relatively new in international summer sports for the disabled. It must therefore be expected that some mistakes will be made during the development. Although the 1980 Olympic Games for the Disabled in Holland had one integrated sport—sitting volleyball—the first larger trial with integration will occur at the 1984 International Games for the Disabled in New York. For the first time on this level, ISOD shooting events, table tennis, and weightlifting will have an integrated classification for amputees and les autres. Anticipated experiences at the Games will indicate the need for changes.

Different sports require different degrees of physical qualities. A sport with a relatively low degree of required locomotive power/ability, for instance, is pistol shooting. A sport requiring a high degree of locomotive power/ability is swimming. Should the CP-ISRA, the ISMGF, and the ISOD therefore choose to jointly organize world championships in air pistol shooting, it is quite probable that they would be able to formulate an integrated classification in about 3–4 classes. If swimming was the sport, it is not likely that the classification could be constructed quickly. Maybe a few of the present separate classes could be combined, but probably an integrated classification for swimming would still consist of 4–5 CP classes, 4–5 paraplegic and tetraplegic classes, 4–5 amputee classes, 1–2 les autres classes, and 4–5 really combined classes. This is still a total of 20–23 classes, but the current program has 31 classes. Undoubtedly experience of swimming competitions with integrated classification would lead to a further reduction of the number of classes without jeopardizing the fairness for the athletes.

Conclusion

There should be freedom of choice among world organizations as to whether their individual members wish to compete according to integrated or diagnosis-oriented classifications. Some athletes may wish to enter both. As Sir Ludwig Guttmann once pointed out, classifications are never static. All involved in disabled sports wish to uphold a fair classification for the athletes whether it is integrated or diagnois-oriented. When the international organizations seek to arrange a joint tournament, they can either agree to a joint integrated classification, or they can agree to organize separate programs at the tournament.

References

Labanowich, S., Karman, P., Veal, L., & Wiley, B.D. (1984). The principles and foundations for the organization of wheelchair sports. *Sports 'N Spokes, 9*(6), 25–32.

Lindström, H. (1983, February). A system presentation of the "integrated classification" concept. *ISOD Circular, 13*, 15-16.

Lindström, H. (1984). Sports for disabled alive and well. *Rehabilitation World, 8*(1-2), 12-16.

PART III

Exercise Physiology Research

13

Dynamic Strength and Physical Activity in Wheelchair Users

Glen M. Davis, Susan J. Tupling, and Roy J. Shephard
SCHOOL OF PHYSICAL AND HEALTH EDUCATION
UNIVERSITY OF TORONTO, ONTARIO, CANADA

Upper-body muscle strength and endurance often are important factors limiting the daily activities of wheelchair-confined people. Whether the cause is neuromuscular disease, infantile atraumatic paraplegia, cerebrovascular "stroke," or traumatic spinal cord injury, all lower-limb disabled people require minimal levels of muscular strength for force generation on wheelchair pushrims (Tupling & Davis, 1983) or for body support using crutches. However, the evaluation of muscle function in this population has previously received little attention.

Although a low correlation seems to exist between the site of spinal cord injury and muscle performance in paraplegics (Kofsky, Davis, Shephard, Jackson, & Keene, 1983), a number of authors (Cameron, Ward, & Wicks, 1977; Grimby, 1980) have reported a significant relationship between habitual physical activity and upper-body isometric strength. It has been demonstrated that the extent of participation in sport and fitness programs is highly correlated with simple isokinetic measures of peak moment (Davis, Kofsky, Shephard, & Jackson, 1981; Davis, Shephard, & Ward, 1984). The present study assessed differences of upper-body isokinetic force, work, and power in highly active versus less active disabled individuals, with a view toward (a) defining the best overall basis of strength assessment in such individuals and (b) determining which movement patterns are enhanced by wheelchair sports.

Methods

Subjects were 30 asymptomatic male volunteers (ages 16 to 42 years), with neuromuscular impairment evaluated according to the International Stoke Mandeville Games Federation grading scheme. Subjects were weighed on a recumbent hospital scale, and height was assessed in the supine position with manual stretching of the limbs. Skinfold fat was measured at four sites (biceps, triceps, subscapular, and suprailiac) using Harpenden calipers.

Subjects were divided into two groups of 15 each, based on their verbally reported physical activity patterns. Group I was highly active (HA), training for provincial or national wheelchair competitions at least four times per week. Group II, the less active (LA) group, participated in regular physical activity less than two times per week.

The peak moment (M), peak power (PP), average power (AP), and total work (W) of shoulder and elbow flexion and extension and shoulder abduction and adduction were assessed on a CYBEX II isokinetic dynamometer at joint velocities of 60, 120, 180, 240, and 300 degrees$\cdot$s^{-1}. Force time curves were digitized (see Figure 1) on a HP9874A Digitizer controlled by a HP9835A microprocessor without application of a gravity correction (Cybex damping = 2). To assess differences of muscular endurance between groups, "dropoff" indices were calculated for each joint movement using the average of the highest

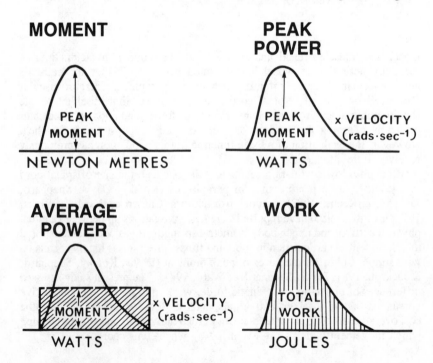

Figure 1. Schematic representation of moment, peak power, average power, and work as determined from Cybex moment-velocity curves

three and lowest three moment scores during 50 repeated biphasic contractions at 180 degrees•s^{-1}.

The physical characteristics of the subjects were compared using an analysis of variance. Since interindividual differences of muscle strength and endurance may be associated with body stature, an analysis of covariance was used to "adjust" group means for the influence of height[2]. Moment-, power-, and work-velocity curves were calculated using standard multiple regression techniques.

Results

The two activity groups did not differ significantly with respect to body size, severity of disability, or length of wheelchair confinement, although the LA group tended to be shorter, lighter, and more obese than the HA group (Table 1).

Table 1. Physical characteristics of spinally paralyzed males with highly active and less active lifestyle patterns

Physical Characteristics	Highly active group (n = 15) M	SE	Less active group (n = 15) M	SE
Age, yr	29.4 ± 1.3		26.8 ± 2.2	
Body height, cm	168.6 ± 4.4		163.2 ± 4.3	
Body mass, kg	64.1 ± 3.5		58.6 ± 3.4	
Sum of 4 skinfolds, mm	32.8 ± 2.8		39.2 ± 5.4	
ISMGF disability classification	3.6 ± 0.2		3.5 ± 0.3	
Number of years disabled	14.4 ± 3.1		14.1 ± 2.6	

Note. No significant differences existed between the groups.

Endurance dropoff scores did not differ between HA and LA subjects; both groups averaged a 47 to 56% decrease in performance over the 50 repeated contractions. However, after strength data were statistically adjusted for intergroup differences of body height, HA subjects displayed significantly greater M (27-50%), PP (22-42%), AP (21-36%), and W (21-46%) at all angular limb velocities relative to LA (see Figures 2A-2D). Differences of shoulder abduction between groups (37-50%; see Figure 3A) were larger than for shoulder and elbow flexion or extension and shoulder adduction.

Discussion

The physical characteristics and disability status of the subjects were similar to those reported in previous cross-sectional investigations (Kofsky et al., 1983; Wicks, Oldridge, Cameron, & Jones, 1983).

Previous authors have used cable tensiometry (Kofsky, et al., 1983), hand grip force (Zwiren & Bar-Or, 1975; Wicks et al., 1983), or measurements of isokinetic moment of the shoulder, elbow, and wrist (Grimby, 1980; Davis et al., 1981; Davis et al., 1984) to assess the muscular performance of wheelchair-dependent individuals. Despite criticisms of its reliability and reproducibility, isokinetic testing is probably the best available laboratory technique for the assessment of upper-body strength. Positive relationships have been observed between M and the level of habitual physical activity (R^2 = .63, Davis et al., 1981) or wheelchair force generation (Tupling & Davis, 1983) of disabled adults. The combined scores of several static strength measures of the wrist, elbow, and shoulder are also well correlated ($r = .82$) with isokinetic total upper-limb strength (Kofsky et al., 1983).

After adjusting strength data for interindividual differences of body stature, LA subjects still displayed significantly poorer M, PP, AP, and W at all joint-specific velocities compared to their athletic counterparts. Differences between groups for shoulder flexion AP (22–34%; see Figure 2A) were generally slightly greater than for shoulder extension AP (24–29%; see Figure 2B), suggesting the HA subjects had benefitted from sport-specific training of shoulder agonists during wheelchair propulsion. On the other hand, differences between HA and

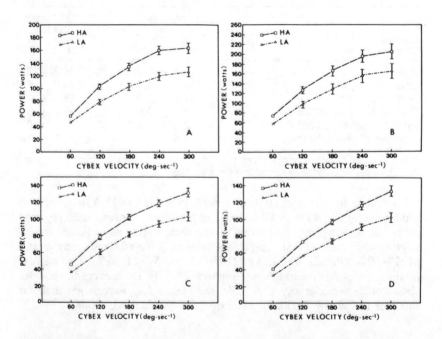

Figure 2. Relationship between Cybex angular velocity and A: shoulder flexion average power; B: shoulder extension average power; C: elbow flexion average power; and D: elbow extension average power for highly active (HA) and less active (LA) disabled males. Values are adjusted means ± SE from analysis of covariance.

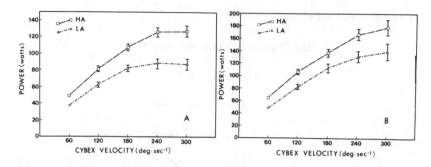

Figure 3. Relationship between Cybex angular velocity and A: shoulder abduction average power and B: shoulder adduction average power for highly active (HA) and less active (LA) disabled males. Values are adjusted means ± SE from analysis of covariance.

LA subjects were similar for elbow flexion versus extension (see Figures 2C and 2D), averaging 24–30% at joint speeds of 60–300 degrees•s^{-1}.

In a concurrent investigation of sedentary disabled individuals who were undergoing forearm-crank training (Davis et al., 1984), significantly greater improvements of elbow extension AP were observed relative to elbow flexion, shoulder flexion, or shoulder extention AP. The differences of elbow versus shoulder trainability between the longitudinal and cross-sectional studies may reflect dissimilarities of sedentary populations in the two studies or an advantage from test-specific conditioning (forearm cranking) in the training study.

The possibility that specific shoulder conditioning has occurred in the wheelchair athletes was further borne out in comparisons of shoulder abductors versus adductors. Differences between HA and LA individuals averaged 37–50% for shoulder abduction AP (see Figure 3A), but only 22–29% for shoulder adduction AP (see figure 3B). The agonists for shoulder flexion and shoulder abduction are anterior and medial deltoid, respectively, and both are probably used in wheelchair competition (Grimby, 1980).

The average power velocity curves for shoulder flexion and elbow extension (see Figure 4) were good predictors of the ability to generate muscular force over the full range of joint movement (R^2 = .77 and .83, respectively). The relative weight of the activity group strongly suggested that AP was a better discriminator between athletic and sedentary subjects than M, PP or W. The recommendation to use average power data concurs with previous findings for disabled subjects undergoing forearm-crank training (Davis et al., 1984). It may be the result of inherent limitations in the measurement of peak forces by isokinetic dynamometry (Sapega, Nicholas, Sokolow & Sarantini, 1982) or it may imply that AP gives a better measure of overall muscular strength than peak moment (a.k.a. peak torque; see Figure 1). The velocity group interaction terms are also significant and the difference of AP between HA and LA subjects is best brought out at higher angular velocities (see Figures 2A–2D, 3A, 3B), suggesting that fast-twitch muscle strength is specifically enhanced by physical activity in disabled adults.

SHOULDER FLEXION AP (Watts) =

$$0.33 \, (\text{CYBEX Velocity, deg} \cdot \text{s}^{-1})$$

$$+ \, 5.82 \, (\text{Activity Group})$$

$$+ \, 0.13 \, (\text{Group} \cdot \text{Velocity})$$

$$+ \, 0.001 \, (\text{Height}^2, \text{ cm })$$

$$- \, 1.00 \qquad\qquad R^2 = 0.77$$

ELBOW EXTENSION AP (Watts) =

$$0.29 \, (\text{CYBEX Velocity, deg} \cdot \text{s}^{-1})$$

$$+ \, 2.00 \, (\text{Activity Group})$$

$$+ \, 0.09 \, (\text{Group} \cdot \text{Velocity})$$

$$+ \, 0.001 \, (\text{Height}^2, \text{ cm })$$

$$- \, 15.52 \qquad\qquad R^2 = 0.82$$

Figure 4. Regression equation for shoulder flexion average power and elbow extension average power. Activity group was coded 0 = LA and 1 = HA. R^2 = coefficient of determination.

References

Cameron, B.J., Ward, G.R., & Wicks, J.R. (1977). Relationship of type of training to maximum oxygen uptake and upper limb strength in male paraplegic athletes. *Medicine and Science in Sports and Exercise, 9*, 58.

Davis, G.M., Kofsky, P.R., Shephard, R.J., & Jackson, R.W. (1981). Classification of psycho-physiological variables in the lower-limb disabled. *Canadian Journal of Applied Sports Sciences, 6*, 159.

Davis, G.M., Shephard, R.J., & Ward, G.R. (1984). Alterations of dynamic strength following forearm crank training of disabled subjects. *Medicine and Science in Sports and Exercise, 16*, 147.

Grimby, G. (1980). Aerobic capacity, muscle strength and fiber composition in young paraplegics. In H. Natvig (Ed.), *Proceedings of the 1st International Medical Congress for Sports for the Disabled* (pp. 13-17). Oslo, Norway: Royal Ministry of Church and Education.

Kofsky, P.R., Davis, G.M., Shephard, R.J., Jackson, R.W., & Keene, G.C.R. (1983). Field testing: Assessment of physical fitness of disabled adults. *European Journal of Applied Physiology, 51*, 109-120.

Sapega, A.A., Nicholas, J.A., Sokolow, D. & Sarantini, A. (1982). The nature of torque "overshoot" in Cybex isokinetic dynamometry. *Medicine and Science in Sports and Exercise,* **14,** 368-375.

Tupling, S.J., & Davis, G.M. (1983). Wheelchair impulse generation and arm strength in the physically disabled. *Canadian Journal of Applied Sports Sciences,* **8,** 228.

Wicks, J.R., Oldridge, N.B., Cameron, B.J., & Jones, N.L. (1983). Arm cranking and wheelchair ergometry in elite spinal-cord injured athletes. *Medicine and Science in Sports and Exercise,* **15,** 224-231.

Zwiren, L.D., & Bar-Or, O. (1975). Response to exercise of paraplegics who differ in conditioning level. *Medicine and Science in Sports and Exercise,* **7,** 94-98.

14

Fitness Classification Tables for Lower-Limb Disabled Individuals

Peggy R. Kofsky, Roy J. Shephard, and Glen M. Davis
UNIVERSITY OF TORONTO
TORONTO, ONTARIO, CANADA

Robert W. Jackson
TORONTO WESTERN HOSPITAL
TORONTO, ONTARIO, CANADA

It is now well established that a sedentary but otherwise healthy individual is capable of increasing cardiorespiratory fitness by 20–30% through an increase in habitual activity (Bailey, Shephard, Mirwald, & McBride, 1974; Shephard, 1977; Shephard, Cox, Corey, & Smyth, 1979). Nevertheless, at least one half and possibly as much as two-thirds of the difference between an average person and an international athlete is constitutionally determined. This makes it quite difficult to assess fitness from measurements of maximum oxygen intake and muscle strength (Shephard, 1978). A paucity of data pertains to physical fitness of disabled people, particularly with respect to the relative importance of habitual activity and the severity of the disability.

Problems of access associated with disability often reduce the desire for exercise and thus restrict physical work performance (Nilsson, Staff, & Pruett, 1975). On the other hand, the life of a handicapped person probably demands a greater level of fitness than is needed by the general population. It is possible that daily wheelchair ambulation may help to sustain such fitness.

Many of the health and longevity problems that plagued earlier generations of physically disabled individuals have been eliminated. Thus, while some disabled individuals are still content to be passive recipients of care, many are now eager to realize their potential, satisfying to the limit of their ability, their special need for upper-body strength (UBS) and cardiovascular fitness.

A need exists to study the influence of levels of habitual physical activity (vigorous, moderate, sedentary) and the severity of the disability (i.e., the amount of paralysis) in relation to fitness goals. In essence, should there be one set of fitness tables for highly endowed athletes and a second for the general population, or should disabled people be judged by the same yardstick? A clear answer to this question would facilitate the prescription of both work and leisure pursuits, with benefit to the patient, athlete, therapist, employer, and coach.

The intent of the present study was thus to examine the fitness status of lower-limb disabled individuals, to develop sex-specific normative data, and to study the impact of intrinsic (spinal cord lesion level) and extrinsic (selective pressures and habitual physical activity) factors upon fitness classifications. The testing methods were derived from a previously developed and validated battery of fitness tests (Kofsky, Davis, Shephard, Jackson, & Keene, 1983) applicable to field, hospital, recreational, and/or home settings.

Method

The subjects involved were 260 lower-limb disabled individuals (163 males and 97 females). They were recruited through contacts from various housing and rehabilitation facilities, organizations, and associations for the disabled such as the Canadian Paraplegic Association as well as various recreational and sporting clubs. In addition, the fitness testing opportunity was advertised in newspapers and bulletins throughout Toronto and the surrounding boroughs. Because of upper-body weakness, 12% of this group were unable to complete the test. The sample for this study thus comprised 146 males ages 16 to 68 ($M \pm SD = 31.4 \pm 11.5$ years) and 83 females 16 to 66 ($M \pm SD = 35.6 \pm 13.5$ years), about one half of the estimated lower-limb disabled population in the Toronto area.

Design and Procedure

Activity Classification

Three broad categories of habitual physical activity were distinguished:

A = Vigorously active subjects who were elite wheelchair athletes of national and/or provincial caliber
B = Moderately active subjects undertaking deliberate vigorous activity at least 1 day per week
C = Sedentary subjects.

Disability Classification

Disability was rated using the International Stoke Mandeville Games Federation (ISMGF) scheme (Jackson & Fredrickson, 1979) as illustrated in Table 1 and Table 2.

This investigation excluded people in Class I (quadriplegia), and Class VI (minimal deficit).

Table 1. Number of male subjects classified by disability level (ISMGF classification) and activity level

Activity level	Disability level (lesion level)			
	II (T1–T5)	III (T6–T10)	IV (T11–L3)	V (L4–S2)
A	6	10	11	10
B	8	13	14	10
C	14	16	18	16
Total	28	39	43	36

Table 2. Number of female subjects classified by disability level (ISMGF classification) and activity level

Activity level	Disability level (lesion level)			
	II (T1–T5)	III (T6–T10)	IV (T11–L3)	V (L4–S2)
A	—	—	3	1
B	1	3	5	6
C	5	14	23	22
Total	6	17	31	29

Aerobic Power

Aerobic power ($\dot{V}O_2$ peak) was predicted from a submaximum, three-stage arm ergometer test (Kofsky et al., 1983, see Figure 1).

Figure 1. Disabled subject performing a submaximal arm ergometer test on a Monark Rehab Trainer. Photo courtesy of M. Durocher.

This procedure was validated in a subsample of 17 male disabled subjects ages 20 to 42 years (M±SD = 30.0±7.3 years). A continuous progressive forearm ergometer test was carried out to voluntary exhaustion, the intensity of effort being further increased at 1-min intervals to voluntary exhaustion ($\dot{V}O_2$ peak). Oxygen consumption was determined using a standard open circuit technique (Andersen, Shephard, Denolin, Varnauskas, & Masironi, 1971; Kofsky et al., 1983). The difference between the field and laboratory tests averaged ±3.9 ml•kg•min^{-1} ($r = .84$).

Upper Body Strength

A Clark cable tensiometer with a supporting frame was used to measure the maximal force of elbow flexion, elbow extension, and shoulder extension with the forearm positioned at 90 degrees in each case (see Figure 2). The score noted for each movement was the maximum of three definitive attempts. The sum of the three force measurements provided an index of total UBS.

Figure 2. Disabled subject performing a static muscle force test. Photo courtesy of the photography department of Toronto Western Hospital.

Body Composition

Height and body fat determined as the sum of four skinfolds (biceps, triceps, subscapular, and suprailiac) were measured as described previously (Kofsky et al., 1983), while body mass was measured on a portable scale designed to weigh the person in a wheelchair (see Figure 3).

Statistical Analysis

The General Linear Models procedure within the Statistical Analysis System (SAS; Ray, 1982) was used to perform analyses of variance for unbalanced data. The significance of differences between activity levels and disability levels was determined, and the Duncan post hoc analysis was applied when significant differences were demonstrated.

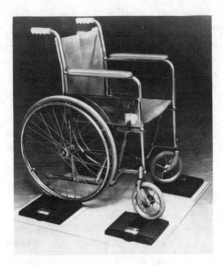

Figure 3. Portable scale designed to weigh the mass of a disabled subject while seated in a wheelchair. Photo courtesy of the photography department of Toronto Western Hospital.

Results

The physical characteristics of the sample were similar to those encountered in the general population of Toronto (males: height 170.0 ± 13.5 cm, body mass 68.4 ± 13.8 kg, and average of four skinfolds 11.5 ± 5.7 mm; females: height 158.2 ± 12.6 cm, body mass 57.8 ± 12.0 kg, and average of four skinfolds 14.5 ± 5.8 mm).

Aerobic Power

Findings were different for males and females with respect to absolute $\dot{V}O_2$ peak and degree of disability. The absolute $\dot{V}O_2$ peak ($1 \cdot min^{-1}$) for the male subjects differed significantly with disability level. Post hoc analysis indicated that males in Class II had lower scores than males in Classes III, IV, and V. Results indicated, however, that females did not differ between Classes II through V. When $\dot{V}O_2$ peak was expressed relative to body mass ($ml \cdot kg^{-1} \cdot min^{-1}$), no differences existed between disability levels for either sex.

Pooled data for ISMGF Classes II through V were thus used to test the effects of activity levels and gender, the latter revealing a 28% advantage in $\dot{V}O_2$ peak ($ml \cdot kg^{-1} \cdot min^{-1}$) for the male subjects. Male elite athletes (Group A) scored significantly higher than either their moderately active (Group B) or their sedentary (Group C) counterparts; however, a significant difference also existed between Group B and Group C ($F = 34.9, p < .001$). Among the female subjects, Groups A and B had similar scores, both having greater scores than Group C ($F = 31.1, p < .001$). We conclude that in the male subjects, significant pressures of athletic selection existed, giving a 29% average boost to the effects of regular physical activity. For males, two sets of fitness classifications are thus presented for the evaluation of fitness status—one for the highly selected athlete (Group A) and one for the general population (Groups B and C). In contrast, one set of normative data (Groups A + B + C) remains appropriate for the females. The five fitness classifications correspond to -3 to -1.8 SD, -1.8 to -0.6 SD, -0.6 to $+0.6$ SD, $+0.6$ to $+1.8$ SD, and $+1.8$ to $+3$ SD as previously proposed by Mathews (1978). No independent age effects existed over the range tested, although over a broader distribution it would plainly be necessary to taper expectations for older individuals (see Table 3).

Table 3. Classification of predicted $\dot{V}O_2$ peak ($ml \cdot kg^{-1} \cdot min^{-1}$) for males and females

Fitness levels	Total group	Females	Elite male athletes	General male population
Poor (−3 to −1.8 SD)	<7.8	<5.4	<17.2	<10.5
Below average (−1.8 to −0.6 SD)	7.8–22.4	5.4–16.2	17.2–31.5	10.5–21.9
Average (−0.6 to 0.6 SD)	22.5–37.1	16.3–27.1	31.6–45.9	22.0–33.4
Above average (0.6 to 1.8 SD)	37.2–51.9	27.2–38.0	46.0–60.3	33.5–44.9
Excellent (1.8 to 3 SD)	>51.9	>38.0	>60.3	>44.9

Upper Body Strength

Findings were again different for males and females. In male subjects a significant difference of UBS existed between lesion levels ($F = 2.48$, $p < .05$); post hoc analysis indicated that Class II differed from Classes III, IV, and V. In female subjects, UBS was unrelated to lesion level. This interpretation of the data was unchanged when results were normalized with respect to body mass. The effects of gender were much as in the able-bodied population, with males being 35% stronger than females. As with aerobic power, males showed significant intergroup differences for all three activity levels ($F = 17.1$, $p < .001$). Similar intergroup differences occurred for the females ($F = 13.0$, $p < .001$). These differences were unchanged when values were expressed relative to body mass. The selective pressures averaged 23% UBS for the men and 17% for the women. Normative tables thus distinguish elite athletes from moderately active and sedentary men, but the three groups have been combined to establish population standards for females. A significant disadvantage (16%) with Level II spinal cord lesions also existed in the men. To simplify interpretation, Level II values were boosted by 16% in calculating the population table (see Table 4); a corresponding discount should be applied in evaluating the potential of such individuals.

Table 4. Classification of upper body strength ($n \cdot kg^{-1}$) of males and females

Fitness levels	Total group	Females	Elite male athletes	General male population
Poor (−3 to −1.8 SD)	<8.2	<1.9	<10.4	<7.1
Below average (−1.8 to −0.6 SD)	8.2–13.8	1.9–7.5	10.4–16.3	7.1–12.6
Average (−0.6 to 0.6 SD)	13.9–19.5	7.6–13.3	16.4–22.4	12.7–18.1
Above average (0.6 to 1.8 SD)	19.6–25.2	13.4–19.0	22.5–28.4	18.2–23.6
Excellent (1.8 to 3 SD)	>25.2	>19.0	>28.4	>23.6

Note. Data for ISMGF Class II males were increased by 16% for the purpose of calculating standard deviations (see text). Male subjects with Class II lesions may be expected therefore to have values 16% lower than shown.

Discussion

Critique of Methods

It is now widely accepted that in able-bodied individuals, the best single measure of cardiorespiratory fitness is directly measured maximal oxygen intake (Davies, 1968). For disabled individuals, many have argued for the use of absolute rather than relative $\dot{V}O_2$max, on the grounds that activity is weight-supported. Nevertheless, the effort required to propel a wheelchair does vary in proportion to the combined mass of the individual, and perhaps 20 kg of chair and the relative units give a better picture of potential mobility than absolute values.

Various problems of technique and safety make direct testing of $\dot{V}O_2$max impractical for a large scale epidemiological study of disabled people. In order to avoid the drawbacks associated with upper-body maximal effort testing, predictions of $\dot{V}O_2$max were made based on responses to submaximal forearm ergometry. The accuracy of individual predictions, about $\pm 15\%$ (Davies, 1968), is clearly less than the precision achieved by direct measurements of young subjects performing leg work. Since no systematic error exists, however, the approach is appropriate for population surveys and to establish community levels of fitness as in able-bodied individuals (Shephard, 1978). In subsequent use of the tables the probable error of a field prediction would be .67 SD $\pm 10\%$ (± 3 ml$\cdot$kg$^{-1}\cdot$min^{-1} in the men and ± 2 ml$\cdot$kg$^{-1}\cdot$min^{-1} in the women). This would enable 73% of the sample to be correctly classified within our fitness tables. It would also demonstrate a 20% training response in 68% of the subjects. We have found some impact of UBS upon the $\dot{V}O_2$ peak of our subjects. However, from the viewpoint of assessing fitness, it is probably preferable to examine $\dot{V}O_2$ peak and UBS independently, while recognizing that some interaction exists between these two variables.

From the viewpoint of constructing fitness classification tables, while convenient, it was surprising that over the Class II through V level range there was so little influence of spinal cord lesion level upon $\dot{V}O_2$ peak or UBS. The degree of disability in each individual was assessed by an experienced technician, using an internationally accepted classification scheme (ISMGF). These findings thus cannot be attributed to a lack of precision in classification. We must presume that forearm power output and UBS of a carefully immobilized subject are not materially affected below T6 (Class III) and that many individuals in Class II have no specific local limitation of function.

Training Versus Selection

The average training response of disabled people is indicated by the difference between Groups B and C in men and the difference between Groups A + B and C in women. This amounts to 34% in the men and 44% in the women—a figure not too dissimilar from that found in able-bodied individuals. A maximum estimate of the effect of competitive selection for men is indicated by the difference between Group A and Group B. In the women, no effect of competitive selection is apparent. This is probably because of the small number of female participants and the nature of many events in ISMGF sports. In contrast, the unusual performances of both men and women encountered in the regular Olympics reflect a competitive searching through a base population of many millions.

In the men, a greater emphasis on endurance events and a larger number of participants has apparently led to a competitive selection factor similar to that in able-bodied athletics. However, the effect may be less than the 14% suggested by our comparison of Groups A and B, since elite athletes were not only selected for their sport, but also were training harder than moderately active disabled people. This finding was different for women; albeit, the relatively smaller number of disabled females in general accounts for rather arduous subgroup comparisons.

The relative importance of nature and nurture is a difficult issue to resolve. Even studies of mono- and dizygotic twins have failed to provide clear-cut answers. Certainly, those disabled individuals who fear they can never emulate top-performers should take heart from a classic study of national swimming champions in Sweden (Åstrand et al., 1963), which demonstrated that 5 years after withdrawal from competition, the fitness level of the elite competitors had already dropped below that of average Swedish housewives.

If genetic endowment of the athlete exists, able-bodied or disabled, this may be more psychological—a willingness to devote long periods of each week to vigorous training, to the exclusion of other pursuits—than physiological. Further research should thus be devoted to differences in the psychosocial background of individuals who fall into each of the three activity groups. It is doubtful whether a personality that is unwilling to train hard can be modified, but this approach could indicate a more effective basis for encouraging physical activity among individuals who resist vigorous training.

References

Andersen, K.L., Shephard, R.J., Denolin, H., Varnauskas, E., & Masironi, R. (1971). *Fundamentals of exercise testing*. Geneva: World Health Organization.

Åstrand, P.O., Engström, L., Eriksson, B., Karlberg, P., Nylander, I., Saltin, B., & Thorén, C. (1963). Girl swimmers. With special reference to respiratory and circulatory adaptation and gynaecological and psychiatric aspects. *Acta Paediatrica, Supplement,* **147**, 1-75.

Bailey, D.A., Shephard, R.J., Mirwald, R.L., & McBride. G.A. (1974). A current view of Canadian cardiorespiratory fitness. *Canadian Medical Association Journal,* **111**, 25-30.

Davies, C.T.M. (1968). Limitations to the prediction of maximum oxygen intake from cardiac frequency measurements. *Journal of Applied Physiology,* **24**, 700-706.

Jackson, R.W., Flynn, C.D., & Oisen, J.S. (1977). *Torontolympiad 1976.* Toronto: 1976 Olympiad for the Disabled.

Jackson, R.W., & Fredrickson, A. (1979). Sports for the physically disabled. *American Journal of Sports Medicine,* **7**, 293-296.

Kofsky, P.R., Davis, G.M., Shephard, R.J., Jackson, R.W., & Keene, G.C.R. (1983). Field testing: Assessment of physical fitness of disabled adults. *European Journal of Applied Physiology,* **51**, 109-120.

Mathews, D.K. (1978). *Measurements in physical education* (5th ed.). Philadelphia: Saunders.

Nilsson, S., Staff, P.H., & Pruett, E.D.R. (1975). Physical work capacity and the effect of training on subjects with long-standing paraplegia. *Scandinavian Journal of Rehabilitative Medicine,* **7**, 51-56.

Ray, A.A. (Ed.). (1982). *SAS user's guide: Statistics.* Cary, NC: SAS Institute Inc.

Shephard, R.J. (1977). *Endurance fitness* (2nd ed.). Toronto, Canada: University of Toronto Press.

Shephard, R.J. (1978). The prediction of athletic performance by laboratory and field tests. In H. Lavallée & R.J. Shephard (Eds.), *Physical fitness assessment.* Springfield, IL: Charles C. Thomas.

Shephard, R.J., Cox, M., Corey, P., & Smyth R. (1979). Some factors affecting accuracy of Canadian home fitness test scores. *Canadian Journal of Applied Sport Sciences,* **4**, 205-209.

15

Physical and Physiological Characteristics of Elite Wheelchair Marathoners

Kenneth D. Coutts
UNIVERSITY OF BRITISH COLUMBIA
VANCOUVER, BRITISH COLUMBIA, CANADA

Wheelchair sports are a relatively recent addition to international sport competitions, with the participation of wheelchair athletes in marathon races initiated within the past 10 years. Within this short time span, performances in wheelchair marathons have improved dramatically. This is a consequence of improved design and engineering of chairs and the improved and increased training of the athletes.

The purpose of this paper is to describe some of the physical traits and physiological responses to maximal wheelchair exercise of a small group of elite wheelchair marathoners. For comparison purposes a group of nonmarathon wheelchair athletes was also studied.

Methods

Three wheelchair marathoners who finished first, fourth, and fifth at the 1983 World Championship race held in Miami, Florida, and three nonmarathon wheelchair athletes who have competed internationally in basketball and other events served as subjects for this study. All subjects were either Class IV or Class V male competitors actively involved in training at the time of the study. The marathoners included two with a spinal cord injury and one with polio, and the nonmarathoners consisted of two with a spinal cord injury and one amputee. These subjects had a mean age of 28 years, with a range of 24 to

36 years. Each athlete completed a battery of tests on a single visit to the laboratory. All subjects had participated in previous studies and were familiar with the test procedures. The tests included measures of peak torque at 0.52 rad/s on a Cybex dynamometer for flexion and extension at the shoulder and elbow. Maximal handgrip strength was measured using a handgrip dynamometer, and the number of dips completed in 1 min from a sitting position was recorded.

To evaluate body composition, skinfold thicknesses were determined at the biceps, triceps, subscapular, and suprailiac sites. At least three determinations were made at each site to achieve consistency in the determinations.

Maximal oxygen uptake was determined using a continuous protocol of increasing power outputs on a wheelchair ergometer. Power output was increased by 4 to 10 watts each minute until subjective exhaustion or failure of the subject to increase power output. Details of the ergometer, recording equipment, and test protocol have been previously reported (Coutts, Rhodes, & McKenzie, 1983). During the minute of exercise when maximal oxygen uptake was recorded, values for power output, heart rate, minute ventilation, respiratory exchange ratio, oxygen pulse, and ventilatory equivalent for oxygen were also recorded.

Average values for each measure were calculated for the marathon and nonmarathon subjects. Additional statistical procedures were considered invadvisable due to the small sample size and incidental nature of the sample. The results, therefore, represent a purely descriptive comparison of the two groups of subjects.

Results

Table 1 presents the basic data and skinfold measures for each subject and the group averages. The marathon subjects are listed in their relative order

Table 1. Basic data and skinfold thicknesses of marathoners and nonmarathoners

Subjects	Mass (kg)	Age (yr)	Biceps (mm)	Triceps (mm)	Subscap (mm)	Illiac (mm)	Total (mm)
Marathoners							
1	63.8	24	3.6	5.2	10.2	6.2	25.2
2	89.4	29	3.6	8.2	15.4	13.0	40.2
3	61.5	28	3.3	5.2	10.4	6.3	25.1
Mean	71.6	27	3.5	6.2	12.0	8.5	30.2
Nonmarathoners							
1	85.0	26	4.2	17.0	14.4	13.6	49.2
2	86.8	36	5.2	13.2	15.0	10.6	44.0
3	53.5	29	5.9	12.0	15.3	9.2	42.3
Mean	75.1	30	5.1	14.1	14.9	11.1	45.2

of finish in the 1983 marathon, while the nonmarathon subjects are in no particular order. Considering the group averages, the nonmarathoners were slightly heavier and older with larger skinfold thicknesses at each of the four sites than the marathoners. The triceps skinfold displayed the largest difference between the groups.

Marathoner 2 had relatively high skinfold thicknesses at the subscapular and suprailiac sites, but he was also the heaviest subject. A valid method for converting skinfolds to the percentage of body fat for this subpopulation is needed to enhance the interpretability of this data.

The strength measures, presented in Table 2, indicate that the marathoners had a greater maximal handgrip and higher peak torques for elbow flexion

Table 2. Strength Measures

Subjects	Dips (#/min)	Handgrip (N) Rt	Lt	Elbow flex (N•m) Rt	Lt	Elbow ext (N•m) Rt	Lt	Shoulder flex (N•m) Rt	Lt	Shoulder ext (N•m) Rt	Lt
Marathoners											
1	88	589	569	70	73	56	42	69	56	137	131
2	30	726	647	71	49	49	38	77	62	119	119
3	78	432	422	78	71	42	58	60	66	108	120
Mean	65	582	546	73	64	49	46	69	61	121	123
Nonmarathoners											
1	22	412	441	52	56	35	49	40	47	87	87
2	44	520	481	66	63	66	42	70	84	126	119
3	32	464	432	36	29	49	45	72	66	90	78
Mean	33	464	451	51	49	50	45	61	66	101	95

and shoulder extension than nonmarathon subjects. While no differences in peak torques for elbow extension and shoulder flexion were apparent, the marathoners were able to complete more dips in 1 min, which basically involves a combination of these two movements.

Table 3 contains the values for maximal oxygen uptake and other concurrent variables. The marathoners displayed a higher maximal oxygen uptake, which was associated with a higher power output, heart rate, minute ventilation, and oxygen pulse and a lower ventilatory equivalent for oxygen. No group difference was apparent in the respiratory exchange ratio when maximal oxygen uptake was achieved.

Discussion

The lower skinfold thicknesses of the marathon group are consistent with findings on able-bodied distance runners (Pollock et al., 1977). The values are similar to those reported by Gass and Camp (1979) on a group of trained wheelchair athletes, and they reflect the consequences of the amount and intensity of training of the athletes.

Table 3. Maximal oxygen uptake and associated variables during wheelchair ergometry

Subjects	Max O$_2$ (1/m)	Uptake (ml/kg/m)	Power (W)	Heart rate (bts/m)	V$_E$ BTPS (1/m)	RER	O$_2$ Pulse (ml/bt)	V$_E$ Eq O$_2$ (1/1)
Marathoners								
1	3.32	52.0	114	192	122	1.22	17.3	36.9
2	2.85	31.9	98	181	108	1.17	15.7	37.8
3	2.94	47.8	90	206	137	1.28	14.3	46.6
Mean	3.04	43.9	100	193	122	1.22	15.8	40.4
Nonmarathoners								
1	2.46	28.9	76	174	71	1.05	14.1	28.9
2	2.42	27.9	102	175	99	1.29	13.8	40.9
3	2.03	37.9	58	201	115	1.29	10.1	57.0
Mean	2.30	31.6	79	183	95	1.21	12.7	42.3

The strength measures of all of the athletes in this study are comparable to values reported on participants in the 1976 Olympiad for the Physically Disabled (Wicks, Oldridge, Cameron & Jones, 1983). The somewhat higher values of the marathon group may be attributable to two factors: the smaller diameter pushrim used on marathon chairs and the inclusion of uphill wheeling as part of their training. The smaller diameter pushrim decreases the mechanical advantage of the system, necessitating a greater force exertion over a smaller linear distance to create the same angular momentum and acceleration of the wheelchair. The uphill training for marathon races would also add to the resistance and create the need for higher force generation. This could explain the higher maximal handgrip exhibited by the marathoners since it would aid in preventing slippage between the hand and pushrim during the higher force applications.

The higher peak torques in the marathoners for elbow flexion and shoulder extension suggest a difference in movement patterns which may also be a consequence of their smaller pushrims (i.e., the normal propulsive movement for a standard or larger diameter pushrim used in basketball and most other sports involves elbow extension and shoulder flexion). In order to even maintain the same time of force application during each push, the marathoner with a smaller diameter pushrim would need to increase the arc when force is applied. Thus the marathoner may include an upward and forward pull on the rims involving elbow flexion and shoulder extension in addition to the more normal forward and downward propulsive push used with standard rims.

The higher maximal oxygen uptake and associated cardiorespiratory responses of the marathoners were expected on the basis of similar findings on able-bodied distance runners (Pollock et al., 1977). The maximal oxygen uptake data for all of the athletes are generally comparable to values reported on similar groups of subjects (Crews, Wells, Burkett & McKeeman/Hopkins, 1982; Gass & Camp, 1979; and Wicks, et al., 1983). The marathoners in this study displayed above-average maximal oxygen uptakes in comparison to these groups of wheelchair athletes that included some data on other marathoners.

The small sample size in this study prohibits drawing general conclusions about the unique characteristics of wheelchair marathoners in comparison with other wheelchair athletes. The growing body of knowledge, however, about this group of athletes suggests that they exhibit many of the same kind of physical and physiological differences noted in able-bodied athletes.

References

Coutts, K.D., Rhodes, E.C., & McKenzie, D.C. (1983). Maximal exercise responses of tetraplegics and paraplegics. *Journal of Applied Physiology: Respiratory, Environmental and Exercise Physiology, 55,* 479–482.

Crews, D., Wells, C.L., Burkett, L., & McKeeman/Hopkins, V. (1982). A physiological profile of four wheelchair marathon racers. *The Physician and Sportsmedicine, 10,* 134–143.

Gass, G.C., & Camp, E.M. (1979). Physiological characteristics of trained Australian paraplegic and tetraplegic subjects. *Medicine and Science in Sports, 11,* 256–259.

Pollock, M.L. (1977). Submaximal and maximal working capacity of elite distance runners. Part I: Cardiorespiratory aspects. *Annals of the New York Academy of Sciences, 301,* 310–322.

Pollock, M.L., Gettman, L.R., Jackson, A., Ayres, J., Ward, A., & Linnerud, A.C. (1977). Body composition of elite class distance runners. *Annals of New York Academy of Sciences, 301,* 361–370.

Wicks, J.R., Oldridge, N.B., Cameron, B.J., & Jones, N.L. (1983). Arm cranking and wheelchair ergometry in elite spinal cord-injured athletes. *Medicine and Science in Sports and Exercise, 15,* 224–231.

PART IV

Biomechanics Research

16

Propulsion of Racing Wheelchairs

Colin Higgs
MEMORIAL UNIVERSITY OF NEWFOUNDLAND
ST. JOHN'S, NEWFOUNDLAND, CANADA

Cine photographs were taken of 16 world class spinally paralyzed athletes (Classes 4 and 5) during competition. Filming was undertaken during track finals of the Olympic competition in Arnham, Holland, during June and July 1980. All athletes were filmed at 36 frames per second over a portion of the track approximately 20 m long. The center of the marked portion of the track was 30 m from the finish line. The sprinters ($n = 8$) were filmed as they approached the finish of their Olympic 200 m finals, while the 1500 m distance racers ($n = 8$) were filmed as they passed the marked portion of track for the second of four times. This was to allow the distance racers to settle into their wheeling patterns, but to prevent them from being filmed during a period of high fatigue when their form might have deteriorated.

Frame-by-frame analysis of the film was made with special reference to the path of the hand as it applied force to the handrim to propel the chair. The distal end of metacarpal three was used as a reference point. Figure 1 shows a typical hand path during one complete propulsion cycle.

Four possible phases can be noted:

I.   Initial contact phase: during this period the hand is in contact with the handrim but is not applying any propulsive force;

II.   Propulsive phase: during this portion of the cycle the hand is in contact with the handrim and is applying a propulsive force;

III. Disengagement phase: during this part of the cycle the hand is still in contact with the handrim but is not in a position to apply any propulsive force, and

IV.   Recovery phase: during this period the hand is not in contact with the handrim and is being positioned so as to be able to restart phase I.

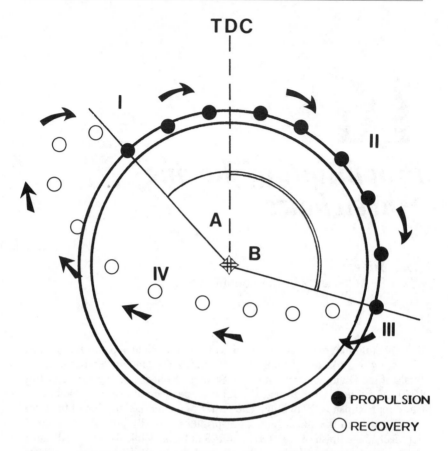

Figure 1. Typical path of hand in the application of propulsive force to wheelchair handrim. (I) Contact, (II) Propulsion, (III) Disengagement, and (IV) Recovery.

Due to the speed of hand movement and the limitations in resolution imposed by the photographic emulsion, identification of phases I and III was extremely difficult. Analysis was therefore restricted to propulsive (phase II only) and nonpropulsive (phases I, III, and IV combined) portions of the cycle only.

The angle from the vertical of the onset and completion of the propulsive phase (A and B respectively, Figure 1) was noted for each subject as were the duration of the propulsive and nonpropulsive phases of the cycle. Total cycle time was then calculated.

Chair velocity was determined by counting the number of photographic frames required for the wheelchair to pass two marked points on the track.

Results

Table 1 shows the times for the propulsive and recovery phases of wheeling cycles for both sprinters and distance racers. It should be noted that while the

Table 1. Propulsive phase, nonpropulsive phase and cycle times for sprint and distance racers (time in seconds)

Racers	Cycle time	Propulsive time	Non-propulsive time
Sprinters			
1	.66	.19	.47
2	.47	.17	.30
3	.83	.28	.55
4	.64	.19	.44
5	.53	.22	.30
6	.61	.17	.44
7	.78	.25	.53
8	.42	.19	.22
M	.62	.21	.41
SD	.14	.04	.12
Distance			
1	.97	.25	.72
2	.55	.28	.28
3	.50	.25	.25
4	.61	.22	.39
5	.75	.28	.47
6	.78	.25	.53
7	.78	.28	.50
8	.58	.25	.33
M	.69	.26	.43
SD	.16	.02	.15

cycle times and the recovery phase times show no significant differences between the sprinters and the distance racers, $t(14) = .929$, the distance racers had a mean propulsion phase time of .26 sec and applied force to the handrim for significantly longer, $t(14) = 3.138, p < .01$, than did the sprinters with a mean time of .21 seconds.

Table 2 gives individual and mean scores for stroke rate, defined as the number of cyclic hand movements completed in 1 min, along with the percentage of stroke cycle time that propulsive force was being applied. In addition, chair velocity as a percentage of the fastest performer (sprinters as a percentage of the fastest sprinter, distance racers as a percentage of the fastest distance racer) is given.

The chair velocities were significantly higher for the sprinters than for the distance racers, $t(14) = 4.925, p < .01$. The stroke rate was 10.46 strokes/min higher in the sprinters than in the distance racers although this difference was not significant, $t(14) = .930$, perhaps because of the high intragroup variance.

Analysis of the point of contact and release of the propulsive phase of the stroke cycle indicated several differences between the sprinters and the distance racers. The sprinters with a mean contact angle of 30.84 degrees before top-dead-center (TDC) started the propulsive phase of the cycle nearer the vertical than did the distance racers with a mean angle of 42.47 degrees. This difference was not significant, $t(14) = 1.66, p < .10$, however the angle of the completion

Table 2. Stroke rate, relative chair velocity, and percentage of time propulsion applied for sprint and distance racers

Athlete	Stroke rate	Propulsion % time	Relative velocity
Sprinters			
1	90.00	29.17	86.26
2	127.60	35.29	77.74
3	72.29	33.00	80.63
4	93.70	30.43	92.44
5	113.21	42.11	94.64
6	98.36	27.27	85.57
7	76.92	32.14	84.61
8	142.80	46.67	100.00
M	101.86	34.51	87.74
SD	24.45	6.67	7.43
Distance Racers			
1	61.86	25.71	61.00
2	109.10	50.00	87.89
3	120.00	50.00	100.00
4	98.36	36.36	81.84
5	80.00	37.04	83.19
6	76.92	32.14	75.96
7	76.92	35.71	85.37
8	109.10	42.86	84.87
M	91.53	38.72	82.52
SD	20.40	8.46	11.05

phase differed significantly, $t(14) = 4.49, p < .01$, between the distance and sprint racers. The sprinters had a mean completion angle of 99.5 degrees while the distance racers continued applying force to the handrim for an additional 31 degrees for a mean completion angle of 130.5 degrees. This combination of slightly earlier contact and later completion angle resulted in a significantly, $t(14) = 4.39, p < .01$, greater contact arc for the distance racers—172.93 degrees as opposed to 130.31 degrees.

Figure 2 allows a comparison of the means (plus and minus one standard deviation) of the two groups for contact and release angle.

In an attempt to identify those factors in the propulsion of a wheelchair that contributed to the speed of the chair on the track, each of the following variables was correlated with wheelchair velocity: (a) percentage of time propulsive force applied during each cycle, (b) stroke rate, (c) time per cycle that propulsive force was applied, (d) time per cycle of nonpropulsive phase, (e) contact arc in degrees, (f) contact angle (degrees before TDC), and (g) completion angle (degrees after TDC). It should be noted that this was done only within each of the two groups (distance and sprint) so as to avoid any spurious correlations caused by the intrinsic differences in velocity between the two groups. Table 3 shows the product moment correlation coefficients between chair velocity and each of the identified variables.

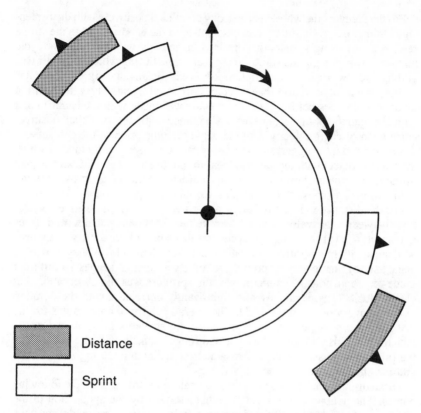

Distance

Sprint

Figure 2. Mean position (plus and minus one standard deviation) for the start and finish of the propulsion phase for sprint and distance racers.

Table 3. Zero order correlations between wheelchair velocity and selected propulsion factors for sprint and distance racers

Factors	Sprint velocity	Distance velocity
Percent time force applied	.6216	.8894
Stroke rate	.5206	.8320
Time force applied per cycle	−.1076	.1751
Nonpropulsive time/cycle	−.5388	−.8984
Degrees contact	−.5469	.5872
Contact angle	−.5672	.6653
Release angle	.3523	.3829

For the sprinters the wheelchair velocity correlated positively with the percentage of time, per cycle, that force was applied to the handrim and to the stroke rate. Not surprisingly, velocity correlated negatively with the time per cycle that force was not applied (i.e., the recovery time during which the chair was gliding and, by virtue of the friction involved, loosing speed). Of particular interest is the observation that velocity correlated negatively with both the number of degrees before TDC that contact was made with the handrim and with the length of the contact arc. Combined with the low, but positive, correlation of chair velocity with the angle of completion of the contact arc, this would seem to suggest that the faster sprinters used a technique in which they made contact with the handrim near to, but preceeding, TDC and pushed through a relatively short arc. This was performed with a high stroke rate and with as rapid a recovery (nonpropulsive) phase as possible.

For the distance racers a different pattern emerges. High positive correlations between chair velocity and (a) stroke rate, (b) contact angle, (c) degrees of contact, and (d) percentage of cycle time that a propulsive force was applied, combined with low positive correlations between chair velocity and (a) release angle and (b) time per cycle propulsive force was applied suggests a different mode of propulsion. In common with the sprinters was the observation that chair velocity was negatively and significantly correlated with the duration of the recovery phase of the cycle. The overall pattern of correlations for the distance racers suggests that compared to the sprinters the fastest distance athletes' propulsion required earlier and longer contact with the handrim in the propulsive phase, while at the same time maintaining a high stroke rate and the shortest possible recovery time.

To aid discussion, the two propulsion techniques were assigned the following names. The actions of the sprinters, characterized by the application of the propulsive force over a restricted segment of the handrim, resembles the back and forth motion of a shuttle. The action of the distance racers over a more extended segment of the handrim approaches a circular motion.

Higgs' (1983) analysis of racing wheelchairs used at the 1980 Olympics showed that the sprinters' chairs were constructed with the seats higher and further forward than the chairs of the distance racers. This would allow better access to the preferred segment of the handrim. The lower, more rearward placement of the seats in the chairs of the distance racers would appear to make a greater proportion of the handrim accesible for the application of propulsive force and suggests that both the techniques and chairs used have been adapted for specific events.

Conclusions

Analysis of hand movements used in the propulsion of racing wheelchairs has identified two types of action: (a) the shuttle action associated with sprinters and (b) the circular action found in distance racers. Inspection of the hand paths of the 16 athletes indicated that many of the actions were wasteful. For both sprinters and distance athletes, chair velocity was correlated negatively with the duration of the nonpropulsive phase of the action. The hand pathways,

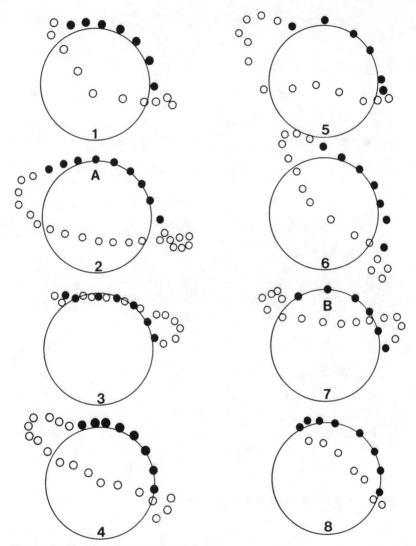

Figure 3. Hand pathways of sprinters

Figures 3 and 4, show that many of the athletes had embellished their actions with nonproductive and time consuming anterior and/or posterior loops (see Figures 3A and 3B and Figure 4C).

These loops contribute substantially to the duration of the nonpropulsive phase, as do some of the indirect recovery pathways. It should be noted that the best of the sprint and distance athletes (as reflected in medals won and world records set), for example Figure 3 sprinter #8 and Figure 4 distance athletes #2 and #5, do not exhibit any of those nonproductive loops. The absence of those loops in the most successful athletes, and the high negative correlation between chair velocity and the duration of the nonpropulsive phase of the wheeling cycle, suggests that athletes strive for the most direct and rapid

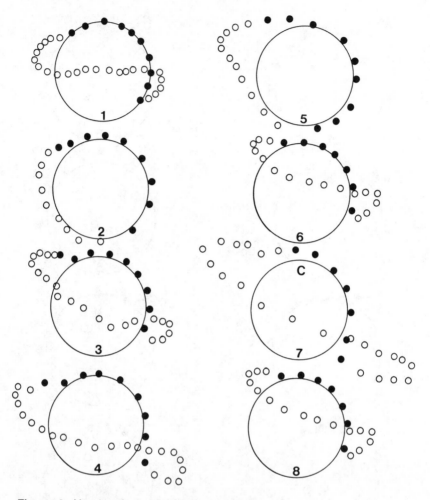

Figure 4. Hand pathways of distance athletes

return of the hand to the start of the propulsive phase. In the case of sprinters this appears to be a straight line; further investigation is required to determine the relative effectiveness of straight line and circle-completion recoveries for the distance racers.

Reference

Higgs, C. (1983). An analysis of racing wheelchairs used at the 1980 Olympic Games for the Disabled. *Research Quarterly for Exercise and Sport, 54*(3), 229–233.

17

Running Gait of the Blind: A Kinematic Analysis

Carol J. Pope
TEXAS WOMAN'S UNIVERSITY
DENTON, TEXAS, USA

Peter McGrain
UNIVERSITY OF NORTH CAROLINA AT CHAPEL HILL
CHAPEL HILL, NORTH CAROLINA, USA

Robert W. Arnhold, Jr.
UNIVERSITY OF ILLINOIS AT CHICAGO
CHICAGO, ILLINOIS, USA

Scientific analysis of sport skills has been conducted for many years. Recently the United States has developed a center for scientific analysis of Olympic sports at Colorado Springs, CO. One of the primary areas of investigation at this center entails the biomechanical analysis of these sports. Biomechanical analysis may involve the determination of kinematic (motion) or kinetic (force) parameters. These types of research projects require cinematographic data collection followed by quantitative reduction of film data. Through these projects the athlete and coach work with the researcher to make the athlete more efficient during performance.

With the advent of competition for the disabled athlete, a growing need exists to apply biomechanical techniques to this population as well. The purpose of this investigation was to determine which kinematic variables contribute to increasing velocity of visually impaired runners during a 50-yd (45.8 m) sprint.

Slocum and James (1968) defined the most commonly observed unit in the run as the *stride*, or a cycle of motion which begins when one foot strikes the ground and continues until the same foot strikes the ground again. Mann and Sprague (1983) noted that average horizontal velocity is the "most obvious measure of success" in sprinting and that "success in producing maximum velocity is dependent upon the ability to produce large amounts of muscle moment in the lower limbs. The greatest contributor to sprint success appears to be muscle activity at the hip'' (p. 309).

Dawson (1981) examined kinematic variables of 7 visually impaired subjects ages 19 to 30 years during walking. Specific variables analyzed included center of gravity motion and limb displacements and velocities. She found that the congenitally blind tended to walk with the head tilted back and use the lead leg as a probe. The adventitious blind, however, walked with the head tilted down as if focusing on the ground in front of their feet.

MacGowan (1983) examined kinematic variables of the walking gait of 18 congenitally blind and sighted children ages 6 to 10 years. When compared with the sighted subjects, the congenitally blind subjects took shorter steps, walked more slowly, and spent more time in the support phase.

Methods

Forty-eight legally blind students from the Parkview School for the Blind in Muskogee, OK, and the Texas School for the Blind in Austin, TX, served as subjects for the study. A total of 29 males and 19 females between 9 years and 28 years of age constituted this sample. The visual classification system developed by the United States Association for Blind Athletes for competition was used in placing the subjects into 3 categories based on their degrees of visual impairment. Subjects consisted of 19 Class B-1 (total blindness or some light perception), 6 Class B-2 (capable of seeing some hand movements with slight visual acuity of up to 20 over 600 with a 0–5 degree visual field), and 23 Class B-3 (restricted visual acuity from 20 over 599 to 20 over 200 and a visual field of 5–20 degrees) (Kosel, 1983). Only four subjects were adventitiously blind; all others were visually impaired from birth (congenital). Film data were collected during a 50-yd (45.8 m) dash with a 16 mm Bell and Howell 70-HR spring wound camera. Tri-X reversal black and white film with an ASA of 200 was used to collect data. The camera was placed perpendicular to the running track at a point 35 yd (32 m) from the starting line and 40 ft (12.2 m) from the track. Two trials were filmed on each subject, but only one was selected for analysis.

The film data were quantified by using a Numonics 1224 digitizer interfaced to a DEC 2050 computer system. The segmental data reported by Clauser, McConville, and Young (1969) and recommended by Hay (1978, p. 136) were used to determine the center of gravity location. An 18-point computer model (McGrain & Arnhold, 1983) served to describe body kinematics during each run for each subject. Joint angles at the hip, knee, shoulder, and elbow were determined trigonometrically by using the proximal and distal joint center locations as well as the center of the joint under investigation. Additionally, the angle of trunk to the horizontal and the angle of the head-neck to the horizontal were investigated (see Figure 1.)

The initial frame digitized for each subject consisted of the first frame in which the subject's left foot touched the ground. The final frame digitized was the frame in which the left foot again made contact with the ground. Therefore one complete cycle (two strides) was analyzed in this study.

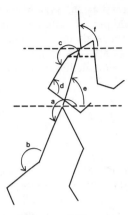

Figure 1. Six angular displacements selected for analysis (a—absolute angular displacement of the right hip joint, b—angular displacement of the knee joint, c—absolute angular displacement of the right shoulder joint, d—angular displacement of the elbow joint, e—angle of the trunk segment to the horizontal, f—angle of the head-neck segment to the horizontal).

Statistical methods consisted of determining the correlation between linear velocity and each selected kinematic variable. A multiple regression analysis was then computed to determine which set of selected kinematic variables could be used to predict running velocity. An F-statistic was used to test if a variable significantly added to the prediction of running velocity. An alpha level of .01 was used for all analyses.

Results

Correlations between running velocity and the selected kinematic variables are presented in Table 1. Six kinematic variables were found to be significantly correlated to running velocity in blind individuals.

Table 1. Relationships between running velocity and selected kinematic variables for blind individuals

Variable	r
Stride length	.92
Right hip joint range of motion	.74
Right knee joint range of motion	.62
Right shoulder joint range of motion	.59
Right elbow joint range of motion	.48
Minimum head-neck angle to the horizontal	−.32

Note. All of the correlation coefficients are significant at $p < .01$ with 46 degrees of freedom.

A step-wise multiple regression analysis was used to develop a set of kinematic variables that would predict running velocity. The combination of stride length and hip joint range of motion significantly predicts running velocity, $F(2, 46) = 48.5, p < .001$. The addition of knee joint range of motion does not significantly add to the prediction ability of running velocity for blind people.

Discussion

The findings for blind runners that stride length is highly correlated ($r = .92$) with running velocity and that hip joint range of motion adds to the prediction of velocity indicate that blind runners are similar to sighted runners in this respect (Mann & Sprague, 1983). Success in sprints is highly related to muscle activity around the hip joint.

It is interesting to note that the correlations between velocity and joint range of motion decrease with the size of the joint. For example, the massive muscles located around the hip generate large torques to help increase running velocity. The range in knee joint angular displacement (also related to running velocity) is due to the flexion occuring during the recovery of the leg followed by an extension prior to contact with the ground. The knee joint range of motion increases as the runner flexes the knee to a greater degree during recovery. This flexion helps reduce the moment of inertia of the lower extremity which makes it easier for the runner to recover the leg faster and contributes to a faster running velocity.

The relationship between the upper extremity joint range of motion (shoulder and elbow respectively) and running velocity can be explained by mechanical principles related to the run. As the left lower extremity is recovered forward, the right upper extremity is brought forward in opposition. This increases linear momentum forward and counteracts the generated angular momentum of the left lower extremity. The implications of increasing joint ranges of motion during running are especially important for blind runners who use assistive devices such as rails or guide wires. The coach should create a movement pattern that increases the range of joint motion yet allows for some tactual feedback with the assistive device. Too much contact reduces the range of motion and linear momentum forward, thus contributing to a lower running velocity.

The head-neck minimum angle to the horizontal is slightly negatively correlated to velocity in blind runners. This finding is consistent with proper mechanics for sighted individuals. It implies that, to run faster, blind athletes should be coached to lean forward and attempt to get the center of gravity forward of the base of support. Dawson (1981) found that congenitally blind people tend to lean the head backward more than adventitiously blind people while walking. In this study the backward lean of the head was characteristic of many of the Class B-1 subjects. Some blind runners obviously must be taught to lean the head-neck segment forward. This mechanical alteration will aid in increasing running velocity.

References

Clauser, C., McConville, J., & Young, J. (1969). Weight, volume and center of mass of segments of the human body. *AMRL Technical Report*. Dayton, OH: Wright-Patterson Air Force Base.

Dawson, M. (1981). A biomechanical analysis of gait patterns of the visually impaired. *American Corrective Therapy Journal, 35*, 66–71.

Hay, J. (1978). *The biomechanics of sports techniques* (2nd ed.). Englewood Cliffs, NJ: Prentice-Hall.

Kosel, H. (Ed.). (1983). *International Blind Sports Association Handbook*. Cologne, West Germany: International Blind Sport Publishers.

Mann, R., & Sprague, P. (1983). Kinetics of sprinting. In J. Terrauds (Ed.), *Biomechanics in sports: Proceedings of the International Symposium* (pp. 305–316). Del Mar, CA: Academic Publishers.

MacGowan, H. (1983). The kinematic analysis of the walking gait of congenitally blind and sighted children: Ages 6-10 years. *Dissertation Abstracts International, 44*, 703-A. (University Microfilms No. DA8318095)

McGrain, P., & Arnhold, R. (1983). *GAIT.FOR* [Computer program]. Denton, TX: Texas Woman's University.

Slocum, D., & James, S. (1968). Biomechanics of running. *Journal of the American Medical Association, 205*, 721–738.

PART V

Sport Sociology and Psychology Research

18

Social Status and Athletic Competition for the Disabled Athlete: The Case of Wheelchair Road-Racing

Gerard A. Brandmeyer and G. Fred McBee
UNIVERSITY OF SOUTH FLORIDA
TAMPA, FLORIDA, USA

Erving Goffman (1963) was among the first to discuss visible physical disabilities as stigmas that are socially discrediting and disqualifying, marking the bearer as one to be avoided, especially in public places. The general question this paper raises is whether athletic activity can be a means of destigmatizing physical disability. Should competitive athletics prove adaptive to this end, then wheelchair road-racing athletes, the population in focus here, would begin to be normalized by the able-bodied; that is, they would be perceived to be physically different, but not socially devalued due to their handicap (Davis, 1964).

Historical Perspective

Competition, including athletics, has been acknowledged since ancient Greek times as a basic means to gain the respect and approval of others (Gouldner, 1965). This approval, which we call *prestige*, is formally defined by sociologist William Goode as "the esteem, respect, or approval that is granted by an individual or a collectivity for performances or qualities they consider above the average" (1978, p. 7). The granting or withholding of approval is basic to the exercise of social control, which, in athletics, is commonly managed through access to participation in events that yield valued awards, prizes, and honors.

Success in athletic competition does more than heighten the prestige of the victor; that is, prestige is more than an end in itself. It is a means to broadened access to opportunity. In a sport context, victories bring prestige and prestige brings invitations, both athletic and social. Prestige enhances symbolic identification as an elite athlete and perhaps instrumental recognition in the form of economic inducements to continue competing. In exchange for having the "right stuff," the winning athlete finds himself or herself subtly deferred to in whim and wish.

Images of this font of prestige are a partial explanation of the appeal of competitive athletics to members of socially disesteemed groups who have become more assertive lately in seeking "overt deference and real respect" (Goode, 1978, p. 376). Is there a more apt illustration of sport anywhere that encourages images of upward mobility for the socially disesteemed than that which U.S. television provides to the black community? Likewise the physically stigmatized have actively turned to sport both for therapeutic reasons and as an opportunity to deal with their prestige deficit.

After World War II, sulfa drugs made spinal cord injury survivable. Soon a variety of recreational sport programs became available. By the 1960s this included short distance racing in "shaking, quaking, rattletrap" wheelchairs (McBee, 1983, p. 6). In the 1970s emphasis shifted from the original investment by health professionals in recreational sports for rehabilitational therapy to competitive sports for athletic prowess. Through sophisticated training regimens and the advent of the racing wheelchair, by 1975 it was possible for Bob Hall to astound the road-racing community with his 2-hr-and-58-min time as an unofficial entrant in the Boston Marathon.

With each subsequent year, racing times for the 10 k and marathon shorten in response to improvements in training methods, racing chair technology, and the quality of competition. By 1978, when George Murray was the first wheelchair racer to beat the able-bodied winner to the finish line in the Boston Marathon, it was apparent that wheelchair road-racing had made rapid progress. Fred McBee racalls "From a bunch of convalescing cripples out for a little recreation, we'd become a bunch of muscled, highly fit gimps out for blood" (McBee, 1983, p. 6).

Today's Road-Racing Disabled Athlete

These developments validate sport sociologist Eldon Snyder's judgment (1984) that the role of the elite disabled athlete embodies those properties that theorist Robert Stebbins (1982) labels "serious leisure"—the development of skill and knowledge, the accumulation of experience, and the expansion of effort— with durable benefits, including heightened self-esteem, deep identification with the athletic role, and a subcultural ethos. Of all the qualities by which Stebbins distinguishes serious from merely casual leisure, *perseverance* personifies the elite wheelchair racer, not only in the face of failure, pain, and embarrassment, but perseverance especially against the resistance of traditionalist elements in road-racing management. In seeking prestige through competitive sports, the interests of wheelchair athletes do not always conform to the interests of race organizers. These events are prestige conferring; some administrators seem to fear that association with the stigmatized would detract from the prestige of the event.

Proponents of wheelchair entry to road races for the able-bodied deny the validity of these fears. They legitimate their access on the widely accepted and precedented principle that participation by disabled athletes represents an extension of the democratic conception of sport as inclusive according to performance levels (Goode, 1978); this is the same basis by which ethnic minorities and women have gained athletic access in the last 50 years. Once convinced that a wheelchair division can be integrated with a minimum of planning and adaptation (e.g., a brief head start) without diluting the quality or detracting from the aesthetics of a road race, officials have generally practiced a bit of creative exceptionalism by including and sometimes even seeking out wheelchair participants (Murray, 1984).

But some people see wheelchairs as a threat to the quality of the foot race, turning the contest into, according to a 1982 London Marathon official, "a multi-purpose jamboree" (Marshall, 1982, p. 27). The race is viewed as a zero-sum game in which prestige is diluted if it must be shared, first with women, now with the disabled. With this zero-sum perspective, these race officials hope to exercise their gate-keeping function in order to contain wheelchair athletes within the disabled community. Fred Lebow, director of the New York City Marathon and a persistent foe of wheelchair accommodation, favors an "exclusive wheelchair marathon" since wheelchairs resemble bicycles in their speed and structural weaknesses and are a safety hazard on the same course with foot racers (Lebow, 1983). Here we have conflicting definitions of justice and fairness which, while simple to understand, resist solution. In the case of the New York City Marathon, the parties once even reached litigation in search of a solution. Lately these race officials have devised tactics to foil, contain, or at least impugn wheelchair participation. Some of those tactics include (a) modifying the entry form to refer to foot racers; (b) discouraging media coverage by requiring the occasional wheelchair entrant forced on them to start after the able-bodied; and, (c) by questioning the sincerity of race officials elsewhere who publicly welcome wheelchair applicants, accusing them of exchanging overt deference for good PR because "no editor can deny a picture of a wheelchair athlete" (Lebow, 1983). However principled or petty the traditionalists are in withstanding the wheelchair incursion, their resistance seems to be based on questions of safety, spectacle, and authenticity as follows:

1. *Safety*: Where race directors have opted to cooperate with the wheelchair athletic movement, establishing rules of the road to fit both the peculiarities of the individual course and prevailing weather conditions, safety has become a nonissue.

2. *Spectacle*: While thousands may be safely accomodated running and pushing side by side in major road races, the mass popularity of these events has introduced the element of spectacle. Officials concerned with spectacle and

media relations are understandably reluctant to see their races used without invitation as platforms for social and political action. Officials are also concerned when their events are used as outlets of expression by individuals disposed to masquerade in all manner of bizarre costume, including one dressed in a waiter's uniform carrying a bottle of wine on a tray. At the once staid Boston Marathon, for example, the *Boston Globe* reported this spring, in its article touting the wheelchair race, on others "running to call attention to causes" (Singelais, 1984, April 15, p. 68). Various contingents entered the race as advocates of issues ranging from world hunger to chiropractic education.

When wheelchair racers first seek unofficial entry into an established race, there has been a tendency for local officials to react to them not as elite athletes seeking to compete on the same basis as do the able-bodied, but rather as on dramaturgic display; perhaps participating to raise money for their good cause as an end-in-itself (Marshall, 1982). According to this definition of the situation, no matter how therapeutic and healthy mainstream participation is for disabled individuals, the fact of their physical limitation dilutes the athletic and status-enhancing potential of the effort, relegating it to the dim, stigmatized life/world of the handicapped. This world is explicitly associated with the symbolism of "special" Olympics.

In working to disavow this image of joyful Special Olympians on display, elite wheelchair athletes seek to establish credentials as a legitimate category within road racing similar to the age and gender divisions. Boxing has long stood as precedent for such equality by athletic excellence through its weight divisions (Lelchuk, 1984, January 15), as indeed wheelchair sports have through classification by degree of spinal cord injury.

3. *Authenticity*: Next, attention turns to the matter of authenticity. Do wheelchairs belong in a footrace, or, as Lebow argues, are they more akin to the bicycle (Lebow, 1983)? A lively discussion of this issue emerged in wheelchair athletic circles when competitive road-racing took hold in the 1970s with the development of the racing chair. The racing chair differs significantly from the regular wheelchair. Its frame and upholstery are made from lightweight materials so that the racing chair weighs less than one quarter of what a standard chair weighs. The size of the pushrims is also reduced so that the racing chair is faster, though harder to push. To achieve stability and power, the racer sits "low between the rear wheels," with chest resting on knees and feet on raised platforms (McBee, 1984, p. 12). These distinctive features aside, the racing chair requires a pushrim form of powering just as the standard "lived in" chair does. From a wheelchair perspective, then, the pushrim chair is to the disabled racer what running shoes are to the able-bodied foot runner—the operative accessory of locomotion.

Advances in Wheelchair Construction

While most members of the road-running community appear to accept this foot/wheel analogy, the issue is complicated by advancing technology that has developed an alternative—the crank-driven racing chair. This is a multigeared device with salient parts, including handlebar and brakes, adapted from the 10-speed bicycle. The operator propels the chair by turning a rachet attached to a wheel hub. Pushrim advocates (Murray, 1982) tend to view the crank-driven chair as an embarrassing threat to their identification with the mainstream road-racing community. By appearing on the race course, crank advocates blur the distinction between the racing chair and the bicycle by increasing the mechanical factor vis-a-vis the foot runner, thereby both giving aid and comfort to the proponents of wheelchair separation and disunifying the disabled athletic community.

Ironically, the technology that has enabled disabled athletes to perform in the road-racing limelight now catches them in a Luddite-like dissociation from the crank-driven chair because here technology threatens to sideline them. Even if affiliation with bicycle racing were technically appropriate and organizationally workable, there seems to be much greater affinity in style between foot and pushrim racing. Furthermore, the growing popularity of jogging and long distance running as serious mass leisure activities has sweetened the prestige pot for all who compete in major road races, regardless of classification. In the U.S. at least, bicycle racing can offer nothing to match the prestige of major races such as the Boston Marathon.

Sharing the Road

Wheelchair athletes have generally achieved peaceful coexistence with the able-bodied on the road. No logic compels this noncompetitive coexistence any more than logic calls for men and women who do not directly compete to run together. In the case of disabled athletes even less comparability exists because the wheelchair confers some energy-saving mechanical advantage. In the absence of a logical imperative for merging these diverse categories of competition, sharing the road at least has not impeded either the pace or progress of able-bodied male runners. Furthermore, the logical difficulty is mitigated by the obvious prestige windfall to women and wheelchair competitors through association with elite male runners in prime events.

Joint performance with elite runners minimizes the differences; this seems to be the most efficient way to confront the discrediting effects of stigmas due to disability. Even though competition is not direct, the opportunity to evaluate oneself in reference to the ''best'' in terms of physical prowess is bound to be status enhancing for wheelchair athletes.

Opportunities to compete jointly allow disabled racers to build a sense of symbolic athletic community with able-bodied runners who, through exposure, come to appreciate the athleticism of their disabled counterparts. Those watching ESPN coverage of this year's Boston Marathon heard world-class runners Greg Myers and Kevin Ryan, serving as commentators, refer to the skill and technique of the wheelchair racers, leaving it to the less aware TV reporters to relate to them solely in terms of inspiration.

Sharing the road as fellow athletes allows the able-bodied to break through the ''zone of first impressions'' (Davis, 1964, p. 120) beyond which spontaneous sociability, even friendship, can replace the sticky and embarrassing discomfort that usually starves relations with those whom we have never previously perceived as "normal."

This normalization process expands opportunities; for example, wheelchair athletes begin to share in sponsorship via selection to prominent racing teams. Victories and honors attract new recruits, justify further commitment of time and energy to the sport (Goode, 1978), and create heroes to celebrate. Surely George Murray would not be one of just six athletes to be pictured in 1984 on the WHEATIES cereal box in General Mills's "Search for Champions" contest had he not first won national media acclaim for his dramatic triumph in the 1978 Boston Marathon. But do these accolades gracing the athletic elite pay off in terms of improved life chances for the broader disabled population? While an answer to that question is beyond the scope of this paper, it is sufficient to note here that experts do not all agree that the disabled community is benefited by this involvement in competitive sports as serious leisure (Hahn, 1984).

For now, an invitation to compete in men's and women's "demonstration" events at the 1984 Summer Olympics represents the ultimate symbolic recognition to date that wheelchair sports have outgrown the "pat on the head" stage. Perhaps, as with poor relations at a wedding party, wheelchair athletes, having now been invited, may someday soon get to dance with the bride (Davis, 1964).

References

Davis, F. (1964). Deviance disavowal: The management of strained interaction by the visibly handicapped. In H.S. Becker (Ed.), *The other side: Perspective on deviance* (pp. 119–137). Glencoe, IL: The Free Press.

Goffman, E. (1963). *Stigma: Notes on the management of spoiled identity.* Englewood Cliffs, NJ: Prentice-Hall.

Goode, W. (1978). *The celebration of heroes: Prestige as a social control system.* Berkeley, CA: University of California Press.

Gouldner, A. (1965). *Enter Plato: Classical Greece and the origins of social theory.* New York: Basic Books.

Hahn, H. (1984). Sports and the political movement of disabled persons: examining nondisabled social values. *The Arena Review, 8,* 1–15.

Lebow, F. (1983). Guest spot: Wheelchairs are welcome everywhere, but do they belong in races? *Runner's World, 18,* p. 178.

Lelchuk, A. (1984, January 15). Prized fighting: A tale of true valor. *The Boston Globe Sunday Magazine,* pp. 8–10, 41–42, 53–58.

Marshall, T. (1982). Marathons and road racing. *Sports 'N Spokes, 8,* 27.

McBee, F. (1983, Fall). The continental quest. *Omnibus: A student newspaper supplement of the University of South Florida,* pp. 6–9, 38–42.

McBee, F. (1984). *The continental quest: An eyewitness account of the first wheelchair crossing of North America.* Tampa, FL: Overland Press.

Murray, G. (1982). Guest editorial: Cranks. *Sports 'N Spokes, 8,* 4.

Murray, G. (1984). Guest spot: The thrill of road racing is a matter of heart, not legs. *Runner's World, 19,* p. 126.

Singelais, N. (1984, April 15). A new beginning for Boston wheelchair racers. *The Boston Globe*, p. 68.

Snyder, E. (1984). Sports involvement for the handicapped: Some analytic and sensitizing concepts. *The Arena Review, 8,* 16–26.

Stebbins, R. (1982). Serious leisure. *Pacific Sociological Review, 26,* 251–272.

19

Sport Socialization of Blind and of Cerebral Palsied Elite Athletes

Claudine Sherrill, Wanda Rainbolt,
Tom Montelione, and Carol Pope
TEXAS WOMAN'S UNIVERSITY
DENTON, TEXAS, USA

Seven sport organizations for disabled athletes are recognized by the United States Olympic Committee under the Amateur Sports Act of 1978. This research focuses upon national level competitors of two of the organizations: the United States Association for Blind Athletes (USABA), founded in 1976, and the National Association of Sports for Cerebral Palsy (NASCP), founded in 1978. Both organizations are attempting to socialize as many disabled people into sport as possible. This report summarizes findings of two separate studies, each based on data collected at a national meet. The purpose of each study was to investigate sport socialization of national level adult competitors with disabilities. The specific hypothesis examined was that the family and home setting are not important variables in the sport socialization of disabled athletes.

Of the several orientations to sport socialization, the social learning approach of Kenyon and McPherson (1973) was selected as the theoretical basis for this study. According to their approach, three general groups of variables determine sport role learning: (a) *personal attributes*, which refers to the characteristics of the individual; (b) *socializing agents*, which refers to significant others and/or reference groups who exert influence on the individual by teaching and modeling behaviors, beliefs, attitudes, interests, and values; and (c) *socializing situations*, which refers to settings and/or opportunities in which sport role learning occurs.

Method

The sample for each study was comprised of approximately one half of the adult population (i.e., athletes 17 years of age or older) who competed. In each study the sample was representative of the population in gender, age, geographical distribution, and visual or sport classification. Sample 1 was 100 blind athletes who competed in the seventh national USABA Games at the University of Montana in 1983. Sample 2 was 201 cerebral palsied (CP) athletes who competed in the fourth national NASCP Games in Fort Worth, Texas, in 1983. Data were collected by interviewing athletes individually at the meets. The Disabled Athlete Sports Inventory (Sherrill, 1983), which included 82 items, provided structure for these interviews. Data concerning selected personal attributes, socializing agents, and socializing situations were treated statistically by means of the frequencies, crosstabs, and breakdown programs of the Statistical Package for Social Sciences (Nie, Hull, Jenkins, Steinbrenner, & Bent, 1975) on a DEC 2050 mainframe computer.

Results

Personal Attributes

Personal attributes reported in this paper include age, gender, onset of disability, and classification. Ages of the blind athletes ranged from 17 to 60 years with a mean of 25.64. Of the 100 athletes, 62% were male and 38% were female. The onset of blindness was 58% congenital and 42% adventitious. Percentages in the three visual classifications used to equalize competition were B-1 (light perception or total blindness), 32%; B-2 (9/600 to 20/600 or field of vision of 5 degrees or less), 30%; and B-3 (legal blindness to 20/599 or field of 20 degrees or less), 38%. Ages of the CP athletes ranged from 17 to 59 years, with a mean of 26.82 years. Of the 201 athletes, 62.7% were male and 37.3% were female. The onset of disability was 91% congenital and 9% adventitious. Rounded-off percentages in the eight functional ability sport classifications used to equalize competition were 9, 14, 14, 10, 17, 14, 16, and 6, respectively. Of these, the first four classifications (47%) were wheelchair users, and the last four classifications (53%) were ambulatory.

Socializing Agents

Socializing agents investigated included (a) the athlete's perception of parental influence on sport socialization, (b) the athlete's perception of athletic ability of father, mother, and siblings, (c) the person who most influenced the athlete to become interested in sport, and (d) the person who gave the athlete most of his or her first sport instruction. For blind athletes, age, gender, and onset of disability made no significant difference in the socializing agents; visual classification made a significant difference in the athlete's perception of parental influence ($F[2] = 4.21, p = .02$). For CP athletes, gender made a difference in one variable—perceived athletic ability of father ($X^2[1] = 6.40, p =$

.01)—and sport classification made a difference in the person who most influenced the athlete to become interested in sport ($X^2[5] = 11.39$, $p = .04$) and in the person who gave the athlete his or her first sport instruction ($X^2[3] = 8.51$, $p = .04$).

The athlete's perception of parental influence on sport socialization was determined by ratings of the following semantic differential scales in response to the question, How would you describe your parents in relation to your learning and competing in sports as a child? (See Table 1)

Table 1. Athlete's perception of parental influence on sport socialization

Influence	Positive			Neutral	Negative			
Proud	7	6	5	4	3	2	1	Indifferent
Encouraging	7	6	5	4	3	2	1	Overly protective
Helpful	7	6	5	4	3	2	1	Not helpful
Same as toward your siblings	7	6	5	4	3	2	1	Different from siblings
Taught you sports	7	6	5	4	3	2	1	Not knowledgeable about sports
Attended your meets	7	6	5	4	3	2	1	Didn't attend
Total score	42	36	30	24	18	12	6	

Total scores ranged from 6 to 40 for the blind athletes, with a mean of 26.56, which can be interpreted as slightly above neutral (24). Total scores ranged from 6 to 42 for the CP athletes, with a mean of 29.06, which can be interpreted as high neutral. For both blind and CP samples, this finding supports the hypothesis that parents do not play an important role in sport socialization.

Motor development texts (Cratty, 1979; Espenschade & Eckert, 1980) typically point out that sport-proficient children come from homes in which parents have been highly active in sport. Research also supports the importance of parents' past athletic experiences as a positive influence on children's sport socialization (McPherson, 1978; Overman & Rao, 1981; Spreitzer & Snyder, 1976). To determine whether these findings applied also to disabled athletes, subjects were asked if they considered their father and mother to be athletic. Both groups overwhelmingly indicated "no." Specifically in relation to their fathers, 62.6% and 70.9% of the blind and CP athletes, respectively, answered no; in relation to their mothers, 85% and 80.9% of the blind and CP athletes answered no. To further explore athletes' perceptions of the family as athletic, subjects were asked how many of their brothers and sisters participated in sport as much or more than they did. Both blind (60%) and CP athletes (49%) indicated that they were more athletic than all or most of their brothers; 23% of the blind and 28% of the CP athletes perceived themselves and their brothers as equally athletic; and 17% of the blind and 23% of the CP athletes had no brothers. Findings were similar for sisters. Both blind (65%) and CP athletes (60%) perceived themselves as more athletic than all or most of their sisters; 8% of the blind and 12% of the CP athletes perceived themselves and their sisters as equally athletic; and 27% of the blind and 28% of the CP had no sisters.

Concerning the person who most influenced the athlete to become interested in sport and who gave the first instruction to him or her, Table 2 presents findings for blind, wheelchair CP, and ambulatory CP athletes. For blind athletes, the physical education teacher was the most important socializing agent for both sport interest and instruction. Generalization for CP athletes as a total group is not appropriate because significant differences existed between wheelchair and ambulatory competitors. For wheelchair athletes, peers/friends (25.8%) were the most significant others who influenced their interest in sport, whereas for ambulatory athletes it was family (32.7%). Nonschool personnel, most of whom were United Cerebral Palsy Associations, Inc. (UCPA) employees, received the second highest percentage for both groups as the significant other who most influenced their interest in sport. As providers of first sport instruction, nonschool (UCPA) and recreation personnel were most important for both wheelchair users (51.5%) and ambulatory CPs (39.4%); the second most important for both groups was peers/friends.

Table 2. Percentage of blind and of cerebral palsied athletes reporting people who most influenced them to become interested in sport and who first taught them sports

Variable	Blind	CP classes*	
		1-4	5-8
Person who most influenced athlete			
PE teacher	32.3	11.3	15.4
Peers/friends	22.1	25.8	17.3
Family	25.3	17.5	32.7
Nonschool personnel	—	19.6	19.2
Recreation spec	13.8	15.5	5.8
Others	6.5	10.3	9.6
Person who first taught athlete			
PE teacher	44.2	22.7	30.8
Peers/friends	18.6	10.3	3.8
Family	15.2	15.5	26.0
Nonschool/recreation	22.0	51.5	39.4

*$X^2(5) = 11.39$, $p = .04$ for person who most influenced athlete
$X^2(3) = 8.51$, $p = .04$ for person who first taught athlete

Socializing Situations

Socializing situations studied included the setting where the first sport instruction occurred, the elementary school placement, and the secondary school placement. The setting in which blind athletes received their first sport instruction was residential school, 33%; home/neighborhood, 25%; mainstream physical education in public school, 15%; separate/adapted class in public school, 7%; park/recreation, 7%; sport club for disabled and mainstream sport club, each 4.5%; and other, 3%. The setting in which CP athletes received their first sport instruction was nonschool sport club for disabled, 28.5%; home/neighborhood, 18.5%; separate/adapted class in public school or residential setting, 17.5%; mainstream class in public school, 16%; mainstream sport club, 12.5%; and other, 7%. Elementary and secondary school physical education placements are depicted in Table 3.

Table 3. Percentage of blind and of cerebral palsied athletes in elementary school and high school physical education placements

Variable	Blind classes*			Blind total	CP classes**	
	B-1	B-2	B-3		1-4	5-8
Elementary school PE placement						
Excused	18	18	12		25.8	18.4
Recess only	—	—	—		8.2	16.5
Separate/public	10	0	0		42.3	22.3
Mainstream/public	24	61	71		20.6	41.7
Residential school	48	21	17		—	—
No response	—	—	—		3.1	1.1
High School PE Placement						
Excused				10.7	47.9	27.9
Separate/public				3.2	27.1	28.8
Mainstream/public				40.9	25.0	42.3
Residential school				45.2	—	—
No response				—	—	1.0

*$X^2(8) = 24.29, p = .002$
**$X^2(4) = 18.35, p = .001$ for elementary school
**$X^2(3) = 10.72, p = .01$ for high school

Visual classifications (B-1, B-2, B-3) and sport classifications (1-4, wheelchair; 5-8, ambulatory) significantly affected elementary school physical education placement for blind athletes ($X^2[8] = 24.39, p = .002$) and CP athletes ($X^2[4] = 18.35, p = .001$), respectively. Most B-1 (totally blind) athletes had received elementary school physical education in a residential school setting (48%), whereas most B-2 and B-3 athletes had received physical education in the public school mainstream (61% and 71%, respectively). It should be noted that 18% of both B-1 and B-2 athletes had been excused from physical education, and 12% of B-3 athletes had been excused.

Most wheelchair CP athletes (42.3%) had received elementary school physical education in a separate/adapted class in public school, whereas most ambulatory CP athletes (41.7%) had been in mainstream classes. Of particular concern is the fact that 25.8% of the wheelchair users and 18.4% of the ambulatory athletes had been excused from instruction.

Visual classification did not influence secondary school physical education placement of blind athletes, but sport classification did significantly affect placement for CP athletes ($X^2[3] = 10.72, p = .01$). Most of the blind athletes had been in residential schools (45.2%) or mainstream public school classes (40.9%). Most wheelchair users (47.9%) had been excused from high school physical education, whereas most ambulatory athletes (42.3%) had received instruction in mainstream physical education. Other placements for wheelchair users included public school separate/adapted class, 27.1%, and public school mainstream, 25%. Other placements for ambulatory athletes had been public school separate/adapted class, 28.8%; excused, 27.9%; and no response, 1%.

To provide insight into the opportunity for sport learning within the elementary and secondary school settings, athletes' perceptions of the quality of instruction received was determined by ratings of three semantic differential scales. Total scores for the quality of elementary school physical education instruction for blind athletes ($n = 91$) ranged from 3 to 21 with a mean of 15.15 (low positive); for CP athletes ($n = 152$) total scores ranged from 3 to 21 with a mean of 13.48 (high neutral). Total scores for quality of secondary school physical education for blind athletes ($n = 93$) ranged from 3 to 21 with a mean of 16.93 (between low and moderate positive); for CP athletes ($n = 132$) total scores ranged from 3 to 21 with a mean of 15.56 (low positive).

Conclusion and Discussion

It was concluded that the family and home are not of primary importance in the sport socialization of blind and CP wheelchair athletes. This corroborates and extends the belief of Sherrill, Rainbolt, and Ervin (1984) that sport socializing agents appear to be different for blind athletes than able-bodied athletes, particularly in relation to the influence of home and family. The findings are mixed for ambulatory CP athletes. The physical education teacher and the school appear most important in the sport socialization of blind athletes but seem to contribute little to that of wheelchair CP athletes. Classification appears more important than gender and the time of onset in the sport socialization of disabled athletes.

References

Cratty, B. (1979). *Perceptual and motor development in infants and children.* Englewood Cliffs, NJ: Prentice-Hall.

Espenschade, A., & Eckert, H. (1980). *Motor development.* Columbus, OH: Charles E. Merrill.

Kenyon, G., & McPherson, B. (1973). Becoming involved in physical activity and sport: A process of socialization. In G.L. Rarick (Ed.), *Physical activity: Human growth and development* (pp. 303–332). New York: Academic Press.

McPherson, B. (1978). The child in competitive sport: Influence of the social milieu. In R. Magill (Ed.), *Children and youth in sport: A contemporary anthology* (pp. 247–278). Champaign, IL: Human Kinetics.

Nie, N., Hull, C., Jenkins, J., Steinbrenner, K., & Bent, D. (1975). *Statistical package for social sciences.* New York: McGraw-Hill.

Overman, S., & Rao, V. (1981). Motivation for and extent of participation in organized sports by high school seniors. *Research Quarterly for Exercise and Sport, 52*(2), 228–237.

Sherrill, C. (1983). *Disabled athletes sports inventory.* Unpublished manuscript, Texas Woman's University, Denton.

Sherrill, C., Rainbolt, W., & Ervin, S. (1984). Attitudes of blind persons toward physical education and recreation. *Adapted Physical Activity Quarterly, 1*(1), 3–11.

Spreitzer, D., & Snyder, E. (1976). Socialization into sport: An exploratory path analysis. *Research Quarterly, 47*, 238–245.

20

Socialization of Wheelchair Athletes

Chris A. Hopper
HUMBOLDT STATE UNIVERSITY
ARCATA, CALIFORNIA, USA

Research concerning wheelchair athletes has focused primarily on physiological response to exercise (Emes, 1977; Mastenbroek, 1979) and upon the rehabilitative effects of sport and physical activity (Guttman, 1973; Weiss & Beck, 1973). Kennedy (1980) attempted the first psychosocial study by describing selected characteristics of the wheelchair athlete. Kennedy concluded that the age of onset of disability and the severity of disability are not significant factors in sport role socialization. This investigation, as an extension of Kennedy's study, attempts to explain selected socialization via sport variables through an analysis of sport socialization variables. Socialization and sport have two perspectives (Loy & Ingham, 1973). The first, socialization into sport, entails a study of socializing agents: family, school, peer group, and community. These can be assessed with respect to who becomes involved in sport, how sport roles are learned, and at what stages in life these roles are learned. The second perspective relates to socialization via sport and assesses the social learning which occurs as a direct consequence of sport involvement.

The purpose of the study was to explain the four variables representing socialization via sport (athletic aspiration, educational aspiration, occupational aspiration, and self-esteem) through an analysis of selected demographic and sport socialization variables. The demographic variables were age, age at onset of disability, and severity of disability as indicated by wheelchair sport classification. The variables that related to wheelchair sport involvement were wheelchair sport socialization, financial outlay, personal commitment, and duration of sport socialization.

Method

The subjects in this study were 87 spinally paralyzed and amputee wheelchair athletes. This represented 67% of a sample invited to participate. Eighty percent of the sample were men and 20% were women. Each athlete had a significant permanent disability, with the severity of impairment ranging from partial quadriplegia to bilateral, lower-extremity amputation. Age and age of onset of disability were obtained from a personal data questionnaire. Severity of disability was determined by a medical examination in which athletes were classified into six competition groups with Class I being the most severely disabled and Class VI being the least disabled. Ages of the athletes ranged from 16 to 60 years with a mean of 27 and a standard deviation of 9.

The Kennedy Hopper Sport Role Socialization Inventory (KHSRSI) was used to assess sport role socialization. Test and retest procedures (Pearson product moment) indicated a reliability coefficient of .72 ($n = 25$). The KHSRSI consisted of 16 items soliciting information on the influence of family, school, peer group, and community upon the athlete's involvement in wheelchair sport. Items also attempted to assess the athlete's active sport involvement. Scores on this Likert-type instrument, which embodied a 5-point rating scale, ranged from 22 to 60 with a mean of 46 and a standard deviation of 8.

Intensity of the sport role socialization experience was represented by the two variables of financial outlay and personal commitment. *Financial outlay* was measured by the amount of money, in dollars, spent per year on wheelchair sport. This ranged from 0 to 3000, with a mean of 581 and a standard deviation of 302. *Personal commitment* was measured by two statements on a 5-point Likert-type scale: wheelchair sport is my primary leisure activity and wheelchair sport is a very important aspect of life. Total scores indicating personal commitment ranged from 1 to 10 with a mean of 6.21 and a standard deviation of 1.32. The duration of socialization was determined by three factors: (a) the number of years participating, (b) the number of hours per week spent training, and (c) the number of miles traveled each week during competition. Each factor was measured by a 4-point scale; these were combined into a composite indicator of duration. Scores ranged from 3 to 11 with a mean of 5.21 and a standard deviation of 2.04.

The Rosenberg Self-Esteem Scale (Rosenberg, 1965) was used to measure the self-acceptance component of self-esteem. Test-retest reliability for this instrument is .85 ($n = 28$). The scale consisted of 10 items answered on a 4-point Guttman-type scale from "strongly agree" to "strongly disagree." Scores ranged from 0 to 5 with a mean of 1.22 and a standard deviation of 1.21.

Educational aspiration was the athlete's anticipated level of achievement in education. If the current educational level was identical with the anticipated level of achievement, a score of 0 was recorded. If the anticipated educational level was higher than the current level, the educational aspiration was recorded in number of years.

Athletic aspiration was determined by comparing the current athletic level with the anticipated level of achievement. All subjects had attained entry to a regional wheelchair meet. Two further levels of wheelchair participation were considered to exist: national and international. Aspiration toward a national meet was scored as 1, and aspiration toward an international meet was scored as 2. If the athlete was content to participate only in regional meets, a score of 0 was given.

The Haller Occupational Aspiration Scale (Haller, 1963), an 8-item multiple choice instrument, was used to measure occupational aspiration. It included items permitting responses at both the realistic and idealistic expression of occupational aspiration. The alternative for each item consisted of 10 occupational titles drawn from among the 90 occupations ranked by the National Opinion Research Center (NORC). An item score of 9 indicated that the respondent had chosen an occupation from the eight highest prestige occupations on the NORC scale. An item score of 0 indicated that one of the eight lowest prestige occupations had been chosen. Multiple regression analyses were used to assess the relationship of demographic and socialization into sport variables with each dependent variable of socialization via sport. The focus was on explanation rather than prediction, and no theoretical basis existed for ordering the variables in the regression analysis. A stepwise regression procedure was used (Nie, Hull, Jenkins, Steinbrenner, & Bert, 1975).

Results

The explanation of athletic aspiration by the independent variables was successful. All variables used to enter the analysis (age, financial outlay, duration, personal commitment, sport classification, sport role socialization) were statistically significant ($p < .01$). Younger wheelchair athletes had higher athletic aspiration (beta $= -.35$, $F = 7.03$, $p < .01$). The wheelchair athletes who spent the greatest amounts of money on their sport had higher athletic aspiration (beta $= .25$, $F = 9.13$, $p < .01$). The longer the athlete's involvement was, the greater his or her athletic aspiration was (beta $= .16$, $F = 7.23$, $p < .01$). More severely disabled athletes had the higher athletic aspirations (beta $= -.06$, $F = 3.77$, $p < .01$). Athletes with lower sport role socialization scores had higher athletic aspirations (beta $= -.02$, $F = 3.20$, $p < .01$).

Table 1. Influence of socialization into sport on athletic aspiration

Variable	Multiple R	R^2	F	Standardized beta coefficient
Age	.276	.076	7.026*	−.353
Financial Outlay	.422	.178	9.130*	.251
Duration	.455	.207	7.234*	.164
Personal Commitment	.481	.213	5.554*	.088
Severity of Disability	.470	.221	3.774*	−.063
Sport Role Socialization	.470	.221	3.205*	−.025

*$p < .01$

The explanation of educational aspiration by the independent variables was successful. Younger wheelchair athletes had the higher educational aspirations (beta $= -.54$, $F = 25.38$, $p < .01$). The lower the sport role socialization score, the higher the educational aspiration (beta $= -.21$, $F = 14.81$, $p < .01$). The greater amount of time spent participating in wheelchair sport, the higher the educational aspiration (beta $= .14$, $F = 10.33$, $p < .01$). As less money was spent on wheelchair sport, more educational aspiration was derived (beta $= .16$, $F = 8.32$, $p < .01$). Wheelchair athletes who acquired their disabilities later in life possessed higher educational aspirations (beta $= .13$, $F = 6.98$, $p < .01$). As wheelchair sports became the primary focus in life for the disabled athletes, educational aspirations increased (beta $= .09$, $F = 5.93$, $p < .01$).

Table 2. Influence of socialization into sport on educational aspiration

Variable	Multiple R	R^2	F	Standardized beta coefficient
Age	.479	.229	25.379*	−.542
Sport Role Socialization	.511	.260	14.814*	−.214
Duration	.521	.271	10.328*	.145
Financial Outlay	.537	.289	8.321*	−.157
Onset of Disability	.549	.301	6.977*	.130
Personal Commitment	.554	.307	5.927*	.092

*$p < .01$

Table 3. Influence of socialization into sport on self-esteem

Variable	Multiple R	R^2	F	Standardized beta coefficient
Duration	.221	.049	4.364*	.215
Onset of Disability	.282	.079	3.543*	.167
Personal Commitment	.316	.099	3.000*	−.154
Severity of Disability	.334	.011	2.572*	.109
Financial Outlay	.346	.120	2.209	.106
Sport Role Socialization	.353	.125	1.607	.024
Age	.354	.125	1.395	−.026

*$p < .05$

Occupational aspiration was not significantly explained by socialization into sport and demographic variables. The analysis showed that only 6% of the variance was accounted for.

The explanation of self-esteem with the independent variables was partly successful. The greater amount of time spent participating in wheelchair sports, the higher the self-esteem (beta $= .21$, $F = 4.36$, $p < .05$). The later in life a person became disabled, the higher the self-esteem (beta $= .17$, $F = 3.64$, $p < .05$). The less personal commitment to sports, the higher the self-esteem (beta $= -.15$, $F = 3.00$, $p < .05$). Those athletes with less severe disabilities possessed higher self-esteem (beta $= .11$, $F = 2.53$, $p < .05$). The remaining variables that were entered into the regression analysis were not statistically significant.

Discussion

The four variables representing socialization via sport (athletic aspiration, educational aspiration, occupational aspiration, and self-esteem) were explained through an analysis of selected demographic and sport socialization variables which accounted for 71.5% of the total variance. Educational aspiration accounted for 31% of the variance; athletic aspiration, 24%; and self-esteem, 12.5%. The explanation of occupational aspiration was not successful with only 6% of the variance accounted for.

The relationship between the independent variables and each dependent variable provided information concerning the life experiences of wheelchair athletes. For both athletic and educational aspiration, age explained the greatest amount of variance. Furthermore, the younger the wheelchair athlete, the greater the educational and athletic aspiration. This seems to suggest that, for the younger athletes, sport involvement and educational and athletic aspiration are related to recent social changes in their status as disabled people. This group of athletes may represent a cohort of disabled people who have become involved in wheelchair sport in the last decade as a result of legislative changes offering sporting opportunities to disabled people.

An inverse relationship between self-esteem and personal commitment to sport occurred in the analysis of self-esteem. Athletes with high self-esteem had a low personal commitment. This suggests that self-esteem is not directly related to success in wheelchair sport but may be related to other factors in life (e.g., relations with spouse, satisfactory career plans).

In the analysis of both athletic and educational aspiration, the less influence of socializing agents, the higher the aspiration. This finding may suggest that disabled athletes follow a different pattern of socialization than able-bodied athletes. Typically, socializing agents have contributed to high athletic aspiration for able-bodied athletes (Kenyon & McPherson, 1973). A similar inverse relationship was revealed between financial outlay on sports and educational aspiration but not athletic aspiration. This may indicate that, as wheelchair athletes become preoccupied with sport, educational aspiration suffers.

References

Emes, C. (1977). Physical work capacity of wheelchair athletes. *Research Quarterly,* **48**, 209–212.

Guttman, L. (1973). Sport and recreation for the mentally and physically handicapped. *Royal Society of Health Journal,* **93**, 208–212.

Haller, A. (1963). *The occupational aspiration scale.* East Lansing: Michigan State University.

Kennedy, M. (1980). *Sport role socialization and attitudes toward physical activity.* Unpublished master's thesis, University of Oregon, Eugene.

Kenyon, G.S., & McPherson, B.D. (1973). Becoming involved in physical activity and sport: A process of socialization. In G.L. Rarick (Ed.), *Physical activity: Human growth and development* (pp. 303–332). New York: Academic Press.

Loy, J.W., & Ingham, A. (1973). Play, games, and sport in the psychological development of child and youth. In G.L. Rarick (Ed.), *Physical activity: Human growth and development* (pp. 257–302). New York: Academic Press.

Mastenbroek, A.C. (1979). *Delta and net muscular efficiency in wheelchair athletes during steady rate exercise in two types of wheelchairs.* Unpublished master's thesis, University of Oregon, Eugene.

Nie, N.H., Hull, C.H., Jenkins, J.G., Steinbrenner, K., & Bert, D.H. (1975). *Statistical package for the social sciences.* New York: McGraw-Hill.

Rosenberg, M. (1965). *Society and the adolescent self-image.* Princeton, NJ: Princeton University Press.

Weiss, M., & Beck, J. (1973). Sport as a part of therapy and rehabilitation of paraplegics. *Paraplegia,* **11**, 166–172.

21

Sport Anxiety
and Elite Blind Athletes

James Vincent Mastro and Ron French
TEXAS WOMAN'S UNIVERSITY
DENTON, TEXAS, USA

> The mind is sport science's last frontier. All other systems have been extensively used to improve athletic performances.
>
> Straub, 1978, p. i

Competitive sport opportunities for blind individuals have rapidly increased in the past decade. Today, with numerous opportunities to compete in a variety of sports, a need exists to develop training techniques to improve the quality of performance during competitive events. One area that is generally overlooked in training blind athletes is psychological preparation, particularly the management of precompetition anxiety.

Anxiety is a common psychological characteristic of all individuals. Spielberger, Gorsuch, and Lushene (1970) have identified two interdependent forms of anxiety. *Trait anxiety* is a reflection of the anxiety-proneness of a person. It represents a rather permanent disposition. In contrast, *state anxiety* reflects feelings of tension, nervousness, and apprehension which occur during a stressful situation such as a competitive event. State anxiety represents a person's reactions to transitory situations or situational stress. A person who is characterized by high-trait anxiety will respond with a high degree of state anxiety in more situations than will an individual with low-trait anxiety (Cratty, 1983; Magill, 1980).

Based on an extensive review of the literature, Morgan (1980) stated that athletes differ from nonathletes in anxiety levels. These differences become more noticeable when elite athletes are considered. It is generally agreed that athletes elicit an optimum level of anxiety prior to competition (Hanin, 1980; Klavora, 1975). Athletes who demonstrate too high or too low precompetition anxiety will probably need assistance in the interpretation of anxiety levels and in management techniques (Ziegler, 1980). The importance of this psychological assistance is clearly evident in a statement by Kozar and Lord (1983): "Virtually all who have been involved in sports either as participants or coaches are well aware that both coaches and athletes have been saying for years that the game is 80–90% mental and 10–20% is physical" (p. 78).

Evaluation of anxiety levels may be more important for blind athletes than for sighted athletes because stress situations may be heightened by lack of visual cues (Hardy & Cull, 1972; Peake & Leonard, 1971; Wycherly & Nicklin, 1970). Anxiety may be acute for athletes who have recently become visually impaired and now must support themselves and, in some cases, a family (Klemz, 1977). Moreover, blind individuals tend to exhibit a higher anxiety level than sighted people when performing physical activities (Buell, 1974; Wycherly & Nicklin, 1970). The performance of motor tasks without visual cues not only increases anxiety but also increases the metabolic requirements of the circulatory, respiratory, and neuromuscular systems (Jankowski & Evans, 1981).

The purposes of this investigation were to (a) analyze the trait and state anxiety levels of elite, male, blind athletes; (b) compare the level of anxiety between athletes who have congenital or adventitious visual impairments; and (c) compare the state anxiety of high and low trait anxious blind athletes.

Methods

Subjects

The subjects were 33 male, elite athletes, ages 16 to 32 years (M = 21.30 yrs). All subjects represented the United States in the 1984 International Games for the Disabled. The onset of blindness was congenital for 17 (52%) athletes and adventitious for 16 (48%) athletes. Degree of blindness varied as follows: totally blind/light perception, 14; motion perception to 20/600 and/or visual field of 5 degrees, 7; and visual acuity of 20/599 to 20/200 and/or visual field of 5 to 20 degrees, 12.

Instrumentation and Data Collection

The State Trait Anxiety Inventory (STAI; Spielberger et al., 1970) was utilized to determine the precompetition anxiety of elite, male, blind athletes. The STAI consists of state and trait subscales, each comprised of 20 items that are presented on a 4-point scale. Spielberger et al. reported test-retest reliability coefficients of .73 and .33 on the trait and state subscales respectively. Since state anxiety is not a persistent characteristic, low state reliability is desirable.

To demonstrate that STAI data are as reliable when a test administrator reads the items as when subjects do their own reading, Mastro, French, Henschen, and Horvat (1984) administered the STAI to undergraduate students in two modalities: auditorially and visually. The resulting r was .85 on the trait subscale and .73 on the state subscale; from this finding it was inferred that the STAI could be read to visually impaired subjects rather than asking them to use Braille or large print format. Both criterion and construct validity also have been calculated for the STAI. These coefficients range from .52 to .80 (Spielberger et al., 1970).

In the present investigation, five research assistants were trained to administer the STAI to insure that procedures used to collect the data were the same for each subject. Both the state and trait subscales were administered individually 6 days prior to the International Games for the Disabled. The state subscale was again individually administered 1 day prior to the start of competition.

Results and Discussion

The blind athletes in this study were easily within the range expected in the general population in both trait (M = 48) and state anxiety (M = 50) on both administrations. Similar mean T-scores have been reported for elite, sighted athletes. For instance, Silva, Shultz, Haslam, and Murray (1981) reported trait and state mean T-scores of 50 and 55 for elite, sighted wrestlers.

The correlation coefficients between the trait anxiety and state 1 anxiety (r = .25, p = .16) and trait anxiety and state 2 anxiety (r = −.20, p = .26) were low for the blind athletes in this study. Spielberger et al. (1970) also reported low correlations between trait and state subscale scores. Changes in state anxiety are apparently unrelated to the level of trait anxiety (Hodges & Spielberger, 1966). This is particularly true when changes in state anxiety are caused by exposure to physical danger or threats to self-esteem.

Mean scores in a stressful condition are generally expected to be significantly higher than in a nonstress situation (Sachs & Diesenhaus, 1969). Huddleston and Gill (1981) concluded that competition, particularly the anticipation of competition, leads to increased state anxiety. The findings of the present investigation did not support this conclusion. Table 1 reveals that no significant difference existed between State 1 and State 2 scores, (F[1,31] = .06, p = .80), collected 6 days before and 1 day before the commencement of international competition.

Several possible explanations are available for this result. First, researchers have indicated that regularly scheduled practices may elicit state anxiety levels similar to those created by a competitive event (Huddleston & Gill, 1981; Klavora, 1975). In the present investigation, athletes were involved in practices and competition both before and during training camp. Most were training intensively for at least two sports. It appears that intensive training immediately before international competition elicits state anxiety levels in blind athletes similar to those reported by Klavora (1975) for sighted athletes. Klavora

Table 1. Comparison of congenitally and adventitiously blind athletes on state anxiety scores over two testing times

Source	df	SS	MS	F	p
Group	1	90.84	90.84	1.17	.88
Time of Testing	1	3.79	3.79	.06	.81
Interaction	1	132.28	132.28	2.08	.16
Error	31	1974.66	63.70		

reported that male high school football and basketball players experience increased state anxiety between practice and the commencement of the playing season but not between the commencement of playing season and the playoffs.

A second explanation for the lack of significant differences between the two state anxiety scores may be that the second test administration was not close enough to the time of competition. Huddleston and Gill (1981) have suggested that the state anxiety measures should be taken immediately before the actual competition (i.e., 45 minutes before the beginning of the event and 5 minutes prior to the first competition). Rules of the International Games for the Disabled did not permit collection of anxiety data so close to the actual competition. The findings of this research also differed from those of Peake and Leonard (1971) and Wycherly and Nicklin (1970), who reported differences in state anxiety levels as measured by heart rate just prior to, during, and after some form of physical activity. Wycherly and Nicklin (1970) suggested that the differences were probably due to psychological rather than physical stress because the motor activity was a walking task over a relatively short distance. Heart rate monitoring may be a more stringent measure of state anxiety than the paper-pencil test used in the present study.

The data were further analyzed to compare the levels of state anxiety between athletes who have congenital versus adventitious visual impairments. No significant differences resulted, $F(1,31) = 1.17$, $p = .29$. However, a trend leaned toward a significant difference on the first administration with adventitious subjects exhibiting lower state anxiety ($M = 34.93$, $SD = 7.48$) than congenital subjects ($M = 40.12$; $SD = 7.24$). This trend was not evident 1 week later on the second test administration: adventitious, $M = 38.25$, $SD = 8.30$; congenital, $M = 37.76$, $SD = 10.01$. The lack of significant difference supports the findings of Dean (1957), who also could not differentiate specific psychological characteristics based on congenital versus adventitious onset of blindness. One reason for no significant difference between the time of onset of visual impairment and the level of anxiety may be that the groups differed in the amount of usable vision, and this variability confounded the findings. Fourteen (82%) of the congenitally blind athletes had visual acuity within the range of 20/200 to motion perception, and only 3 had no vision. In contrast, 11 (60%) of the adventitiously blind athletes had no vision. A chi-square test indicated that the difference in usable vision in the two groups was significant, ($\chi^2[1] = 8.81$, $p < .01$). Another reason for no significant difference may be the similarities in childhood opportunities to learn sports. The congenitally blind athletes, most of whom had some usable vision, may have been provided comparable opportunities to participate in sports and athletics as the adventitiously blind whose average age of onset of visual impairment was 12.9 years. Most of the congenitally blind athletes had enough usable vision to participate in a regular physical education environment. Thus most of the athletes (both congenitally and adventitiously blind) may have had opportunities to participate in a regular physical education environment before the age of 12.9 years, the mean age for onset of blindness.

To compare the state anxiety levels of high- and low-trait anxious blind athletes, the trait anxiety scores of the upper third ($n = 11$) and lower third ($n = 11$) of the sample were compared on State 1 and 2 scores. When the

Table 2. Comparison of high- and low-trait anxiety blind athletes on state anxiety scores over two testing times

Source	df	SS	MS	F	p
Group	1	63764.20	5.11	.11	.74
Time of Testing	1	1.11	1.11	.02	.94
Interaction	1	102.02	102.02	1.42	.25
Error	20	1437.36	71.87		

subjects were grouped by level of trait anxiety, no significant difference existed between State 1 and State 2 anxiety scores ($F[1,20] = .02$, $p = .94$). This finding differs from that of research on sighted athletes (Magill, 1980).

Also, no significant differences existed between state anxiety scores of blind athletes classified as high- and low- trait anxious ($F[1,20] = .11$, $p < .74$). The high-trait anxiety group did not exhibit the high state of anxiety that characterizes the high-trait anxiety sighted population (Magill, 1980). This lack of difference may have occurred because the data were not collected close enough to the competitive event.

Another possible explanation is that high- and low-trait anxiety blind athletes do not exhibit extreme enough scores to be truly classified as high anxious or low anxious. Hall and Purvis (1980) classified trait scores of more than 45 (upper 20th percentile) as high-trait anxiety and less than 31 (lower 23rd percentile) as low-trait anxiety. Other classification techniques are even more restrictive. In the present investigation the high anxious subjects' trait scores were higher than 38 (upper 50th percentile of normative sample) and the low anxious subjects' trait scores were below 31 (lower 23rd percentile of normative sample).

Conclusion

Based on the findings of this investigation, blind athletes, regardless of congenital or adventitious onset, exhibit similar anxiety levels when compared to the general population and specifically to sighted athletes. Blind athletes classified as high- and low-trait anxious do not exhibit differences in state anxiety. This finding is generally in contrast to results reported in the literature for sighted athletes. Physical educators and coaches should not have preconceived notions about the anxiety levels of blind athletes but should plan training programs based on the psychological characteristics of each athlete.

References

Buell, C.E. (1974). *Physical education for blind children* (2nd ed.). Springfield, IL: Charles C. Thomas.

Cratty, B. (1983). *Psychology in contemporary sport* (2nd ed.). Englewood Cliffs, NJ: Prentice-Hall.

Dean, S. (1957). Adjustment testing and personality factors of the blind. *Journal of Consulting Psychology, 11*, 171–177.

Hall, E., & Purvis, G. (1980). The relation of trait anxiety and state anxiety to competitive bowling. In W. Straub (Ed.), *Sport psychology* (2nd ed.) (pp. 250–256). Ithaca, NY: Mouvement Publications.

Hanin, Y. (1980). A study of anxiety in sports. In W. Straub (Ed.), *Sport psychology* (2nd ed.) (pp. 236–249). Ithaca, NY: Mouvement Publications.

Hardy, R.E., & Cull, J.D. (1972). *Social and rehabilitation services for the blind.* Springfield, IL: Charles C. Thomas.

Hodges, W., & Spielberger, C. (1966). The effects of threat of shock on heart rate for subjects who differ in manifest anxiety and fear of shock. *Psychophysiology, 2*, 287–294.

Huddleston, S., & Gill, D. (1981). State anxiety as a function of skill level and proximity to competition. *Research Quarterly for Exercise and Sport, 52*, 31–34.

Jankowski, L.W., & Evans, J.K. (1981). The exercise capacity of blind children. *Journal of Visual Impairment and Blindness, 75*, 248–251.

Klavora, P. (1975). Application of the Spielberger trait-state anxiety model and STAI in pre-competition anxiety research. In D. Landers (Ed.), *Psychology of sport and motor behavior II* (Pennsylvania State HPER Series No. 10, pp. 141–144). State College: Pennsylvania State University.

Klemz, A. (1977). *Blindness and partial sight.* Cambridge, Great Britain: Woodhead-Falkner.

Kozar, B., & Lord, R. (1983). Psychological considerations for training the elite athlete. In E.R. Hall and M. McIntyre (Eds.), *Olympism: A movement of the people: Proceedings of the United States Olympic Academy VII* (pp. 78–96). Lubbock: Texas Tech University.

Magill, R. (1980). *Motor learning concepts and applications.* Dubuque, IA: Wm. C. Brown.

Mastro, J., French, R., Henschen, K., & Horvat, M. (1984). *Use of the State-Trait Anxiety Inventory with visually impaired athletes.* Unpublished manuscript, Texas Woman's University, Denton.

Morgan, W. (1980). The trait psychology controversy. *Research Quarterly for Exercise and Sport, 51*, 50–76.

Peake, P., & Leonard, J.A. (1971). The use of heart rate as an index of stress in blind pedestrians. *Ergonomics, 14*, 189–204.

Sachs, D., & Diesenhaus, H. (1969). *The effects of stress and order of administration on measures of state and trait anxiety.* Unpublished manuscript, New Mexico State University, Las Cruces. Cited in C. Spielberger, R. Gorsuch, & R. Lushene (1970). *STAI Manual.* Palo Alto, CA: Consulting Psychologists Press, Inc.

Silva, J., Shultz, B., Haslam, R., & Murray, D. (1981). A psychological assessment of elite wrestlers. *Research Quarterly for Exercise and Sport, 52*, 348–358.

Spielberger, C., Gorsuch, R., & Lushene, R. (1970). *STAI Manual.* Palo Alto, CA: Consulting Psychologists Press, Inc.

Straub, W. (1978). *Sport psychology: An analysis of athletic behavior.* Ithaca, NY: Mouvement Publications.

Wycherly, R.S., & Nicklin, B.H. (1970). The heart rate of blind and sighted pedestrians on a town route. *Ergonomics, 13*, 181–192.

Ziegler, S. (1980). Meditation and sports performance. In W. Straub (Ed.), *Sport psychology* (2nd ed.), (pp. 257–264). Ithaca, NY: Mouvement Publications.

PART VI
Applied Research

22

Survey of Wheelchair Athletic Injuries—Common Patterns and Prevention

Kathleen A. Curtis
MOUNT ST. MARY'S COLLEGE
LOS ANGELES, CALIFORNIA, USA

Deborah A. Dillon
INSTITUTE FOR MEDICAL RESEARCH
SAN JOSE, CALIFORNIA, USA

An estimated 4000 to 5000 physically disabled individuals are involved in organized athletic competition within the United States. A large number also participate in recreational sports. The scope of wheelchair athletic participation includes swimming, track and field, road racing, archery, weight lifting, table tennis, tennis, basketball, winter sports, bowling, billiards, boating, and many other recreational and competitive sports.

Although numerous publications in recent years have addressed injury prevention and treatment for the able-bodied athlete, little information is available on injuries sustained by the wheelchair athlete. Jackson (1979) reported that 184 athletes were treated for a variety of injuries at the 1976 Torontolympiad for the Physically Disabled. Corcoran (1980) addressed the potential risks of wheelchair marathon racing. In addition, chronic shoulder problems have been identified as a complication of long-term wheelchair use, especially with increasing age (Nichols, 1979).

The purpose of this study is to determine commonly experienced athletic injuries, sport participation, and training patterns associated with injuries among wheelchair athletes. This paper addresses implications for injury prevention.

This research was supported in part by the Northern California Regional Spinal Injury System, Grant No. G008435010, Project No. 128EH40013, from the Rehabilitation Services Administration, U.S. Department of Education, Washington, D.C. 20202.

Method

A questionnaire was distributed to over 1200 disabled athletes participating in regional wheelchair athletic competition. Information was collected regarding each individual's disability, wheelchair sport participation, use of protective gear, and history of injuries sustained during these sport activities.

Results

Subjects

One hundred and one men (79%) and 27 women (21%) responded. The mean age of respondents was 29.25 ± 7.59 years with a range of 14 to 53, and athletes averaged 14.13 ± 10.39 years since the onset of disability. Disabilities included 65% spinal cord injury, 13% post-polio, 9% congenital disorders, 3% amputations, and 10% other neuromuscular and musculoskeletal disorders. A breakdown by neurological level using National Wheelchair Athletic Association (NWAA) Classification shows that Class IV (T-10 to L-2 paraplegia) was the largest group for both men and women, comprising 28% of the total group.

Wheelchair Sport Participation History

Thirty-two different sports were listed by the athletes responding to the questionnaire. The largest percentages of athletes were involved in track (79%), basketball (71%), swimming (61%), field events (60%), and road racing (57%).

Both males and females reported an average sport participation of 4.35 ± 1.76 days per week. Athletes reported training from 0 to over 25 hours per week, with the most common time being from 6-10 hours (36%). Of all who responded, 69% reported using protective gear such as gloves, safety glasses, or helmets during sport participation to minimize the risks of injury.

Sport Injuries

Seventy-two percent of all athletes responding reported at least one injury from the time of initial participation in wheelchair sports, with some reporting as many as 14 injuries. The 93 athletes who reported injuries sustained a total of 291 injuries. Common injuries reported are listed in Table 1. The most prevalent were soft tissue injuries (33%), blisters (18%), and skin lacerations/abrasions (17%).

Soft tissue injuries, including muscle pulls, strains, sprains, bursitis, and tendonitis, were frequently reported at shoulders, elbows, wrists, and hands. Many of these injuries were recurrent. Few athletes reported seeking medical attention or treatment and tended to use self-treatment for these injuries. Blisters of the hands and fingers and skin lacerations of the hands, fingers, and arms also occurred commonly.

Table 2 indicates that the majority of injuries were associated with track (26%), basketball (24%), and road racing (22%). Injury risk level has been calculated for all sports in which at least 30 athletes indicated that they par-

Table 1. Common wheelchair athletic injuries

Injury	Percentage of all injuries reported (n = 291)
Soft tissue injuries[a]	33
Blisters	18
Lacerations/abrasions/cuts[b]	17
Decubitus/pressure areas	7
Arthritis/joint disorders	5
Fractures	5
Hand weakness/numbness	5
Temperature regulation disorders	3
Head injury/concussion	2
Dental injury	1
Miscellaneous Other (less than 1% each)	4

[a]Soft tissue includes sprains, strains, muscle pulls, tendonitis, and bursitis.
[b]Lacerations includes skin infections and other subsequent complications.

Table 2. Injury patterns among five highest risk sports

Sport	Number of injuries reported	Percent of total injuries reported (n = 291)	Percent of athletes participating (n = 128)
Track	93	26	79
Basketball	84	24	71
Road racing	77	22	57
Tennis	20	6	33
Field events	15	4	60

ticipated (Figure 1). The three highest risk sports for injury in this sample were road racing, basketball, and track. Very low injury risk sports included pool, bowling, archery, slalom, and table tennis.

For the five highest risk sports, individual sport injury patterns varied somewhat. Soft tissue injuries accounted for 33-53% of all injuries in each of the highest risk sports except track, where blisters accounted for 29% of injuries, and soft tissue injuries followed with 27%. Blisters of the hands were a significant problem (20-30% of all reported injuries) in road racing, basketball, track, and tennis.

Those athletes involved in a higher number of sports over their participation history reported a significantly higher number of injuries (p < .0001).

Similarly, a higher number of hours per week spent training was related to a higher number of injuries reported (p < .02). A higher than expected proportion of injuries (p < .01) was found in the 21-30 years age group.

No significant relationship was apparent between sex or age and training patterns, nor was there any difference between males and females and the number of injuries reported. Also, disability type and NWAA classification were not related significantly to the number of injuries reported.

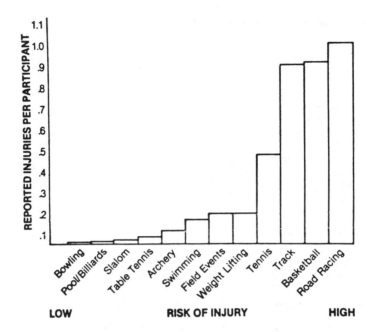

Figure 1. Relative occurrence of reported injuries by sport involvement. Road racing, basketball, and track injuries account for 72% of all reported injuries.

Discussion

A fairly consistent pattern among the high-risk repetitive wheelchair pushing sports (road racing, basketball, track, and tennis) were soft tissue injuries, blisters, abrasions, lacerations, and hand weakness/numbness. These findings may indicate an overuse phenomenon, with injury resulting from continuous work of the arms to push the wheelchair. Of particular concern are the soft tissue injuries and hand weakness/numbness which may become chronic problems.

Ligamentous sprains, tendonitis, and bursitis may result in chronic problems if treated improperly (O'Donaghue, 1976). Preventive measures should be taken to decrease the risk of further injury. As performance can be altered drastically by a recurrent injury, it is in the athlete's best interest to rest an injury, seek medical attention, and slowly start on a program of progressive strength, endurance, and power training before returning to a full workout or competitive schedule.

Hand weakness and numbness, commonly associated with carpal tunnel syndrome, may be caused by the constant trauma and compression of the heel of the hand for each arm stroke on the pushrim. Pain or tingling in the thumb and first two fingers should be signs for the athlete to seek proper diagnosis and treatment.

Mechanisms of common injuries and means of prevention are described in Table 3. The high number of soft tissue injuries, blisters, and lacerations point to the need for intervention and active means of education for wheelchair athletes and coaches.

As a pilot investigation, this study provides subjective, historical information from athletes, not a diagnosis or injury registry by sport medicine professionals. The sample responding to the survey was biased as they were most likely individuals either concerned enough about their injuries to report them or more likely to respond because they had sustained injuries. The intent of the survey was to gather information about trends seen in athletic injuries of wheelchair athletes.

In summary, it may be helpful for future research in this area to be conducted on the basis of information reported by health professionals, to focus

Table 3. Injury causes and prevention in wheelchair athletics

Causes	Prevention
Soft tissue injuries	
Ligamentous injury (falls, physical contact)	Routine stretching, warm-up, cool-down
Overuse muscles, tendons	Protection of old injuries (splinting, taping)
Overexertion without warmup	Slow progression of conditioning program
	Rest, proper treatment of recurrent injuries
Blisters	
Friction (hands on wheelchair pushrim)	Encourage callous formation
Friction (back) on upholstery and/or seat post	Tape fingers; wear gloves
	Pad seat post; wear shirt
Abrasions/lacerations	
Finger contact with brake, armrest socket, or pushrim	Remove hazardous wheelchair parts
Scraping inner arms on tires	Wear arm guards—upper arms
Trapping fingers between wheelchairs (basketball)	Camber wheels
Decubitus/pressure areas	
Friction, pressure buttocks/sacrum	Adequate cushioning under buttocks
Wheelchair design (knees elevated)	Skin checks, weight shifting
Sweat, moisture	Nutrition, hygiene
	Absorbent clothing
Temperature regulation disorders	
Exposure to heat/cold	Insulating clothing
Inadequate autonomic regulation (SCI)	Assisted heat convection
Fluid loss/inadequate intake	Minimize exposure
	Replace fluids

on determining the incidence of injury by using a random sample, and to include criteria for ranking the severity of a particular injury (i.e., days missed from training).

Summary

Road racing, basketball, and track showed the highest percentage of wheelchair athletic injuries. Athletes, coaches, and trainers need to be aware of the causes and means of prevention of common wheelchair sports injuries. Good coaching, attention to equipment maintenance, good officiating, and good health supervision can all optimize performance and prevent injury.

References

Corcoran, P.J. (1980). Sports medicine and the physiology of wheelchair marathon racing. *Orthopedic Clinics of North America, 11*(4), 697–716.

Jackson, R.W. (1979). Sports for the physically disabled, the 1976 Olympiad (Toronto). *American Journal of Sports Medicine, 7*, 293–296.

Nichols, P.J. (1979). Wheelchair user's shoulder? Shoulder pain in patients with spinal cord lesions. *Scandinavian Journal of Rehabilitation, 11*, 29–32.

O'Donaghue, D.H. (1976). *Treatment of injuries to athletes (3rd ed.).* Philadelphia: W.B. Saunders.

23

Blind Athletes Successfully Compete Against Able-Bodied Opponents

Charles Buell
CALIFORNIA ASSOCIATION FOR BLIND ATHLETES
SAN JUAN CAPISTRANO, CALIFORNIA, USA

To better understand how blind athletes successfully compete in the mainstream in many sports, some misconceptions widely held must be corrected. It is generally believed that blindness and sightlessness refer to the same condition. This is not true. According to United States law, blindness is defined as 20/200 or 1/10 or less of normal vision. Actually, at least 80% of blind people have some useful vision. This, of course, makes it easier for them to compete against sighted opponents. Many totally blind individuals, however, are successful also. This paper has three general purposes: (a) to briefly describe conditions currently faced by blind individuals in regular athletics; (b) to list a few efforts being made to improve conditions; and (c) to cite examples of sightless and low vision athletes competing in the mainstream.

Barriers to Full Participation

The greatest barrier to blind athletes competing against opponents who have normal vision is the widespread existence of misconceptions (Buell, 1982). It is common practice to excuse blind students, even those with useful vision, from physical education classes or to overprotect them during physical education instruction, insisting that they keep score or sit on the bench while their sighted peers engage in vigorous exercise. Physiologically, however, no reason exists to explain why blind students should not compete on interscholastic and intercollegiate athletic levels. The present writer, legally blind since birth, competed in integrated high school sports in the 1930s and went on to become a physical education teacher and coach. His biography, written by Whitley (1980), shows the importance of supportive attitudes on the parts of both family and teachers.

Recent research indicates that many blind people feel that their parents are overprotective in regard to their learning and participating in sports (Sherrill, Rainbolt, & Ervin, 1984). Whereas the family is overwhelmingly the most significant factor in sighted children becoming interested in sport, a study of 133 elite blind athletes indicated the following as the most influential: physical education teacher/coach, 41%; family, 15%; self, 11%; friends, 8%; combinations of factors, 29%; other, 6% (Sherrill, Pope, & Arnhold, in press). Thus blind children and youth are not socialized into sport in the same ways and by the same significant factors as sighted youngsters. While many blind people do compete in individual and team sports, it is estimated that two blind individuals are not being given the opportunity to learn and engage in sport for every one blind individual who is (Buell, 1983).

Efforts Being Made to Improve Conditions

Athletics and physical fitness are just as important for blind individuals as for their sighted peers. The only way physical fitness can be attained is by vigorous exercise. Several U.S. laws have been enacted to assure the rights of the blind, as well as other disabled individuals, to the fitness and health that sport participation affords. Among these are the Rehabilitation Act (1973) and the Education for All Handicapped Children Act (1975). Additionally, a little known provision of the Education Amendments (1972) to the Elementary and Secondary Act of 1965 is important to blind people who wish to enroll in physical education classes. Section 904 of this law states the following:

> No person in the United States shall, on the ground of blindness or severely impaired vision, be denied admission in any course of study by a recipient of Federal financial assistance for any education program or activity.

Section 504 of the Rehabilitation Act states the following:

> No otherwise qualified handicapped individual in the United States, as defined in section 7 (6), shall, solely by reason of his handicap, be excluded from the participation in, be denied the benefits of, or be subjected to discrimination under any program or activity receiving Federal financial assistance.

PL 94–142 states that all handicapped students shall receive physical education instruction in the least restrictive environment. For most blind children this is the mainstream (Buell, 1982).

Litigation is also being used to improve conditions for blind people in regard to sport participation. Appenzeller (1983) reviews numerous court cases litigated for all alleged violations of these laws. The following are illustrative of these:

> The mother of a blind student alleged that her son, Michael, was not permitted to participate fully in a game of "goal line soccer" during a physical education class. An investigation revealed that Michael had fully participated in "goal line

soccer" on Tuesday of the week in question without injury. His teacher moved him to the sidelines on Thursday to avoid possible injury. Michael's mother complained that the teacher's failure to permit her son to fully participate in "goal line soccer" violated Section 504 of the Rehabilitation Act. The complaint was upheld and the school notified that Michael must be allowed to take part fully in all physical education activities. (Appenzeller, 1983, p. 8)

An outstanding Pennsylvania high school running back was recruited to play intercollegiate football at Columbia University. The University's physician recommended that he not be allowed to play since he had only one eye. The court found that the University's action in prohibiting the student from participating in football to be in violation of Section 504 of the Rehabilitation Act of 1973. (Appenzeller, 1983, p. 9)

Most teacher training programs now include knowledge of laws and litigation in courses that physical education majors take. With increasing knowledge, attitudes are changing with regard to participation in athletics by blind people.

Another effort has had some impact in improving conditions in athletics for blind individuals. In January of 1977 the President's Commission on Olympic Sports published a 613-page report. Some of the sections were devoted to sports for the handicapped. One of the recommendations made was "to foster the incorporation of sports programs and opportunities for the various handicapped groups into the overall athletic environment" (President's Commission on Olympic Sports, 1977, p. 118). As a result of this report and the efforts of advocates for opportunities for blind people, the National Federation of High Schools has made two modifications in its rule books. The Wrestling Rule Book says, "In matches involving a sight-handicapped wrestler, the finger touch method shall be used in the neutral position and initial contact shall be made from the front" (McGuinness, 1983, p. 20). Interpretations of this rule indicate that contact must be maintained until a break for a takedown is made. Initial movement on the break must be forward. The Track Rule Book now permits a blind athlete to be guided physically by a sighted partner (Frederick, 1984, p. 21). Many marathons and distance runs now make provision for and include blind runners.

Blind Athletes in the Mainstream

This section of the paper is devoted to descriptions of blind athletes competing in the mainstream. Sports included are contact sports, water sports, track and field, distance running, powerlifting, gymnastics, skating, biking, mountain climbing, distance walking, sailing, football, golf, and sky diving. It is hoped that some of the misconceptions concerning blindness can be eliminated by disseminating such information.

More blind athletes have demonstrated their capabilities to compete equally against opponents with normal vision in wrestling than in any other sport. Each year it is estimated that 5,000 sighted wrestlers compete against opponents who are sightless or have low vision. For many years blind wrestlers have won state high school wrestling championships. In 1984 blind wrestlers won state championships in Alaska and South Carolina. Keith West, 54.0 kg (119 lbs), won an individual championship in the Alabama State meet. In the finals he defeated a two-time state champion. He finished the season with a record of 29–1. In South Carolina sightless Lonzy Jenkins won an individual state championship. In the process he defeated a two-time state champion. Jenkins posted a 17–1–1 season. James Mastro, 89.8 kg (198 lbs), who now lives in Texas, has only light perception vision. In 1976 he wrestled in the finals to qualify for the Olympics despite a broken arm and subsequently was selected as an alternate on the U.S. Wrestling Team, which competed in the Montreal Olympics.

In 1980 sightless Anthony Maczynski, Delaware, won a black belt in judo. A few years ago he placed sixth in a national karate championship.

Trischa Zorn is one of the top 15 backstrokers in the U.S., blind or sighted. She has times of 59.46 sec for 91.4 m (100 yds) and 2:06.64 for 182.8 m (200 yds) in the backstroke. At the 1984 Big 8 Conference Swim Meet she placed second in the 182.8 m (200 yd) backstroke with a time of 2:08.32. She also swam the backstroke leg of the University of Nebraska 182.8 m (200 yd) medley relay team, which placed second. At Mission Viejo High School, California, Zorn was selected three times on the All-America High School Female Swim Team. When she graduated she was offered 12 full athletic scholarships. She selected the University of Nebraska and has completed her sophomore year there. Zorn has 1/30 normal vision, but she makes good use of it. She can see the markings on the bottom of the pool to some degree and uses them for guidance. In swimming on her back, she uses the flags stretched across the pool to help her make good turns. Of course the thousands of laps that she has completed in 9 years of double daily workouts have helped her to better judge distances and make good turns. In practice her teammates tell her how much time remains on the clock.

After sustaining a detached retina, John Morgan believed he could no longer swim competitively. Eventually he entered a swim meet of the California Association of Blind Athletes and qualified to compete in the United States Association for Blind Athletes (USABA) Championships. His confidence was greatly improved because he did so well in these competitions, so he entered a 5,000 m (3.1 mi) ocean swim. A buddy swam alongside on a surf board, giving him directions from time to time. In the field of 135 swimmers, Morgan placed 10th. Thus, in a year's time, Morgan's life was completely turned around. During the spring of 1984 he was a member of the swim team of Golden West College, California. Because of the retinal condition, his doctor recommended that he start all races in the water. In doing so, he loses a second or two, compared to a diving start; nevertheless he swam 1508.76 m (1650 yds) in 16:30 sec and qualified for the California State Meet for 2-year colleges. There he was seeded third. Starting in the water, Morgan has a time of 59.2 sec for the 100 m freestyle.

Several blind people have distinguished themselves in water sports. In September of 1983 Harry Cordellos water skied from Long Beach, California, to Avalon, Catalina Island, a distance of about 50 k (31 mi). Gerald Price and Nigel Verbeeck water skied across the English Channel in 1981. Eight years earlier, Dennis Moore paddled a canoe alone across the Channel. He followed a boat with a radio playing loudly.

Some blind athletes have been members of university eight-oared crews. In 1963 John Kavanaugh was stroke for the Stanford University freshmen crew.

Oral Miller competed on the Princeton University crew during the 1950s. As a sightless oarsman he used a thumb tack on the handle of the oar to locate the direction of the blade. His teammates selected him to receive a trophy for rowing in the 1955 season.

Paul Smith, with less than 1/10th normal vision, is a member of the El Camino College track team, California. In a recent meet against Long Beach City College he ran a 100 m dash in 10.7 sec. At Narbonne High School he set a school record of 10.8 sec for 100 m. He has long jumped 6.4 m. His limited vision enables him to see the lanes in sprinting, a bright-colored baton in relay running, and the take-off board in the long jump. Under some lighting conditions Smith places a bright-colored flag at the end of the take-off board for the long jump.

In 1984 Leamon Stansell, running for Santa Monica College, California, turned in a time of 16:03.1 in the 5000 m run against Long Beach City College. In a meet against Pasadena City College he ran 1500 m in 4:17.6. Although he has less than 10% normal vision, he is able to judge when it is appropriate to pass opponents.

With less than 10% normal vision, Janet Rowley has cleared 1.55 m (5 ft, 1 in.) in the high jump. John Orcutt has a mark of 2.09 m (6 ft, 10.5 in.) in the high jump. These jumpers recently competed for Boston University and South Carolina University respectively.

At the 1983 World Masters Games in Puerto Rico, Fritz Assmy of West Germany defeated Payton Jordan in two of three races. Sightless Assmy won the 200 m and 400 m events, while former worldclass sprinter Jordan won the 100 m dash. Assmy ran in lane 8 with a short rope tethered to the wrist of his 27-year-old son/guide. The West German has run 100 m in 12.5 sec. He has inspired crowds to standing ovations.

Individuals with as little as 3% normal vision can safely run around a track which has been cleared of hurdles and other obstacles. With a little more vision, runners can participate in road races. Those who have very low or no vision participate in distance running using a sighted guide. Runners may be tethered together with a short rope. Some prefer to touch elbows from time to time. Sometimes it is better to hold hands, particularly if the terrain is rough. The best known sightless distance runner is Harry Cordellos of California (Cordellos, 1981). In 1975 he ran the Boston Marathon with a sighted partner in 2 hrs, 57 min, 42 sec. At age 46, he has run 85 marathons. Usually he places in the top 30% or higher, whether hundreds or thousands of runners are competing in the field. He has run 80.4 km (50 mi) in less than 8 hrs and has competed in the Iron Man Triathlon in Hawaii, swimming 3.9 km (2.4 mi), biking 180.3 km (112 mi), and running a marathon.

Although Carlos Talbert of Florida has less than 10% normal vision, he has run the Boston Marathon in 2 hrs, 23 min. In December of 1983, he finished third in a field of 700 in the National Super Energy Triathlon in St. Petersburg, Florida. He swam 804.7 m (1/2 mi) in the ocean, biked 32.2 km (20 mi), and ran 10 km (6.2 mi).

John Stratford ran from Wellington to Auckland in New Zealand 675.4 km (420 mi) in an elapsed time of 61.5 hrs. This was a great run for anyone, sightless or sighted. Stratford is sightless and ran the distance to show his fellow citizens that blind people can be very capable.

For blind contestants, powerlifting rules need no modification. At the 1983 Drug Free Powerlifting Championships in New Jersey, Lisa Mellea won the 46.3 kg (102 lbs) championship. She had a deadlift of 129.3 kg (285 lbs) and a total lift of 283.5 kg (625 lbs).

In the early 1980s sightless Gail Castonquay won letters in gymnastics at Weymouth South High School, Massachusetts. Pita Quintana, with 10% vision, placed second in vaulting and fifth in all-around at the 1979 New Mexico State Gymnastics Meet.

Among the visually impaired people who skate are Michael Lawson and Elwin Kelsey. Lawson skated in the 1981 Alaska State Disco Roller Derby Meet and went on to place 11th in the Western Regional Competition. In 1964 Kelsey and his partner placed fifth in the National Junior Pairs Ice Skating Competition. He subsequently became a professional with an ice follies show.

A number of blind people have tandem-cycled across the U.S. with sighted partners. One of them was legally blind 71-year-old Tom Dickey. In 1981 he biked coast to coast across the U.S. to attend the reunion of his class at Amherst College, Massachusetts. The finish of the trip was featured on television.

In July 1981 five blind climbers, an amputee, a person with epilepsy, and two deaf hikers reached the 4,392 m (14,410 ft) peak of Mt. Rainier in Washington. The group was led by expert mountain climbers. The chief purpose of the climb was to dispel the mistaken notion that the horizons of the handicapped are limited. This purpose was achieved because the climb received worldwide media coverage. In addition, more media coverage occurred when the group went to the White House to visit President Ronald Reagan.

In the fall of 1983 Bill Morgan walked across the U.S. from west to east. His road companion was a 4-year-old guide dog. They walked on the shoulder of the road. About 7 miles ahead of them was a van carrying a sign warning of a blind walker.

In August 1983 Hank Decker, with less than 10% vision, sailed 3,862 km (2,400 mi) in 23 days from San Francisco, California, to Honolulu, Hawaii. He used braille charts, a braille compass, a "talking clock," and a navigational system that read his position aloud. Shortly after starting, his radio went dead, and he was unable to communicate and get weather forecasts. So he had no warning of a tropical storm which overturned his boat for 20 min. The swirling sea finally uprighted the boat, and Decker was able to complete the journey.

A number of high school and college football players have had 10% or less vision. Keven Szott, 111.1 kg (245 lbs), is the first string center on a very good St. Lawrence University football team in Canton, New York. He played on the 1982 team which reached the Division III finals.

In the 1984 Bob Hope Tournament in Palm Springs, California, John Mahaffey and Jim Simons were tied at the end of the 90-hole event. Simon's scores were 69-63-70-69-69. In the play-off, Simons missed a 3-foot putt on the second hole. As the winner of second place, he collected $43,200. Simons is legally blind and wears heavy contact lenses. Using coaches to help them, sightless golfers have sometimes turned in scores in the upper 80s and low 90s. Charles Boswell, a blinded veteran of Birmingham, Alabama, was the leading sightless golfer for many years.

Even sky diving can be a sport for blind individuals. Among the best known sightless skydivers is Mike May of California. After a 4-hour training course in 1982, he safely parachuted from an elevation of 914 m (3000 ft) in 12 min. During the dive he was in two-way radio communication with his instructor, Bill Dawes.

Conclusion

Blind individuals have clearly demonstrated that they can participate in a variety of sports. In many sports they successfully compete with opponents who have normal vision.

Still, hundreds of high schools and colleges, at the very least, continue to excuse blind students from physical education classes. Others do not encourage participation of blind students in school and community competition.

In light of what blind athletes have accomplished, it is evident that a great injustice is being done to thousands of sightless and low vision young people. Hopefully the evidence presented here will convince administrators in schools and colleges that blind people have the right and the capabilities to compete in mainstream sports.

References

Appenzeller, H. (1983). *The right to participate: The law and individuals with handicapping conditions in physical education and sport.* Charlottesville, VA: The Michie Company.

Buell, C. (1982). *Physical education and recreation for the visually handicapped* (2nd ed.). Reston, VA: American Alliance for Health, Physical Education, Recreation, and Dance.

Buell, C. (1983). *Physical education for blind children* (2nd ed.). Springfield, IL: Charles C. Thomas.

Cordellos, H. (1981). *Breaking through.* Mountain View, CA: Anderson World.

Education Amendments of 1972, title IX, § 901–907, 20 U.S.C. 1681–1686, 29 U.S.C. § 203 and 213, and 42 U.S.C. § 2000c, 2000c-6, 2000c-9, and 2000h-2 (1982).

Education for All Handicapped Children Act of 1975, Pub. L. No. 94–142, 20 U.S.C. § 1232, 1400, 1401, 1405, 1406, 1411–1420, 1453 (1982).

Frederick, T. (Ed.). (1984). *Track and field rule book.* Kansas City, MO: National Federation of State High School Associations.

McGuiness, F. (Ed.). (1983). *Official high school wrestling rules.* Kansas City, MO: National Federation of State High School Associations.

President's Commission on Olympic Sport (1977). *Report of President's Commission on Olympic Sport.* Washington, DC: U.S. Government Printing Office.

Rehabilitation Act of 1973, 29 U.S.C. § 701–796i (1982).

Sherrill, C., Pope, C., & Arnhold, R. (in press). Sport socialization of blind athletes: An exploratory study. *Journal of Visual Impairment and Blindness.*

Sherrill, C., Rainbolt, W., & Ervin, W. (1984). Attitudes of blind persons toward physical education and recreation. *Adapted Physical Activity Quarterly,* 1(1), 3–11.

Whitley, P. (1980). *Dr. Charles Buell: Leader in physical education for the visually impaired.* Unpublished doctoral dissertation, University of North Carolina at Greensboro.

24

Physically Disabled Athletes Successfully Compete

Thomas L. Montelione and Ron Davis
TEXAS WOMAN'S UNIVERSITY
DENTON, TEXAS, USA

How is success measured? Is it through the attainment of one's personal goals, or the betterment of a standard set by others? While the former definition is acceptable in most instances of competition, the latter holds true for elite athletes. An elite athlete is one who attains a level of competition at or near national standards (Kenyon & McPherson, 1973).

Physically disabled people have increasingly been able to claim success under both definitions. They are athletes in the strictest sense of the word, familiar with the dedication, determination, and physical and mental toughness necessary to succeed. They are individuals accustomed to the hours of practice, sweat, and pain that are part of striving to be a champion. They are familiar also with the need to risk and sometimes fail.

How should society view these physically disabled athletes? Elite athletes who are disabled seek the "hero worship" and accompanying privileges that are accorded the stars in any sport. Illustrative of the feelings of many disabled athletes is the following:

> This is an opportunity for me to show people who stare at me every day what I can do. Once they see us compete, there will be no doubt in their minds that they're watching athletes. It breaks down the stereotypes. That's not my goal—my goal is to beat the best in the world—but it's a positive side-effect. Kris Lenzo, amputee wheelchair racer. (Rosner, 1984, June 10, p. 3WC)

Similar feelings have been expressed by other athletes (Crist, 1984, June 30). They want the same respect for their massive biceps, superb upper-body build, and other outstanding physical characteristics that able-bodied athletes receive. The athlete is telling us once again, "focus on my ability, not my disability."

Purpose

The purpose of this paper is to give recognition to some of the many athletes whose successes have led to wider acceptance of physically disabled people by society. These athletes are to be admired not only for their achievements in relation to a particular physical limitation but also for their meeting or surpassing previous athletic standards.

As is the case with boxing and wrestling weight divisions, in order to ensure equal competition, athletes with different disabilities compete against other athletes within the same disability/classification category. In sports for those with cerebral palsy, for example, a person who is a minimally affected hemiplegic, a Class VIII, competes against others who are in the same class.

The number of athletes with various disabilities who successfuly compete in a myriad of different sports precludes the possibility of citing all of their accomplishments. It is hoped that the personalities and accomplishments presented on the pages that follow are representative of the athlete who is physically disabled. The athlete who is blind has been discussed elsewhere (Buell, 1986). Therefore this paper will focus primarily on athletes with other physical disabilities.

Sporting Events

Archery

Archery is a sport in which individuals with certain physical disabilities can compete with able-bodied athletes. Neroll Fairhall, a wheelchair athlete from New Zealand, competed at the 1984 Los Angeles Olympic Games in archery.

Baseball

Baseball has had its share of athletes with physical disabilities who have achieved success at the major league level. Pete Gray played center field for the St. Louis Browns in 1945. Gray's right arm was amputated at the shoulder. Monty Straton and Burt Shepherd pitched for the Philadelphia Athletics and Washington Senators, respectively, in the 1930s and in 1945. Straton and Shepherd each had a prosthetic leg.

Cross Country Treks

Phil Carpenter and George Murray, two wheelchair athletes, pushed better than a marathon a day in crossing the United States in 1981, the International Year of Disabled Persons. These men were both paralyzed below the waist as a result of spinal cord injuries. Their trip, chronicled in *The Continental Quest* (McBee & Ballinger, 1984), took them 155 days of which 62 were no-push days. In pushing from Los Angeles to New York, Carpenter and Murray traveled across the Rocky Mountains, the Mojave Desert, and the Mississippi River.

Terry Fox, a below-the-knee amputee as a result of cancer, ran across a large part of Canada in 1981 raising money for cancer research. Though Terry died from cancer before he could complete this journey, his efforts heightened awareness of abilities of disabled people.

Dave Kiefer rode his bike 2,962 mi in crossing the United States in June 1984. Kiefer, whose left leg was amputated as a result of a motorcycle accident, averaged 190 mi a day in completing his cross country ride from Los Angeles to New York City.

Equestrian Events

Elizabeth Hartel of Denmark has long served as an inspiration competing in equestrian events. Hartel overcame polio to win a silver medal in the 1952 Olympic games in Helsinki. Mikko Mayeda competes in the les autres (other locomotor impaired) classification in equestrian events. Mayeda, who has multiple sclerosis and is blind, received a gold medal in obstacle course maneuvering and a silver medal in equitation at the International Games for the Disabled on Long Island in 1984.

1500 M

No distance has ever held the racing mystique that the mile has had. Roger Bannister became internationally famous for being the first to break the 4-min barrier. In Olympic competition the 1500 m replaces the mile as the standard by which distance runners are judged. The first wheelchair athlete to push 1500 m in under 4 min was Dan Westley of Canada who turned in a time of 3:57.2 in 1983. Five other athletes finished in under 4 min in the same race.

Football

Tom Dempsey, born with only half a right foot and without functional use of his right arm, successfully competed as a field goal kicker for the New Orleans Saints in the National Football League (NFL). In 1970 Dempsey set the NFL record for the longest field goal kicked—63 yds. That record is unbroken to this day.

Other athletes with physical disabilities have played professional football. They include Larry Brown, a former running back with the Washington Redskins, and Rocky Blier, a running back with the Pittsburgh Steelers. Brown had a hearing impairment, whereas Blier had lost a part of his foot because of a war injury. Both played during the late 1960s and the 1970s.

Marathon Running

Bob Hall, the first wheelchair athlete to compete in the prestigious Boston Marathon, finished with a time of 2:58:0. George Murray won the 1978 Boston Marathon in a time of 2:26:53. In doing so he was the first wheelchair athlete to come in ahead of the able-bodied competitors. Other wheelchair marathoners are now consistently breaking 2 hrs in competition. In 1983 when Jim Knaub won the Boston Marathon in a record time of 1:47:1, seven other wheelchair racers finished with a time of under 2 hrs.

The world record in the men's wheelchair marathon is 1:42:47, set by Rick Hansen of Canada in 1982. Candace Cable of the USA holds the women's record with a time of 2:08:15.

Mountain Climbing

On July 3, 1981, in an example of cooperation among people with different disabilities, Mt. Rainier in Washington was scaled. The ascent was completed by five climbers who were blind (Justin McDevitt, Kirk Adams, Sheila Holzworth, Frederick Noeser, & Douglas Wakefield), two who were deaf (Alec Naimen & Paul Stefurak), one who had epilepsy (Richard Rose), and one who had a leg amputation (Chuck O'Brien). On July 18, 1982, Don Bennit, another person with an amputated leg, also scaled Mt. Rainier.

1984 Summer Olympics

Two wheelchair races, the Women's 800 m and Men's 1,500 m, were included as demonstration events in the 1984 Summer Olympics at Los Angeles. Sixteen wheelchair athletes representing seven countries had earned the right to participate in this Olympiad by virtue of their performances at the Olympic trials held in conjunction with the 1984 International Games for the Disabled. The importance of this event in increasing the knowledge level of the able-bodied population cannot be overestimated. Therefore, all of those who competed in these races are deserving of recognition.

Sharon Rahn Hedrick (USA) took home the gold in the Woman's 800 m race with a time of 2:15.73. Monica Saker (Sweden) was second finishing with 2:20.86, whereas Candace Cable (USA) was third with 2:28.37. Other competitors in this historic race were Sacajawea Hunter (USA), Anna-Marie Orvefers (Sweden), Angela Ieriti (Canada), Connie Hanson (Denmark), and Ingrid Lauridsen (Denmark).

In the Men's 1,500 m, Paul Van Winkle of Belgium took first place with a time of 3:58.50. Randy Snow's (USA) time of 4:00.02 was good enough for second place while Andre Viger of Canada (4:00.47) took third. Other competitors included Mel Fitzgerald (Canada), Juergen Gelder (France), Peter Trotter (Australia), Rick Hanson (Canada), and Jim Martinson (USA).

The over 80,000 people in the stands and the untold millions in front of television sets that watched the wheelchair races at the 1984 Los Angeles Olympics had the opportunity to observe athletes at their best. These races will undoubtedly serve as inspiration for future athletes.

Weight Lifting

Charles Reid, a 24-year-old with cerebral palsy, competes in the bench press. Reid won a gold medal at the International Cerebral Palsy Games in Denmark in 1982 and in the 1984 International Games for the Disabled. In addition to competing against other individuals with cerebral palsy, Reid also competes in Amateur Athletic Union (AAU) meets. He placed sixth in the 1982 USA AAU Bench Press championships. Reid has bench pressed 485 pounds, which is more than three times his body weight.

Athletes

Arnie Boldt, a Canadian athlete whose right leg was amputated above the knee, high jumps by hopping six steps to the bar. Boldt has high jumped 6 ft 8-1/2 in. in competition with other disabled athletes and 6 ft 11 in. in competition with able-bodied athletes.

The long jump is a second event in which Boldt competes. In fact, Boldt won gold medals in the A-2 amputee (single amputation above the knee) class in both the high jump and long jump in the 1976, 1980, and 1984 International Games for the Disabled in Canada, Holland, and the United States, respectively.

Linda Down, a marathoner with spastic cerebral palsy (Class V, i.e., ambulatory with crutches), achieved national recognition with her performance in the 1982 New York City Marathon. Her time was 11 hrs 15 min for the 26.2-mi trek. Though her time was not a standard setter it was remarkable in view of the severity of her condition and her lack of proper training. Today Linda runs the marathon in 8 hrs 45 min (Burfoot, 1984).

Illustrative of athletes who participate in life to its fullest is Scott Sneider. A white water canoer, Sneider also snow skis using an Arroya sled (Taylor, 1984 and participates in organized sports in the les autres category. Sneider, who has muscular dystrophy, received a silver medal for his efforts in the 400-m race at the International Games for the Disabled in 1984.

Among the other multi-talented athletes who competed at the 1984 International Games for the Disabled was Nancy Anderson. Anderson is classified as a Class II (upper) athlete for her participation in cerebral palsy sports. She won gold medals in individual bocce, wheelchair slalom, and 20-m wheelchair dash, breaking the world's record in the latter two events. She also won a silver medal for the 25-m freestyle swimming, a bronze medal as part of team bocce, and finished fourth in the shot put in her class.

John Jerome, classified as A-1 amputee (double above knee), won gold medals in the shot put, discus, and javelin in the 1976 International Games for the Disabled held in Toronto. He repeated this feat at the World Amputee Games in Stokes-Manville, England, 1979, and in 1980 at the International Games for the Disabled in Holland.

Any listing of great athletes whose determination transcended their physical limitations would be incomplete without mention of Wilma Rudolph. A triple gold medalist in the 1960 Rome Olympics in the 100-m, 200-m, and 400-m relays, Rudolph achieved greatness despite both birth defects and polio.

Conclusion

Athletes who are physically disabled have shown their ability and determination in events ranging from bocce to basketball, from swimming to skydiving, and from mountain climbing to marathoning. Some participate for the sheer joy of it and some feel that anything less than first place means leaving the athletic field a loser. In short, anything that can be said about athletics for the able-bodied, pro or con, can be said about athletics for the disabled.

Sport serves as a socializing agent in every society. The advantages of participating in sport are many, but two stand out. First, the skills learned on the playing field allow both disabled and able-bodied individuals to function better as part of a team, a necessary skill in any society. Second, sport achievements help the able-bodied population to see past the disability and recognize the ability of the person competing. If involvement in sports helps to erase a stereotype, then that athlete has been successful.

References

Buell, C. (1985). Blind athletes successfully compete against able-bodied opponents. In C. Sherrill (Ed.), *Sport and disabled athletes: Proceedings of the 1984 International Scientific Congress*. Champaign, IL: Human Kinetics.

Burfoot, A. (1984). The long run of Linda Down. *Runner's World, 19*(10), 72-76.

Crist, S. (1984, June 30). Pride without pity. *New York Times*, p. 33.

Kenyon, G., & McPherson, B. (1973). Becoming involved in physical activity and sport: A process of socialization. In G.L. Rarick (Ed.), *Physical activity: Human growth and development* (pp. 303-332). New York: Academic Press.

McBee, F., & Ballinger, J. (1984). *The continental quest*. Tampa, FL: Overland Press.

Rosner, D. (1984, June 10). Only athletes need apply. *World Class Commemorative Edition, Newsday*, pp. 3WC, 7WC.

Taylor, P. (1984). People in sport: Peter Axelson. *Sports 'N Spokes, 8*(6), 28-30.

25

Normative Health-Related Fitness Data for Special Olympians

Glenn M. Roswal and Peggy M. Roswal
JACKSONVILLE STATE UNIVERSITY
JACKSONVILLE, ALABAMA, USA

Aidan O. Dunleavy
LOCKHEED-GEORGIA COMPANY
MARIETTA, GEORGIA, USA

Since its inception in 1968, the Special Olympics have served to promote the physical development and learning of mentally retarded individuals. Specifically, through programs of physical fitness and athletic opportunities, the Special Olympics provide a physical learning and performance environment within which the trained special educator promotes self-concept development and learning enhancement through athletics. Teachers and coaches of Special Olympians find considerable use in learning and performance norms. Unfortunately, much of the normative data currently available to the Special Olympics educator has been developed on populations that may not be representative of the Special Olympics athlete, thereby limiting the utility of this otherwise useful information within the realms of the Special Olympics. Specifically, placement on the normative table is relative to the population examined. For example, in the area of health-related physical fitness, a mentally retarded athlete compared with AAHPERD health-related physical fitness norms would be placed at a lower percentile ranking than if compared to his or her Special Olympics peers. This may result in (a) misleading training information for the teacher, (b) underestimation of potential, and/or (c) a decrease in teacher or athlete motivation.

This study was supported by a faculty research grant from Jacksonville State University.

Research suggests that mentally retarded individuals have lower physical capacities than their nondisabled peers (Bundschuh & Cureton, 1982; Eichstaedt & Wang, 1981; Londeree & Johnson, 1974; Rarick, 1980; Rarick, Dobbins, & Broadhead, 1976). If this is indeed the case, then it follows that performance norms for the disabled population must be generated from the population itself, that is, norms are population specific. Sufficient evidence exists to suggest that the Special Olympics athlete is representative of a different population than the mentally retarded population as a whole, and thus normative data should be generated specific to the Special Olympics population.

Additionally, there is a paucity of literature regarding the health-related physical fitness of mentally retarded individuals in general and Special Olympians in particular. Health-related physical fitness relates primarily to functional health (cardiorespiratory function, body composition, and abdominal and low back-hamstring musculoskeletal function) and is distinct from performance-related physical fitness which includes abilities that enhance sport-related activity (strength, endurance, flexibility, power, agility, and balance). Although present physical fitness norms are available for mentally retarded individuals (AAHPERD, 1976; AAHPERD, 1977) and health-related physical fitness norms are available for nondisabled individuals (AAHPERD, 1980), health-related physical fitness norms for a mentally retarded population in general and specifically a Special Olympics population are currently unavailable. This needed contribution to the available battery of AAHPERD physical fitness norms was the focus of the present research.

Method

The sample subjects consisted of 887 mentally retarded individuals, aged 8 to 68 years, participating in the Alabama Special Olympics program. Subjects were selected from athletes competing in state-level competition in basketball, bowling, swimming, and track and field. Table 1 shows the number of subjects by age, gender, and class.

Three items of the AAHPERD Health-Related Physical Fitness Test were administered. Those items included: (a) modified sit-ups, (b) sit and reach, and (c) body composition (triceps, subscapular, and sum). Data were collected across five independent variables: (a) age (8-15 years, 16-19 years, 20 years and over), (b) gender, (c) class (mild or moderate), (d) event (basketball, bowling, swimming, track and field), and (e) region (rural or urban). Age

Table 1. Numbers of subjects by age, gender, and class

| Age | Male | | Female | |
	Mild	Moderate	Mild	Moderate
8-15	196	81	131	35
16-19	161	59	41	27
20-68	15	80	23	38
Total	372	220	195	100

classifications corresponded to 1983 Special Olympics Summer International Games age groupings. Class grouping was in accordance with the Alabama Special Education categories of mildly mentally retarded (IQ 50-75) and moderately mentally retarded (IQ 25-49). Subjects were classified urban if they resided in a city of 35,000+ population.

Data were collected by a team of specially trained Jacksonville State University students. Students were specifically trained in the procedures of the AAHPERD Health-Related Physical Fitness Test. Observations were taken on 887 subjects participating in state-level Alabama Special Olympics championship events in basketball, bowling, swimming, and track and field in Spring 1983.

The project and analytic flow is depicted in Figure 1. The present study was Phase I of a multiphasic project directed toward the development of physical fitness norms for Special Olympians. Given the state of knowledge about the health-related physical fitness of this population, a preliminary tailoring study was justified. The fundamental goals at Phase I were (a) exploration of the influence of selected independent variables on exemplar physical fitness parameters, (b) development of preliminary norms for this special population, and (c) comparison of these norms with AAHPERD Health-Related Physical Fitness Test norms. The independent variables, age, gender, region, event, and class were examined to ascertain their importance in identifying mean-

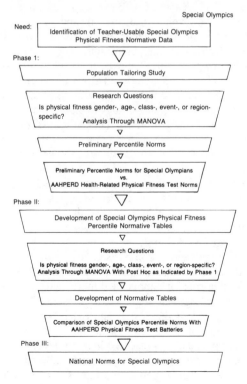

Figure 1. Project and analytic flow.

ingful differences within the Special Olympian population (i.e., is physical fitness performance gender-, age-, class-, event-, or region-specific).

The design of Phase II of the multiphasic project—development of normative data on a comprehensive physical fitness test battery with Alabama Special Olympians—will incorporate the implications of Phase I. Phase III will extend the project to a national sample.

Through the use of multivariate analysis of variance procedures, significant differences were identified within the sample. The implications of these differences for future manipulation of the selected variables were noted. For example, the need to account for age and gender differences in developing normative data for mentally retarded populations was examined. Subsequently, preliminary percentile norms on the dependent variables, with suggested independent variable grouping, were developed. These norms were then compared to AAHPERD Health-Related Physical Fitness Test norms for nonhandicapped populations.

Results

With events (basketball, bowling, swimming, track and field) at four levels, age at three levels (8-15 years, 16-19 years, 20 years and over), gender at two levels, region at two levels (rural, urban), and class at two levels (mild, moderate), and across the five dependent variables MANOVA provided estimates of the differences among performance scores due to each source of variance within the design. Table 2 shows the level of significance for each source of variation within the design. With alpha (α) at .10 it is apparent that each variable, by itself and in combination with other independent variables to a fourth order of interaction, contributes to significant variance within the sample of observations. For example, in the test item sit-ups, with the source of variation being class, $\alpha = .001$, for age $\alpha = .001$, for the class/age interaction $\alpha = .001$, and for the region/class/age interaction $\alpha = .071$. This significant interaction effect for region, class, and age suggests that sit-up performance is a function of the region that the athlete is located within, the athlete's class, and the athlete's age. It also indicates that these three factors are not independent of each other in explaining variance within the data presented here. Similar conclusions may be drawn with regard to gender, event, and region as indicated in Table 2.

Tables 3, 4, and 5 present a comparison of preliminary normative data generated within the present study and data from the AAHPERD Health-Related Physical Fitness Test norms for nondisabled individuals. AAHPERD data was modified to allow direct age and gender comparisons. Table 3 shows sit-up performance norms, Table 4 depicts sit and reach performance norms, and Table 5 shows the sum of skinfolds (triceps and subscapular) performance norms. Special Olympics data is presented in three developmental age groups as distinct from the chronological age groupings utilized by AAHPERD in developing the nonhandicapped population norms. Examination of Tables 3, 4, and 5 reflect apparent differences between the populations.

Table 2. MANOVA table (α levels)

Source of variation	Sit-ups	Sit & reach	Body composition Triceps	Subscap	Sum
Event (E)	.00*	.00*	.64	.42	.00*
Region (R)	.01*	.17	.26	.01*	.00*
Sex (S)	.00*	.00*	.04*	.17	.00*
Class (C)	.00*	.10*	.09*	.00*	.00*
Age (A)	.00*	.01*	.54	.53	.00*
E X R	.04*	.87	.88	.68	.44
E X S	.00*	.32	.66	.21	.03*
E X C	.69	.65	.83	.25	.40
E X A	.02*	.75	.19	.10*	.15
R X S	.02*	.87	.27	.60	.90
R X C	.42	.35	.97	.62	.01*
R X A	.08*	.36	.44	.14	.28
S X C	.14	.29	.62	.03*	.14
S X A	.64	.32	.04*	.36	.18
C X A	.00*	.01*	.28	.92	.22
E X R X S	.14	.74	.83	.56	.47
E X R X C	.60	.07*	.01*	.86	.04*
E X R X A	.04*	.39	.43	.58	.45
E X S X C	.19	.23	.26	.08*	.15
E X S X A	.36	.19	.05*	.09*	.33
E X C X A	.47	.88	.94	.34	.63
R X S X C	.83	.84	.28	.22	.59
R X S X A	.50	.41	.01*	.91	.31
R X C X A	.06*	.53	.15	.90	.18
S X C X A	.63	.19	.89	.05*	.09*
E X R X S X C	.84	.81	.58	.33	.12
E X R X S X A	.90	.59	.61	.82	.20
E X R X C X A	.31	.72	.82	.99	.37
E X S X C X A	.38	.49	.20	.43	.50
R X S X C X A	.21	.82	.47	.66	.13

*$p < .10$

Table 3. Special Olympics preliminary percentile norms for sit-ups

Percentile	Mild Age 8-15	Mild Age 16-19	Mild Age 20+	Moderate Age 8-15	Moderate Age 16-19	Moderate Age 20+	Nonhandicapped* Age 8-15	Nonhandicapped* Age 16-19
Male								
95	48	58	29	40	43	36	54	62
90	44	50	28	37	36	33	49	59
75	39	44	28	33	32	25	38	52
50	35	39	23	25	25	20	37	46
25	29	34	16	17	20	14	31	28
10	25	29	8	8	16	10	25	31
5	22	24	7	9	13	6	20	25
Female								
95	40	44	31	35	44	29	49	54
90	38	41	26	30	38	26	46	50
75	34	34	23	26	33	20	40	43
50	27	32	18	21	26	16	33	35
25	24	27	18	15	13	11	27	30
10	20	22	14	12	11	9	21	24
5	17	18	7	7	9	4	17	20

*Adapted from AAHPERD Health-Related Physical Fitness Test Manual (1980).

Table 4. Special Olympics preliminary percentile norms for sit and reach

Percentile	Mild Age 8-15	Mild Age 16-19	Mild Age 20+	Moderate Age 8-15	Moderate Age 16-19	Moderate Age 20+	Nonhandicapped* Age 8-15	Nonhandicapped* Age 16-19
Male								
95	48	41	37	37	40	39	36	44
90	44	39	35	36	36	37	34	42
75	39	34	27	29	33	29	30	38
50	35	29	18	21	27	21	26	32
25	29	22	11	17	20	15	22	27
10	25	15	7	12	9	8	17	21
5	22	11	5	5	9	6	14	13
Female								
95	40	40	35	40	44	41	39	45
90	37	38	34	38	39	40	38	43
75	32	34	28	30	33	33	34	40
50	27	30	23	27	27	30	30	35
25	21	24	18	20	13	23	28	31
10	15	17	12	13	12	16	39	24
5	9	11	6	11	9	12	21	18

*Adapted from AAHPERD Health-Related Physical Fitness Test Manual (1980).

Table 5. Special Olympics preliminary percentile norms for sum of skinfolds

Percentile	Mild Age 8-15	Mild Age 16-19	Mild Age 20+	Moderate Age 8-15	Moderate Age 16-19	Moderate Age 20+	Nonhandicapped* Age 8-15	Nonhandicapped* Age 16-19
Male								
95	10	11	10	10	11	14	9	9
90	11	12	10	11	11	17	10	10
75	13	14	15	14	16	24	12	12
50	16	17	25	20	22	36	26	32
25	21	21	39	33	38	50	22	27
10	29	29	50	50	59	62	30	30
5	38	42	55	59	67	81	38	38
Female								
95	12	11	—	16	19	19	11	15
90	15	15	20	17	20	23	13	16
75	18	20	36	22	39	33	16	20
50	25	26	41	33	45	42	20	26
25	34	39	53	41	58	55	27	35
10	44	54	67	62	72	66	39	46
5	49	58	69	65	77	78	46	58

*Adapted from AAHPERD Health-Related Physical Fitness Test Manual (1980).

Conclusions

Data generated suggest that percentile norms in the format of present AAHPERD fitness norms (i.e., gender, age, class categories) should be appropriate for use with the Special Olympics population. However, the comparison of preliminary Special Olympics percentile normative data with AAHPERD Health-Related Physical Fitness Test norms suggests that the performance standard of Special Olympians, within these categories, is meaningfully lower than those of a nonhandicapped population as reflected in AAHPERD norms. Phase II will further investigate those sources of variation examined in the present study and their contribution toward explaining performance variance among this handicapped population. Physical fitness performance norms will be developed across an expanded battery of test items on a statewide level. Phase II is intended, therefore, to produce a set of teacher-usable physical fitness performance norms for use by teachers and coaches of Special Olympics athletes.

References

American Association for Health, Physical Education, Recreation. (1976). *Motor fitness testing manual for mildly mentally retarded persons.* Washington, DC: Author.

American Association for Health, Physical Education, Recreation. (1977). *Special fitness test manual for mildly mentally retarded persons*. (rev. ed.). Washington, DC: Author.

American Alliance for Health, Physical Education, Recreation. (1980). *Health related physical fitness test manual*. Reston, VA: Author.

Bundschuh, E.L., & Cureton, K.J. (1982). Effect of bicycle ergometer conditioning on the physical work capacity of mentally retarded adolescents. *American Corrective Therapy Journal, 36,* 159-163.

Eichstaedt, C., & Wang, P. (1981). *A study of physical fitness levels of mentally handicapped children and adolescents in Illinois*. Paper presented at the 1981 AAHPERD National Conference, Boston, MA.

Londeree, B.R., & Johnson, L.E. (1974). Motor fitness of tmr vs emr and normal children. *Medicine and Science in Sports, 6,* 247-252.

Rarick, C.L. (1980). Cognitive-motor development in the growing years. *Research Quarterly for Exercise and Sport, 51*(1), 174-192.

Rarick, G.L., Dobbins, D.A., & Broadhead, G.D. (1976). *The motor domain and its correlates in educationally handicapped children*. Englewood Cliffs, NJ: Prentice-Hall.

26

The Performance of Adolescents With Cerebral Palsy on Measures of Physical Fitness

Francis X. Short and Joseph P. Winnick
SUNY COLLEGE AT BROCKPORT
BROCKPORT, NEW YORK, USA

Sport participation by people with cerebral palsy (CP) is increasing in the United States. Since physical fitness is important in the performance of most sports and games, it is necessary to better understand the fitness of individuals with cerebral palsy.

This study was designed to investigate the performance of adolescents (i.e., 10-17 years old) with CP on field-based measures of physical fitness. The specific purpose was to examine the effects of gender and age on the fitness of CP adolescents and, where appropriate, to compare fitness performance with that of able-bodied (AB) youngsters of the same gender and age.

Procedures

Subjects

The subjects for this study included 396 CP and 1192 AB adolescents. All subjects were in the 10-17 year age range (CP age: $M = 13.1$, $SD = 2.2$; AB age: $M = 13.2$, $SD = 2.1$). For the CP group, only individuals who had been previously diagnosed by medical personnel as having cerebral palsy were included in the study. All CP subjects were free of mental retardation and other significant handicapping conditions. CP subjects were subclassified based on an eight-category functional profile provided by the National Association of Sport for Cerebral Palsy (NASCP) sport classification system (NASCP, 1979).

All subjects were tested in schools and agencies throughout the United States by competency-trained field testers.

Measures of Physical Fitness

Physical fitness was conceptualized as consisting of both health-related and performance-related components. Selected test items measured one of six hypothesized factors of physical fitness. The 17 test items selected for the study, categorized by hypothesized factor, included (a) body composition: triceps, abdominal, and subscapular skinfolds; (b) muscular strength/endurance: flexed knee sit-ups, timed leg raise, timed trunk raise, grip strength (right and left hand), flexed arm hang, pull-ups, standing broad jump, and softball throw; (c) speed: 50-m dash; (d) agility: mat creep and shuttle run; (e) flexibility: sit and reach; and (f) cardiorespiratory endurance: long distance run (ages 10-12 ran for either 1.61 km or 9 min and ages 13-17 ran for either 2.42 km or 12 min). Readers desiring a complete description of test procedures and modifications are referred to Winnick and Short (1982).

Although efforts were made to modify test items as necessary for CP subjects, all items were not appropriate for, and therefore were not administered to, all CP subjects. Testers consulted a participation guide (Winnick & Short, 1982) that was used to standardize procedures for the modification or elimination of test items. The participation guide indicated which items were appropriate for CP subjects in each of the eight subclassifications.

Data Analysis

Since all CP subjects did not take all test items, a multivariate data analysis was obviated. Data were analyzed using univariate analyses of variance and covariance. The .01 level of significance was adopted for all univariate analyses to reduce experiment error. The Scheffé procedure and graphic analysis (a comparison of plotted means with 99% confidence intervals) were utilized for post hoc comparisons. Performance data of CP subjects were entered into each analysis based upon the CP participation guide.

For 12 items, scores were analyzed using a three-way ANOVA with gender, age, and condition (CP vs. AB) as the independent variables. Comparisons between CP and AB subjects were not made on five items, however, because of major differences in test procedures. Where procedures were modified for CP subjects, the modification was dictated by the severity of the condition (indicated by the subclassification of the subject). Some CP subjects, for example, performed the running items in wheelchairs because they were incapable of independent ambulation. Therefore the effects of gender and age on the mat creep, shuttle run, 50-m dash, softball throw, and long distance run were analyzed with the effect of the severity of the condition controlled, or more precisely, the eight-category subclassification covaried.

Results

The results of the three-way univariate ANOVAs are presented in Table 1, and the results of the two-way univariate ANCOVAs are presented in Table 2.

Table 1. Univariate F values for AB and CP adolescents by gender, age, and condition

Item	AB N	CP N	Gender	Age	Condition	Gender × age	Gender × condition	Age × condition	Gender × age × condition
Tricep	1067	386	23.87*	3.27*	.09	4.01	7.27*	.71	1.65
Abdominal	1063	384	14.05*	6.91*	.63	2.13	.18	1.41	.78
Subscapular	1064	380	5.76	7.44*	3.38	.73	1.23	.90	1.39
Sit-up	1162	297	59.92*	1.07	2410.77*	3.26*	13.53*	6.80*	.11
Leg raise	1148	285	9.95*	3.96*	288.44*	.95	5.25	3.15*	.65
Trunk raise	1120	127	.86	.62	93.79*	.59	.01	1.19	.73
Right grip	1041	308	155.37*	95.52*	720.18*	10.79*	30.68*	12.21*	1.77
Left grip	1039	316	158.12*	80.47*	460.43*	10.98*	19.75*	9.46*	2.78*
Arm hang	1109	209	44.28*	1.06	100.93*	.89	10.93*	.90	.40
Pull-up	1114	211	143.39*	3.61*	82.51*	6.40*	42.83*	1.19	1.33
Broad jump	1120	130	81.90*	9.83*	1235.00*	4.14*	3.27	4.43*	1.66
Sit and reach	1159	175	28.09*	3.72*	191.74*	1.95	10.21*	3.25*	1.75

*p < .01

Table 2. Univariate F values for CP adolescents by gender and age, with severity of condition covaried

Item	N	Covariate	Gender	Age	Gender × age
Softball distance	324	83.10*	53.15*	1.63	1.49
Dash	274	49.89*	9.37*	2.43	2.55
Shuttle	295	151.37*	6.42	1.39	1.41
Mat creep	297	63.68*	6.38	2.39	.80
Long distance run	181	73.93*	5.66	.53	1.45

*$p < .01$

The Influence of Condition

No significant differences were found between AB and CP subjects on the three skinfold measures. With one exception the scores of AB subjects were significantly higher than those of CP subjects on the other nine performance items where such comparisons were made. In fact regardless of gender, significant differences between CP and AB subjects were found at virtually every age for eight of the nine performance items analyzed. For the exception, pull-ups, a significant difference favoring AB males was found, but the difference between AB and CP females was not statistically significant.

The Influence of Gender

Gender had a similar, but not identical, influence on skinfold measures for AB and CP subjects. CP females had significantly larger triceps and abdominal skinfolds than CP males. AB females had significantly larger abdominal skinfolds than AB males, but the difference on the triceps skinfold was not significant at the .01 level. Gender was not a significant factor for either AB or CP subjects on the subscapular skinfold.

Gender did not have a similar influence, however, on most of the performance items for AB and CP subjects. The significant interactions in Table 1 indicate that on the sit-ups, sit and reach, right hand grip strength, left hand grip strength, and pull-up tests AB males made significantly higher scores than AB females; however, the gender difference for CP subjects was not significant for each of these items. Both CP and AB males, however, scored significantly higher than their female counterparts on timed leg raise, flexed arm hang, and standing broad jump. Gender was not a significant factor for either group of subjects on the timed trunk raise.

Of those items analyzed separately for CP subjects (see Table 2), gender was found to be a significant factor on only two: the 50-m dash and the softball throw. In both cases performance differences favored the males.

The Influence of Age

In general, age was found to have a similar influence on the skinfold measures of both AB and CP subjects. Where differences were significant, older subjects had significantly larger skinfolds than younger subjects at the abdominal and subscapular sites. Age was also a significant factor on the triceps skinfold although it did not have the same influence on males and females. Where differences were significant, older females had larger measures and older males smaller measures than their younger counterparts.

Age had differential effects on the nine performance items. Age was found to be a significant factor for both AB and CP subjects on the grip strength tests. Where differences were significant older subjects had significantly higher grip strength scores than did younger subjects. Both AB and CP males also showed a significant improvement with age on the pull-ups; however, no significant age differences were found between AB and CP females on this item. Age was not a significant factor for either group of subjects on the timed trunk raise or the flexed arm hang. On the sit-ups, timed leg raise, sit and reach, and standing broad jump, age was found to be a significant factor for AB subjects (older subjects generally made higher scores than younger subjects). Age, however, was not a significant factor on these items for CP subjects. In addition, data from Table 2 indicate that age was not a significant factor on any of the five items analyzed separately for the CP group.

Discussion

While CP subjects were significantly behind AB subjects on virtually all performance measures, they compared favorably on skinfold measurements. This is in contrast to previous research which has established that handicapped subjects generally have larger skinfolds than nonhandicapped subjects. This finding has been reported for educable mentally retarded subjects (Rarick, Dobbins, & Broadhead, 1976) and for sensory impaired (Winnick & Short, 1982) and paraplegic spinal neuromuscular subjects (Winnick & Short, 1984). In the absence of a metabolic explanation, significant differences in skinfolds in the literature have been attributed to lower levels of physical activity of the handicapped group (Rarick et al., 1976). CP individuals in many cases must expend a great deal of energy to perform even simple voluntary movements (Kalakian & Eichstaedt, 1982); therefore their energy consumption may approximate that of AB people resulting in comparable skinfold measures. In addition, some types of cerebral palsy, especially spasticity, are characterized by chronic muscular hypertonicity which may create a higher energy demand even at rest for certain CP individuals.

Previous research with educable mentally retarded subjects (Rarick et al., 1976), visually impaired subjects, and auditory impaired subjects (Winnick & Short, 1982) demonstrated that although the fitness performance of the handicapped group is generally inferior to that of the nonhandicapped group, the variables of gender and age have similar, significant influences on the fitness performance of both groups. In general, however, this familiar developmental profile was absent for CP subjects in the present study. Of the 14 performance items, gender was found to be a significant variable on only five. The fact that gender was generally not a significant factor on the performance of CP subjects may have been due, at least in part, to the possible severity of condition differences between males and females which were uncontrolled in the three-way ANOVAs. Also, the rigorous standard for significance may have masked some true gender differences. Gender, for example, was a significant factor at the .02 level for shuttle run, mat creep, and long distance run.

Perhaps the finding of greater importance is that the performance of the CP group generally did not improve with age. Of the 14 performance items, age was a significant factor on only three: right hand grip strength, left hand grip strength, and pull-ups (males only). Since it has been demonstrated that the physical fitness of CP subjects can be improved with appropriate training (Lundberg, Ovenfors, & Saltin, 1967; Ekblom & Lundberg, 1968), it is suggested that the failure of the older CP subjects to surpass the performance of the younger CP subjects may be due in part to educational and/or therapeutic approaches that do not emphasize the development of physical fitness. The need for appropriate individualized programs of physical fitness for youngsters with cerebral palsy is apparent. It is suggested that physical educators and coaches assume the responsibility of developing and implementing these programs.

References

Ekblom, B., & Lundberg, A. (1968). Effect of physical training on adolescents with severe motor handicaps. *Acta Paediatrica Scandinavica, 57*, 17-23.

Kalakian, L.H., & Eichstaedt, C.B. (1982). *Developmental/adapted physical education*. Minneapolis, MN: Burgess.

Lundberg, A., Ovenfors, D., & Saltin, B. (1967). Effect of physical training on school children with cerebral palsy. *Acta Paediatrica Scandinavica, 56*, 182-188.

National Association of Sports for Cerebral Palsy. (1979). *Constitution, rules, classification, and national records sports manual*. New Haven, CT: Author.

Rarick, G.L., Dobbins, D.A., & Broadhead, G.D. (1976). *The motor domain and its correlates in educationally handicapped children*. Englewood Cliffs, NJ: Prentice-Hall.

Winnick, J.P., & Short, F.X. (1982). *The physical fitness of sensory and orthopedically impaired youth*. Brockport, NY: SUNY College at Brockport. (ERIC Document Reproduction Service No. ED 240 764)

Winnick, J.P., & Short, F.X. (1984). The physical fitness of youngsters with spinal neuromuscular conditions. *Adapted Physical Activity Quarterly, 1*, 37-51.

27

Characteristics of Physically Disabled Riders Participating in Equestrian Competition at the National Level

Natalie Bieber
COORDINATOR OF EQUESTRIAN EVENTS, NASCP
LYME, CONNECTICUT, USA

Horseback riding is a recreational and therapeutic option for people with and without disabling conditions. As a competitive endeavor, however, riding attracts only a small percentage of individuals involved in equestrian programs and places special demands on those who choose to compete. Although equestrian competition for able-bodied riders has long been widely available, only during the past 30 years has competition for riders with disabilities received recognition (Heipertz, 1981). Stellar riders with disabilities, such as Liz Hartel of Denmark, have been able to compete against able-bodied riders. Hartel, a superb horsewoman before contracting polio, won a silver medal in dressage in 1952 at the Olympic Games in Helsinki, Finland (Davies, 1967). Although her achievement focused attention on the therapeutic aspects of horse sports, it had little influence on competitive opportunities for disabled people.

The Scandinavian countries and Great Britain have been leaders in the field of therapeutic riding (Bauer, 1972). In 1953 Norah Jacques began a therapeutic riding program for spastic children; the program grew into the Riding for the Disabled Trust of the United Kingdom (Davies, 1967). This work spurred the organization of other programs and brought professionalism and standardization to the concept. On this continent, the North American Riding for the Handicapped Association (NARHA) and other groups have provided therapy, recreation, and training for riders with a wide range of disabling conditions. In Colorado, Mary Woolverton was instrumental in establishing horse show classes for Vietnam veterans who were amputees (Bieber, 1967). It was not until 1979, however, that competitive opportunities for riders with physical disabilities were formalized and incorporated into the events of a national sport organization for disabled athletes, the National Association of Sports for Cerebral Palsy (NASCP). NASCP equestrian events are now open to any rider with a physical disability who is able to meet the competitive standards for his or her functional profile.

Articles have been written detailing the achievements of isolated elite athletes (Bond, 1974; Dana, 1975, December; Hinkamp, 1975; Mayeda, 1984; Schofield, 1973, May), but no specific investigation has ever been undertaken to describe riders who compete against one another in events tailored specifically for disabled people. With this in mind, the performance characteristics of riders who participated in the equestrian events of the NASCP National Games in 1981 and 1983 were studied to examine (a) the competitors as a group and (b) individual riders who achieved success and placed well. Of particular interest then and now are the factors that combined to enable some individuals to be repeated winners.

Methods

The subjects ($N = 79$) included all participants in the riding events of the two NASCP National Games. Twenty-six competed in RI at the 1981 NASCP Games, and 63 competed at the 1983 Games in TX. Of these, 10 riders participated at both sites. The 79 individuals studied ranged in age from 9-56 years with a mean of 27.7 years. The competitors had a wide range of physical disabilities but were cognitively intact. They represented 13 states and Canada; 40 were female and 39 were male. The equestrian events—dressage, equitation, obstacle course, relay race, and jumping—were based on those included in American Horse Show Association recognized horse shows. NARHA safety guidelines were followed.

Data were gathered by mail through the administration of the Rider's Profile (Glasow, 1980). This form is required of riders in NASCP competitions. An item added to the Rider's Profile was whether the rider was mounted on a familiar or assigned/borrowed horse. The NASCP classification system for riders (NASCP, 1982) was used to define the level of physical function. This system groups riders in three categories: (a) those with cerebral palsy or nonprogressive brain damage with locomotor dysfunction either congenital or acquired; (b) those with spina bifida, spinal cord injuries, amputations, and postpolio; and (c) those with muscular dystrophy, multiple sclerosis, arthrogryposis, and les autres (the others). The three categories are divided into eight classes for the purpose of grouping athletes in a way that allows for competition against those with a similar degree of disability.

Class 1: Severe quadriplegic/triplegic. Severe control problems necessitating use of motorized wheelchair or personal assistance.

Class 2: Severe quadriplegic. Normally propels wheelchair with legs. Better upper-extremity range of motion and coordination than Class 1. More athetosis prevalent.

Class 3: Weak quadriplegic, triplegic, or moderate hemiplegic. Wheelchair.

Class 4: Paraplegic. Good upper-extremity strength and control. Wheelchair.

Class 5: Paraplegic, diplegic, moderate hemiplegic. Ambulates without wheelchair in regular daily activities. May or may not use assistive device for ambulation.

Class 6: Quadriplegic athetoid, ataxic, severe triplegic. Usually ambulates without walking aides.

Class 7: Moderate hemiplegic or moderate to minimal quadriplegic.

Class 8: Minimal handicap group.

Slides and a videotape of the TX competition were used to further validate data collected by the questionnaire. Performance characteristics were determined by the criteria and standards in the NASCP Sports Manual; riders were designated as first, second, and third place winners, or as nonwinners.

Results

NASCP equestrian competitions are held every 2 years. The first was in 1979 in New Haven, Connecticut. No data were collected at that time. The competition held in Rhode Island in 1981 thus was the second opportunity for CP athletes to compete and the first time for riders with other disabilities to be represented. Of the 26 riders participating in 1981 (Table 1), 10 were female and 16 were male. The average age for the female riders was 34.3 as compared with 22 for the male riders. The number of riders more than doubled between 1981 and 1983. Of the 63 riders entered, 33 were male and 30 were female. Again the mean age of the males, 20.3, was much younger than that of the females, 34.3. In both 1981 and 1983 more medals (places first through third) were awarded to male riders than female. More significance can be attributed to gender when examining the 1981 data—male riders comprised only 38% of the total—than in 1983 when they were 52% of the total.

Age was not a significant factor for the male riders in either 1981 or 1983. Winners' ages reflected a wide range—11 to 44 years in 1981, and 9 to 41 years in 1983. However, age did seem to be a factor for the female riders; most of the women who received medals in both 1981 and 1983 clustered in the range of 25 to 34 years, and thus were not representative of the total spectrum of age. No significant correlation was apparent between the length of time the person had been riding and superior performance. This may be a factor of the quality of riding time and instruction rather than the quantity of time.

At the Rhode Island Games, 22 riders had cerebral palsy and 4 had other disabilities: postpolio involvement, spina bifida, and a viral paralysis resulting in a clinical profile very similar to CP. In Texas, although riders with cerebral palsy were in the majority ($n = 47$), 16 non-CP riders also participated. Included among these were three with spinal cord injury, two with multiple sclerosis, two with neurological impairments, and nine others, each with one

Table 1. Characteristics of disabled riders in two national competitions: Rhode Island (1981) and Texas (1983)

Variables	Rhode Island		Texas	
	M (n = 10)	F (n = 16)	M (n = 33)	F (n = 30)
Age				
Range	11-44	17-44	9-56	9-56
Mean	22	34.3	20.3	34.2
Years riding experience				
Range	.5-15	1-10	1-15	1-10
Mean	3.8	5.3	4.3	3.7
Disability				
CP	9	13	29	18
Other	1	3	4	12
NASCP Class				
1	0	1	5	1
2	1	2	1	2
3	1	2	1	3
4	1	1	1	4
5	2	4	7	8
6	1	2	6	6
7	2	4	10	4
8	2	0	2	2
Horse				
Own	3	9	11	11
Winner	2	4	5	6
Nonwinner	1	5	6	5
Assigned	7	7	22	19
Winner	5	2	10	6
Nonwinner	2	5	12	13

Note. Of the 26 competitors in Rhode Island and 63 competitors in Texas, 10 riders competed at both sites.

of the following: muscular dystrophy, arthritis, postpolio, amputation, stroke, scoliosis, spina bifida, closed head injury, and viral paralysis. The winners were divided between CP and non-CP individuals because, in most events, separate medals were awarded for CP and non-CP places.

The data indicated that most of the riders were from classifications 1 through 7, with the repeated winners predominantly in Classes 1, 3, 4, 5, and 7. The low number of athetoid CP riders, Classes 2 and 6, among the "superstars," is an indication of the specific interference presented by this condition for riders. The spastic rider (Classes 1, 3, 4, 5, and 7) is usually better able to ride with "quiet hands" and thus more subtly control a horse. The true paraplegic rider also has an advantage over one with hemiplegia or mixed CP involvement because despite limited use of the lower extremities, trunk control is not a problem, nor is there overflow from abnormal reflexes. The low number of minimally involved riders (Class 8) who entered in the competition is probably the result of those individuals being able to compete in the mainstream if they so chose. This information supports the need for a classification system based on functional profile to equalize competition.

Of the 13 people who placed first through third in the 1981 equestrian events, 8 were mounted on their own or familiar horses and 5 were on assigned, unfamiliar mounts. In 1983, 28 of the 63 riders took all of the medals for first through third place. Less than half of that number, 11 riders, were on familiar horses. The results indicate that being mounted on an assigned or unfamiliar horse is not a disadvantage to a good rider. The disabled rider's ability to perform under circumstances that would tax most able-bodied horse show competitors is impressive.

Conclusions

The criteria and performance standards included in the NASCP Sports Manual are appropriate for most of the riders. Some, however, were able to far exceed the qualifying standards for their classifications. Gender may favor male riders since male riders took a disproportionate share of the awards. Among the females, a correlation existed between a specific age group and winning performance. The one factor that was unmeasurable is probably the one that most influences the disabled rider's performance: the ability to totally concentrate his or her physical energies in a productive manner, maximizing functional strengths while inhibiting abnormal reflex patterns.

Addendum

On June 22, 1984, the first truly international competition for riders with physical disabilities was included as part of the International Games for the Disabled held in New York. The United States contingent consisted of 6 riders on the CP team and 9 non-CP riders, all of whom qualified for selection based on their performances in the U.S. National Games in 1983. Although North American equestrian competitions have existed since 1980 and regional competitions have been available for Scandinavian riders for several years, this was the first time that an international sport governing body (i.e., CP/International Sports and Recreation Association) sanctioned riding competition on a global scale.

Representatives of six nations (Canada, Denmark, Great Britain, Norway, Sweden, and the United States) participated in the equestrian events; eight male and 16 female riders ranged in age from 12 to 47 years. Although there were twice as many female as male riders, the males won 10 of the 19 gold medals. All of the foreign riders and six of the Americans rode unfamiliar horses. The most consistent winners were an American CP Class 1 male (two gold, one silver), an American spinal cord injured Class 4 female (three gold), a Swedish Class 6 male (two gold, one bronze), and a Danish Class 7 male (three gold, one silver). All but the American women were on assigned horses.

References

Bauer, J. (1972). *Riding for rehabilitation: A guide for handicapped riders and their instructors*. East Toronto, Canada: Canadian Stage and Arts Publications, Ltd.

Bieber, N. Personal observations. Denver, 1967; Kingston, RI, August 1-4, 1981; Ft. Worth, TX, July, 30-31, 1983.

Bond, M. (1974). Winning at the brass ring. *The Western Horseman, 36*, 142-144.

Dana, C. (1975, December). Horses give them a leg up on life. *Horseman. The Magazine of Western Riding*, pp. 4-14.

Davies, J.A. (1967). *The reins of life: An instructional and informative manual on riding for the disabled*. London: J.A. Allen.

Glasow, B. (1980). The rider's profile (Available from N. Bieber, 78 Town Woods Road, Lyme, CT 06371).

Heipertz, W. (1981). *Therapeutic riding*. Ottawa: Greenbelt Riding Association for the Disabled.

Hinkamp, C. (1975). Blind rider shows in open classes. *The Chronicle of the Horse, 38*(15), 45-47.

Mayeda, M. (1984). Horseback freedom: What it takes to be a champion. *Ability Magazine, 4*, 22-25.

National Association of Sports for Cerebral Palsy. (1982). *Classification and Sports Rules Manual* (2nd ed.). New York: United Cerebral Palsy Associations, Inc.

Rosenthal, S. (1970). RE-Risk exercise. *The Chronicle of the Horse, 34*(4), 44.

Schofield, S. (1973, May). The wonders of disabled riding. *Light Horse*, pp. 17-19.

28

The 1984 International Games for the Disabled

Michael Mushett
DEPARTMENT OF PARKS AND RECREATION
WESTLAND, MICHIGAN, USA

On a May morning in 1982, Ben Lipton walked into Nassau County Executive Francis Purcell's Mineola, New York office looking for a home for what promised to be the second largest international sports event in the world in 1984. Cities in South Carolina and California had already been ruled out. Lipton, one of the fathers of sports for the disabled and a neighbor of Purcell's in the tiny hamlet of Malverne, asked Purcell to host the third International Games for the Disabled in Nassau County.

Purcell liked the idea. "Ben explained some of the possible problems of holding the Games here," said Purcell. "But I thought it would be worth the trouble." After that meeting, government workers, private business people, and slews of volunteers hustled to prepare for the onslaught of 1,800 athletes from 45 countries (see Table 1).

In early fall of 1982 the Games Director, Michael Mushett, was hired and a tiny headquarters was opened in Eisenhower Park in East Meadow, New York. Mushett's task as director was to bring together all facets of the community, the sponsoring organizations, and fund-raising groups, as well as to coordinate the actual competition. The Organizing Committee had 2 years to complete the 4-year task of gearing up for the games, and work began at a back-breaking pace. In time, the office would burgeon with people, desks, chairs, computers, constantly ringing phones, and mounds of paper.

With help from Nassau government leaders, the Games director set about building an elaborate organization of workers. In November 1982, Bud Cosgrove, a top parks official, Tom Darcy, a county management expert, and

Special thanks to Geraldine Baum and Joe Kurpinski for their contributions.

Table 1. Countries competing in the 1984 international games for the disabled

Argentina	Italy
Australia	Japan
Austria	Kenya
Belgium	Korea
Brazil	Kuwait
Burma	Liechtenstein
Canada	Luxembourg
China	Mexico
Denmark	Netherlands
Egypt	New Zealand
Faroes	Norway
Federal Republic of Germany	Poland
Finland	Portugal
France	Spain
German Democratic Republic	Sweden
Great Britain	Switzerland
Hong Kong	Thailand
Hungary	Trinidad and Tobago
Iceland	United States
India	Venezuela
Indonesia	Yugoslavia
Ireland	Zimbabwe
Israel	

Mushett spent several days discussing ideas, needs, and names—names of people who could be drafted to work and would come through.

The planning began with what Cosgrove called a "mission" statement—a two-page explanation of the purpose of the games. From that flowered a "Games Master Plan" and then a flow chart including seven key leaders to organize different aspects of the Games, such as security, fundraising, and public relations. At the top of the chart was the nine-person Games Executive Board. It was a mad scramble, but the goal to make everything come together by June 16, 1984 was achieved.

Athletic Selection

The participating athletes were selected through qualifying trials held in their home countries. In conjunction with the three host organizations—the National Association of Sports for Cerebral Palsy (NASCP), the U.S. Amputee Athletic Association (USAAA), and the U.S. Association for Blind Athletes (USABA)—

the international governing bodies for disabled sports established the rules and classification systems for the 1984 Games.

The international contenders participated in 18 sports, including track and field, swimming, weight lifting, archery, wrestling, cycling, wheelchair soccer, table tennis, and horseback riding. In each of the events, athletes were classified by the nature and degree of their physical disabilities. For example, blind athletes competed in three different classes, based on their degree of visual impairment, amputee athletes in nine, and athletes with cerebral palsy in eight.

These classifications were set in order to ensure an even balance of competition among disabled athletes of world-class caliber and as familiar with the thrill of victory and the agony of defeat as their able-bodied counterparts. According to experts, participation by a disabled person in sports has particular social and thereapeutic value in the total rehabilitative process. But some of the disabled athletes who took part in the 1984 Games had no special interest in academic theory.

Janet Rowley is a legally blind 24-year-old shot put, discus throw, and high-jump expert. Already the possessor of over 30 medals won in world-class competition, she added several more to her collection at the 1984 International Games for the Disabled. Rowley said, ''I hate to see newspaper headlines that read: 'Rowley Overcomes Blindness.' We disabled athletes go in for athletics for exactly the same reasons as nondisabled people. We have fun in athletic competition and we need an outlet for our competitive instincts.''

Rowley's feelings are shared by many disabled athletes. The determination, stamina, and will to win were as much in evidence at the International Games for the Disabled as at any able-bodied athletic event. Acts of competition are essential to the development of all people, whatever their particular disabilities.

The International Games for the Disabled were established in 1976 to increase awareness and expansion of competitive sports programs for the physically disabled, and to demonstrate to the world that these athletes can— and do—participate in sports events.

Adopting the same 4-year cycle and host countries as the Olympic Games, the International Games for the Disabled first took place in Toronto in 1976. The 1980 Games were held in Arnhem, Holland.

The Location

After 2 years of planning, fundraising, and sweat, the starting gun sounded in Nassau County for the 1984 International Games for the Disabled. In addition to the complex logistics involved in setting up the game sites themselves, arrangements had been made to house and feed the 1,800 athletes, their coaches, and staff members from the 45 nations.

The hub of athletic activity was the new $11-million Mitchell Park athletic complex, which boasts a lighted nine-lane oval track surrounded by seating for 15,000 spectators, and an ultramodern pistol and rifle range. The opening and closing ceremonies took place at the west end of the oval, where the Games' touch burned for 15 days. Nearly all the action took place within a 1-mile radius of the new complex, including events at Nassau Community College, Hofstra University, and Eisenhower Park. The only exception was the horseback riding, which was held at Caumsett State Park on Lloyd Neck.

Just north of Mitchell Park was a small tent city known as Olympic Plaza. Here were located support facilities (first-aid, wheelchair repair, etc.), an information center, and ticket booths. There was a large tent (nicknamed the Cabaret International) which was reserved exclusively for the athletes as a social gathering place, and a video games tent. A special post office, bank, and telephone facilities, as well as an interfaith chapel and food and souvenir concessions, were also in the plaza.

Events not scheduled for Mitchell Park took place in surrounding facilities: Court games were held in the field house and gymnasium of Nassau Community College's physical education center; swimming events at the Hofstra University Swim Center, one of the few Olympic-sized pools in the United States; and lawn bowling, cycling, and cross country track in Eisenhower Park.

The athletes, trainers, and staff were housed in the Hofstra University residence towers, which were very accessible to the handicapped. In accordance with a $1.3-million contract with the Games board, Hofstra provided the athletes and their 700 aides with room and board during their stay. Besides the essential facilities and services, a variety of other ornaments were built at the Games' sites, including a 64-foot-wide archway to the Village and the 22-foot-high Olympic-style torch which is a now permanent monument to the Games.

Security

When George Maher first heard that an international group of disabled athletes would come to Nassau County for 2 weeks, the police chief wasn't too worried. Securing the big event sounded like just another extra duty for his county force.

That was April, 1983. But as the weeks went by and the meetings began to add up, so did Maher's concern. "I had no idea it would snowball into what it did," said Maher, recalling the day when he first asked to arrange security for the International Games for the Disabled at Mitchel Park and other sites.

For the 2 weeks of the Games—June 16 to June 30—about one-third of Nassau County's 3,000-person force was assigned to the Games. Officers were guarding the athletes' living quarters, patrolling all the facilities, escorting groups to airports and beaches, and monitoring the movement of the 80,000 spectators who attended the games.

On top of that, turmoil and politics in countries such as the Soviet Union and China were the concern of the top brass in the county police headquarters in Mineola. Suddenly terrorists and defectors were a potential problem. Suddenly a civil war in Sri Lanka and bombings in the Persian Gulf were being monitored in Mineola. "We kept constant watch on these matters," said Maher. "We needed to be able to react."

To complicate security matters, President Reagan and many other dignitaries attended the opening ceremony on Sunday, June 17. In planning for the visits of the athletes as well as these dignitaries and spectators, the Nassau police coordinated their efforts with the Federal Bureau of Investigation, the State Department, the Secret Service, and the Whitehouse Advance Team.

In the past, U.S. presidents and other international figures had visited Long Island, but "we had never had this type of job before," said Maher, adding, "for that matter no one else in this country has had to worry about that many foreigners, disabled people, and that much potential controversy in the same place at the same time."

To get advice on how to prepare for the event, the Nassau chief sent envoys to Los Angeles, which played host to the Olympics, and to police headquarters in Toronto, where the first disabled games were held in 1976. Maher also wrote to his counterpart in Arnhem, Holland, where the last games were held in 1980. The Dutch chief responded at length, Maher said: "He recommended that we demand a good press card system so we could keep a handle on the press. He also told us to really get involved in the original planning: Don't let them plan anything that will come back to haunt you later on."

The groundwork was extensive and the cost high, according to county officials. The county had budgeted $3.5 million for officers' overtime during the games, but security costs overall ran almost $5 million. "The real cost was manpower," said Deputy County Executive Owen Smith. "We wanted to be prepared for anything."

The potential for terrorists to lash out at the athletes was real. "You had all the components for an international incident," said Maher. "And never mind the international terrorists, we had our own local nuts to worry about."

Nassau had its own specially trained tactical officers to handle those kinds of situations. In addition, officers had to be aware of the special problems of the disabled. The police department set up a precinct at the Games' central site at Mitchel Park. From computers to a desk sergeant and a squad of detectives, the precinct had all the trappings of the county's eight permanent precincts. Ambulances and helicopters, radios and patrol cars were available exclusively for the games.

A 12-level security system also had been set up so that about 10,000 people—everybody from the 2,500 volunteers to the 500 reporters—were assigned identification cards before they set foot on the Games' grounds. People with Level 1 cards, for example, could enter all facilities, including the athletes' dorms. Reporters, who were assigned Level 6 cards, couldn't enter the dorms at Hofstra University. All I.D. card holders were screened by the police. "We really couldn't take the chance of issuing an I.D. card to somebody that had a record of the crimes we consider potentially dangerous," said Maher. "Whatever you were convicted of that kept you from getting a pistol license would bar you from getting an I.D. card." The police plan began with the arrival of the first athletes and their staffs on June 8, and lasted until July 5.

Fundraising

One of the toughest jobs in getting the 1984 Games on track fell to Long Island's Michael Manzer, who took over the fundraising leadership in November, 1983. His job: Luring corporate support, mostly through promotional packages.

In the short time that he had to accomplish this, the Melville-based expert put together a marketing strategy to get companies to take out ads in the official programs as well as to give financial support. But still, the fundraising remained a team effort.

While several national, regional, and local companies gave money, a large portion of the funding for the games came from government. The federal government, via the U.S. Information Agency, provided an $850,000 allocation, and the state of New York provided $550,000, plus $263,000 for National Guard support.

Nonprofit groups as well made sizeable contributions. They included: the U.S. Olympic Committee, $50,000; United Cerebral Palsy Associations, Inc., $50,000; the N.Y. Arrows Soccer Club, $5,000; J.M. Foundation, $20,000; Herman Goldman Foundation, $25,000; U.S. Wheelchair Sports Fund, $10,000; U.S. Association for Blind Athletes, $5,000; The Knights of Columbus regionally, $19,000; Lions Clubs of New York State, $6,000.

The corporate world showed its support with contributions of cash and services: Grumman contributed $25,000; Pepsi Cola, $100,000; Newsday, $65,000; Genovese Drug Stores and Eastman Kodak, $50,000 each; European American Bank, $25,000; Lumex Corporation, $25,000; Avon, $20,000; William Street Brokers, $10,000; Rolex Watch Co., $5,000; New York Telephone, $25,000; Long Island Trust, $5,500; Villa Banfi Wines, $10,000; Red Lobster, $10,000; National Football League, $5,000; Olsten Corporation, $5,000. IBM, Wang, Motorola, Avis and several other companies donated equipment, and Mobil Corporation ran a $150,000 program to publicize the Games and to bring disabled children in the area to the Long Island events.

Other major fundraising included "the Torchlight Ball," which produced $80,000, and the "Sponsor an Athlete Program" spearheaded by Long Island Trust Vice President Dick Hamber, which generated approximately $150,000. The preceeding programs, supplemented by ticket sales, entry fees, softball tournaments, and numerous grass roots programs, allowed the Organizing Committee to raise approximately $3.5 million for the Games.

The Competition

The 1984 International Game for the Disabled were really many games in one.

There were four groupings for the athletes and classifications within each grouping, so that everyone could be as fairly and evenly matched in the various competitions as possible.

The official groupings were: Amputee; Blind; Cerebral Palsy; and Les Autres (French for "the others") which included such functional disabilities as osteogenesis imperfecta (brittle bones), muscular dystrophy, dwarfism, Guillain's Syndrome (a neurological disorder) and arthrogryposis (stiff joints). The groupings and classifications were made systemically, based upon scientific fact, medical examination, and functional ability.

Before any of the atletes got onto a field, court, or track, they underwent a thorough classification exam, which was given by a team of up to 50 doctors, optometrists, and technical medical officers during the three days before the start of the Games. Each athlete was accompanied by a coach or trainer while undertaking the exam.

"There is an intricate system of classification in disabled sports," said Fred Koch of West Hempstead, the director of physical education for United Cerebral Palsy in New York City, who served as the coordinator of competition for the Games. "It is important that the various athletes be carefully matched according to their comparative disabilities. This will ensure fair and equitable competition for everyone."

Amputee

Amputee athletes were classified by the degree of amputation. (AK stands for a leg amputation above or through the knee joint, BK for a leg amputation below the knee joint. AE stands for an arm amputation above or through the elbow, BE for an arm amputation below the elbow.)

A-1 was the designation for an athlete with a double AK, or who had both legs amputated above the knee. An athlete classified A-2 had a single AK and an A-3 athlete a double BK. A-1, A-2, and A-3 athletes competed as wheelchair athletes in track events or were ambulatory. A-2 athletes competed as ambulatory athletes in field events, such as long jump or discus, with the use of a prosthesis, or artificial leg.

A-4 signified a single BK, an athlete who had one leg amputated below the knee and who was ambulatory by means of a prosthesis.

Other ambulatory classifications were A-5 through A-8. An athlete classified A-5 had a double AE arm amputation, A-6 a single AE, A-7 a double BE, and A-8 a single BE. An athlete classified A-9 had combined upper and lower limb amputations.

Track and Field

Amputee athletes competed in a wide variety of track and field events. There were dashes of 60 and 200 meters for women, and 100 and 400 meters for men. There was also a long-distance race of 800 meters for woman wheelchair contestants, and 1,500- and 5,000-meter events for ambulatory men. There were also relay races (4 × 100 and 4 × 400) in several of the classifications.

The field events for both men and women included shot put, discus, javelin and long jump. The men also competed in the high jump. The shot put, discus, and javelin throws were contested by both wheelchair and ambulatory athletes.

Swimming

There was a full range of swimming contests, covering distances of 100, 200, and 400 meters. There was competition in the freestyle, backstroke, breaststroke, butterfly stroke, and individual medley (a combination of strokes) events. Swimmers in the wheelchair classifications started from positions in the water, while the ambulatory swimmers used the traditional diving start. The swimming competition also included men's and women's relays among combined-classification teams.

Lawn Bowling

This sport, popular in the English-speaking countries, was contested on a specially laid-out green at Eisenhower Park. Wheelchair and ambulatory contestants alike put plenty of concentration, and their own distinctive body English, into their efforts to win.

Blind

There were three classifications for the blind athletes. B-1 was the classification for athletes who were totally blind by medical standards. B-2 indicated vision of light and shadows. These athletes could make out silhouettes but could not distinguish visual details. B-3 was for those with so-called "tunnel vision." These athletes had a limited scope of sight, enabling them to negotiate everyday life as sighted persons. They could distinguish images, but not clearly, and without full peripheral vision.

Experienced optometrists used approved professional tests to determine the classifications of the athletes in this grouping during the three-day examination period before the start of the Games.

Track and Field

The totally blind athletes competed in the same wide range of running events as those men and women with light/shadow vision or tunnel vision. There were races at 100 meters, 400, 800, 1,500, 3,000, and 5,000 meters.

The B-1 runners competed individually with guide ropes on either side. B-2 athletes ran in heats with two lanes at their disposal. They were allowed a caller on visual cues. B-3 athletes ran essentially as able-bodied individuals.

There is a Russian sprinter in the B-2 classification who can see only some light and shadows, with 11.05-second speed in the 100-meter dash. He runs toward a caller giving auditory signals at the finish line. This speed puts him in the same category of ability as a world-class able-bodied athlete.

Middle and longer distances (from 400 meters to 5,000 meters) were run with a second, sighted person at the athlete's disposal. Pacing and coaching by the sighted guide were forbidden during a race.

Athletes in all three blind classifications also competed in the field events of long jump, triple jump, high jump, discus, shot put, and javelin, as well as the pentathlon, a group of five track and field events that test an athlete's versatility.

Swimming

Swimming was another of the sports in which the blind athletes excelled despite their disability. The water was the great equalizer as they competed in freestyle, backstroke, breaststroke, butterfly stroke, and individual medley events from 50 to 400 meters long. The athletes showed an uncanny ability to negotiate the turns smoothly and without losing a stroke. The highlight of this sport was the relay races of combined classifications.

Wrestling

This sport was for the blind athletes only. There was competition in 10 weight classes, ranging from 48 kilograms (105.6 pounds) to more than 100 kilograms (220 pounds). The nature of the contact sport allowed athletes in all three classifications to compete against each other.

Goal Ball

Goal Ball is a sport that belongs to blind athletes. Those with limited vision are included with a rule that calls for everybody wearing a blindfold. A team of three players tries to roll, or otherwise move along the floor, a soccer-sized ball that is weighted like a medicine ball and equipped with a bell inside. The defensive team protects a net that spans the width of the court (9 meters, or 27 feet) on their hand and knees, lunging at the sound of the approaching ball. Spectators are not allowed to root (except after a goal is scored), because the athletes require silence to use their hearing as part of the sport. There was both men's and women's goal ball competition in the Games.

Cerebral Palsy

The athletes with cerebral palsy were classified by the severity of their disability, which was determined by functional ability in scientific terms and measurements by medical doctors and sport technicians.

CP-1 was the classification given the most severely disabled athlete who used an electric wheelchair for mobility. CP-2 indicated an athlete with moderate to severe disability in all four extremities who used a manual wheelchair. This classification was further delineated by whether athletes used their arms or their feet to move their manual wheelchairs. "There are some amazing athletes in these events who use their feet to push the wheelchair with speed and accuracy," Koch said.

CP-3 indicated the athlete who had moderate use of two or three limbs, including use of hands to grasp or release, and a full range of motion in the shoulders and arms. The CP-4 athlete had good strength, speed, and control in the upper extremities but none in the lower extremities. This was the highest-functioning, strongest, and most mobile of the wheelchair cerebral palsy athletes.

The CP-5 classification was given to the so-called "crutches ambulate," an athlete with the strength and control of CP-4, but who could walk with crutches. CP-6 indicated an athlete with moderate to severe disability in all four extremities, like CP-2, but who could walk rather than use a manual wheelchair.

The CP-7 athlete was the athlete who like CP-3 had moderate use of at least two or three limbs, but who could walk, usually with a noticeable limp. These athletes had some limitation in control of their upper and lower extremities. An example of a CP-7 athlete would be a hemiplegic, someone who had suffered a stroke and thus had paralysis or limited control of one lateral half of the body.

The CP-8 was the most minimally disabled athlete, who had good balance and motor control and a wide range in motion. "These are the highest-functioning athletes with very subtle problems, " Koch said. "From their endeavors and abilities on the athletic field, they are hardly distinguishable from able-bodied athletes."

Track and Field

The track events for cerebral palsy athletes began with various slalom events for the CP-1 through CP-4 classes, an exercise in maneuverability and control in an electric or manual wheelchair around an obstacle course that called for full turns, half turns, and sudden changes into reverse. The course included four reverse gates, a full circle, a figure eight, and a raised ramp to negotiate.

The races for CP-2 athletes over 60 and 200 meters featured the unusual sight of several athletes speeding backward by pushing their wheelchairs with their feet. They didn't look where they were going, concentrating instead on staying within the white lines of their lanes, knowing they'd finished only when the finish line appeared in their wake.

Also featured was a relay event for three CP-2 and CP-3 athletes, racing 60 meters each in their wheelchairs.

The field events included the shot put, discus, and javelin, and the severely disabled athletes and those with limited use of both upper extremities also threw soft shots (resembling beanbags) or clubs (such as those used in gymnastics exhibitions) for both precision and distance.

There was also a long jump for the highest-functioning cerebral palsy athletes.

Swimming

Some of the most inspiring events included 25-meter races in which CP-1 and CP-2 athletes used flotation aids to complete the course. The other cerebral palsy athletes competed in freestyle, backstroke, breaststroke, and butterfly stroke races of from 50 to 200 meters. There were also medley relays for combined classifications.

Soccer

There were both wheelchair soccer and ambulatory soccer matches, made even more interesting by the use of coed teams in combined classifications. In the wheelchair version, passes and shots were made with both hands and feet, in a way similar to team handball. The ambulatory game, played only with the feet, featured much of the same dexterity and ball control as in able-bodied soccer matches.

Boccia

Competition in both individual and team events was held indoors at the Nassau Community College field house. The court was marked off by lines, but did not contain sideboards or backboards. The boccia balls, including the target ball (jack), were handmade of leather. Men and women competed together.

Air Rifle

Shooting events were divided differently by classification because of the amount of dexterity necessary in the upper extremities. Men and women competed separately, with CP-3 and CP-6 athletes in one division and CP-4, CP-5, and CP-7 athletes in another. Participants fired .77-caliber pellets at targets 10 meters away.

Horseback Riding

This sport earned a spot in the Games for cerebral palsy riders after a group of four American equestrians put on an exhibition at the International Cerebral Palsy Games in Denmark two summers ago. It included combinations of classifications (CP-1 and CP-2, CP-3 and CP-6, CP-4 and CP-5, CP-7 and CP-8) with coed competition in all divisions. There was also a world cup event for riders with other disabilities, including amputees.

Table Tennis

There was both wheelchair and ambulatory competition, starting with a men's event for CP-3 athletes who had limited use of two or three limbs.

Archery

Wheelchair and ambulatory athletes competed together, classified by the amount of upper extremity involvement. In this contest, one entrant could be seen sitting in a wheelchair shooting at one target, while the contestant next to him shot from a standing position. Men and women competed separately.

Cycling

The CP-7 and CP-8 athletes competed on bicycles while CP-5 and CP-6 athletes, those with more severe disability in the upper extremities, competed on specially designed tricycles to offset the need for perfect balance. The pure exhilaration of "Break Away" was present in both divisions of competition.

Cross Country

This excursion over a rolling course was for the CP-6, CP-7, and CP-8 athletes, who ran either 1,000 or 1,500 meters, with separate events for men and women.

Power Lifting

With the implementation of more and more properly equipped gyms, power lifting has become a fast-growing sport in cerebral palsy programs, one that has become very popular with athletes in all classifications and quite an attention-getter with spectators. Power lifting was done from a bench-press position using the Universal bench-press machine, thus eliminating the balance variable for cerebral palsy athletes with control problems. The body weight of the competitors, ranging from 52 kilograms (114.4 pounds) to more than 90 kilograms (198 pounds), was the sole criterion in classifying the athletes, providing they had 190 degrees' range of motion in their upper extremities.

Les Autres

This was the first year of competition for les autres, aptly named in French as "the others." While the official groupings of previous Games for the Disabled had clearcut categories for amputee, blind, and cerebral palsy athletes, there was no previous opportunity for athletes with other functional disabilities to compete. They were trapped in an athletic limbo.

These other disabilities included osteogenesis imperfecta (brittle bones), muscular dystrophy, dwarfism, Guillain's Syndrome (a neurological disorder) and arthrogryposis (stiff joints), to name a few. The team of medical personnel determined the eligibility of Les Autres athletes after precise examination.

"The definition for les autres reads like a medical book," Koch said. "Generally speaking, this is not a spinal-cord injured disability group and it does not include the mentally disabled. We are obliged to make the distinction that this is not the Special Olympics."

The classifications in Les Autres were made according to the degree of functional problems that the athlete lived with. The L-1 classification was for wheelchair athletes with reduced functioning, problems in mobility, and poor balance. L-2 was also a wheelchair athlete with poor to moderate sitting balance, although the athlete had a dominant arm or hand. The L-3 athlete had good sitting balance in a wheelchair.

The L-4 athlete was ambulant, with or without crutches and/or braces. They had a weakness in the dominant arm, causing reduced functioning. The L-5 athlete was similar to L-4, with normal function in the dominant arm, but generally had a problem with hip rotation. The L-6 athlete had minimal trunk or lower limb disability.

Track and Field

The wheelchair events for L-1 though L-3 athletes ranged from 60 meters to 400 meters, with men and women competing separately. The events for the athletes in the ambulatory classes went from 100 meters to 1,500 meters. The field events included shot put, discus, javelin, and club throws. There were no jumping events—yet.

Swimming

The swimming had a full range of events, starting at 25 meters and extending to 200-meter medley races. The competition was in freestyle, backstroke, breaststroke, and butterfly stroke. There were also relays combining various classifications.

Integrated

In order to provide more sports for the athletes with disability in the lower limbs and to incorporate the les autres athletes with other competitors, an integrated grouping of amputee and les autres athletes was established for a variety of sports.

Air Pistol

The qualifying standard for competition was 480 points for men and 320 points for women.

Air Rifle

This was a new sport for the integrated grouping. Men and women competed separately.

Archery

The men competed with a qualifying standard of 954 points, and the women with a qualifying standard of 894 points. There was also a team competition for men of combined classes.

Basketball

There was a demonstration in both wheelchair and standing basketball. The sport was for men only this year.

Table Tennis

The competition was both in wheelchairs and ambulatory. There were singles and doubles events in the various men's and women's classifications.

Volleyball

There was sitting volleyball for men, and standing volleyball for coed teams.

Weight Lifting

Weight lifting in the integrated sport grouping was the same as power lifting in the cerebral palsy competition, entailing lifting from the bench-press position. The integrated weight lifting used the standard Olympic bar and weights.

Results

The competition results were too numerous to list here. The official results book fills four volumes, with over 900 sets of medals (gold, silver, and bronze) having been awarded. However, Table 2 represents a sampling of some of the outstanding performances.

A wheelchair event was included in the Olympics for the first time in 1984, and trials to pick the top wheelchair athletes from around the world to compete in Los Angeles were held concurrently with the International Games for the Disabled.

The Olympic trials for the 1,500-meter race for men and the 800-meter race for women took place on Friday, June 29 at the Mitchel Park athletic complex. Eight men and eight women and two alternates were selected to compete in Los Angeles August 11.

"There is no better example of the Olympic spirit than these athletes who have overcome considerable odds to achieve highly competitive times in the worldwide sports communities," said Peter V. Ueberroth, president of the Olympic Organizing Committee and now commissioner of major league baseball.

"These athletes will represent sports for the disabled to the world. Their recognition in the Olympic games is a great achievement," said Ueberroth.

The Olympic competitors were determined after two rounds of competition. They were previously nominated by the Cerebral Palsy-International Sports and Recreation Association, the International Stoke-Mandeville Games Federation, and the International Sport Organizations for the Disabled.

In Los Angeles, Paul Van Winkel won the 1,500 meters in 3:58.50, Sharon Hedrick claimed the gold medal in the 800 meters in a world-record time of 2.15.73. These results were achieved before 75,000 spectators and worldwide TV.

Media Coverage

The 1984 International Games for the Diabled was the most widely covered event in the history of disabled sports. Not only was there tremendous media coverage in the United States, but also around the world. The heaviest day of coverage was the opening ceremonies, during which 500 newspaper, radio, television, and magazine reporters from the four corners of the world observed as President Reagan opened the games. The outstanding public relations effort was spearheaded by Carl Byoir & Associates, a New York public relations firm.

Extensive coverage of the games was provided by Cablevision/Sports Channel, Channel 21 Public Television, ABC's "Nightline" and "Good Morning America," NBC TV, CBS TV, WNBC Radio, *The New York Times*, Long Island's *Newsday*, and "Voice of America," as well as BBC TV, Dutch TV, West German TV, and Swedish radio and TV. This major coverage was supplemented by hundreds of stories in all media, around the world.

Table 2. Outstanding performances

Event	Name	Grouping/Class	Country	Sex	Result
Power lifting (bench press)	Charles Reid	Cerebral Palsy/3	United States	M	215K (473 lbs.)
100 meters (wheelchair)	Merja Jaarda	Cerebral Palsy/4	Sweden	F	21.24 seconds
100 meters	Antonio Carlos Martins	Cerebral Palsy/8	Portugal	M	12.82 seconds
100 meters (backstroke)	Trischa Zorn	Bline/2	United States	F	1.13.87 minutes
100 meters	Winford Haynes	Blind/1	United States	M	11.78 seconds
100 meters	Paul Smith	Blind/3	United States	M	11.19 seconds
400 meters	Lucien Quemond	Blind/3	France	M	50.53 seconds
Discus	Karen Farmer	Amputee/4	United States	F	33.04 meters
High jump	Arnie Boldt	Amputee/2	Canada	M	1.95 meters
Long jump	Ronnie Alsup	Amputee/4	United States	M	5.54 meters
100 meters (wheelchair)	Jim Martinson	Amputee/1-3	United States	M	17.34 seconds
400 meters	Harri Jauhiainen	Amputee/6	Finland	M	49.81 seconds
Weight lifting (lt. hvy. wt.)	Bernard Barberet	Integrated	France	M	185.00K (407 lbs.)
800 meters (wheelchair)	Sharon Hedrick	Olympic Trial	United States	F	2:22.4 seconds
1500 meters (wheelchair)	Paul Van Winkel	Olympic Trial	Belgium	M	4.07.2 minutes

By spreading the news of this quadrennial Olympic-style competition throughout Long Island, the United States, and the world, the Games' organizers achieved one of their major goals. That was to communicate to the general public that these athletes were world-class athletes—who happened to have a disability. This event for the first time presented to disabled youngsters athletic role models, and a chance to identify with sport stars who themselves are physically challenged.

Summary

The 1984 International Games for the Disabled was the second largest sporting event in the world in 1984, second only to the Los Angeles Summer Olympic Games. The Organizing Committee, at its peak, included more than 3,000 staff members and volunteers and generated more than $3,000,000 to fund the games in only 18 months.

The Organizing Committee is extremely proud of the efforts put forth by the people of Long Island and other parts of the United States which made the 1984 International Games for the Disabled one of the great sporting events in modern history.

PART VII

Appendices:
Classification Systems and
Supplemental Information

APPENDIX

Disability Classification for Competition

In each category of disability represented in the International Games for the Disabled, there are classifications for competition to insure that each athlete is vying with others equally. These categories are described below in material prepared by Fred Koch, Competition Director.

Cerebral Palsy

Class 1 — Severe involvement in all four limbs. Limited trunk control, unable to grasp a softball. Poor functional strength in upper extremities, necessitating the use of an electric wheelchair.

Class 2 — Severe to moderate quadriplegic, normally able to propel wheelchair with legs or if able, propels wheelchair very slowly with arms. Poor functional strength and severe control problems in the upper extremities.

Class 3 — Moderate quadriplegic, fair functional strength and moderate control problems in upper extremities and torso. Uses wheelchair.

Class 4 — Lower limbs have moderate to severe involvement. Good functional strength and minimal control problems in the upper extremities and torso. Uses wheelchair.

Class 5 — Good functional strength and minimal control problems in upper extremities. May walk with or without aids, but for ambulatory support.

Class 6 — Moderate to severe quadriplegic. Ambulates without walking aids, less coordination balance problems when running or throwing. Has greater upper extremity involvement.

Class 7 — Moderate to minimal hemiplegic. Good functional ability in nonaffected side. Walks/runs with a limp.

Class 8 — Minimally affected hemiplegic. May have minimal coordination problems. Able to run and jump freely. Has good balance.

Amputee Based Classification System

The system is based on acquired and congential amputations.

Abbreviations

AK — Above or through knee joint
BK — Below knee, but through or above talocrural joint
AE — Above or through elbow joint
BE — Below elbow, but through or above wrist joint

Classification Code

Class A1 — Double AK
Class A2 — Single AK
Class A3 — Double BK
Class A4 — Single BK
Class A5 — Double AE
Class A6 — Single AE
Class A7 — Double BE
Class A8 — Single BE
Class A9 — Combined lower plus upper limb amputations

Les Autres Classifications

L1 — Wheelchair bound. Reduced functions of muscle strength, and/or spasticity in throwing arm. Poor sitting balance.

L2 — Wheelchair bound with normal function in throwing arm and poor to moderate sitting balance. Or reduced function in throwing arm, but good sitting balance.

L3 — Wheelchair bound with normal arm function and good sitting balance.

L4 — Ambulant with or without crutches and braces; or problems with the balance together with reduced function in throwing arm.

Note: An athlete is allowed to use orthosis or crutches if he so wishes. The throw can be done from a standstill or moving position in L4 and L5.

L5 — Ambulant with normal arm function in throwing arm. Reduced function in lower extremities or balance problem.

L6 — Ambulant with normal upper extremity function in throwing arm and minimal trunk or lower extremity disability. A participant in this class must be able to demonstrate a locomotor disability which clearly gives him/her a disadvantage in throwing events compared to able-bodied sports men/women.

Blind Classifications

B1 — No light perception at all in either eye up to light perception, but inability to recognize objects or contours in any directions and at any distance.

B2 — Ability to recognize objects or contours up to a visual acuity of 2/60 and/or a limitation of field of vision of 5 degrees.

B3 — 2/60 to 6/60 vision and/or field of vision between 5 and 20 degrees.

APPENDIX B

Classifications

Class IA

All cervical lesions with complete or incomplete quadriplegia who have involvement of both hands, weakness of triceps (up to and including grade 3 on testing scale), and with severe weakness of the trunk and lower extremities interfering significantly with trunk balance and the ability to walk.

Class IB

All cervical lesions with complete or incomplete quadriplegia who have involvement of upper extremities but less than IA with preservation of normal or good triceps (4 or 5 on testing scale) and with a generalized weakness of the trunk and lower extremities interfering significantly with trunk balance and the ability to walk.

Class IC

All cervical lesions with complete or incomplete quadriplegia who have involvement of upper extremities but less than IB with preservation of normal or good triceps (4 or 5 on testing scale) and normal or good finger flexion and extension (grasp and release) but without intrinsic hand function and with a generalized weakness of the trunk and lower extremities interfering significantly with trunk balance and the ability to walk.

Class II

Complete or incomplete paraplegia below T1 down to and including T5 or comparable disability with total abdominal paralysis or poor abdominal muscle strength (0-2 on testing scale) and no useful trunk sitting balance.

Class III

Complete or incomplete paraplegia or comparable disability below T5 down to and including T10 with upper abdominal and spinal extensor musculature sufficient to provide some element of trunk sitting balance but not normal.

Class IV

Complete or incomplete paraplegia or comparable disability below T10 down to and including L2 without quadriceps or very weak quadriceps with a value up to and including 2 on the testing scale and gluteal paralysis.

Class V

Complete or incomplete paraplegia or comparable disability below L2 with quadriceps in grades 3-5.

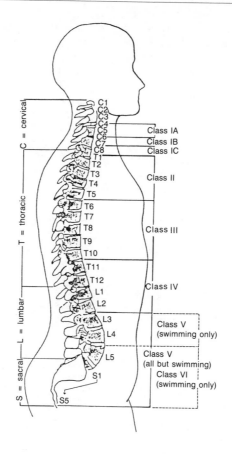

APPENDIX C

Major Magazines and Journals Which Feature Sports for Disabled Athletes

Ability, official publication for the U.S. Amputee Athletic Association, P.O. Box 5311, Mission Hills, California 91345.

Able Bodies, official newsletter of the American Alliance for Health, Physical Education, Recreation, and Dance, 1900 Association Drive, Reston, Virginia 22091.

Adapted Physical Activity Quarterly, Human Kinetics Publishers, Inc., Box 5076, Champaign, Illinois 61820.

The Deaf American, 814 Thayer Avenue, Silver Spring, Maryland 20910.

NWAA Newsletter, 2107 Templeton Gap Road, Suite C, Colorado Springs, Colorado 80907.

Palaestra, Challenge Publications, LTD, P.O. Box 508, Macomb, Illinois 61455.

Sportsline, official newsletter of the National Association of Sports for Cerebral Palsy, UCP, Inc., 66 E. 34th Street, New York, New York 10016.

Sports 'N Spokes, 5201 North 19th Avenue, Suite 111, Phoenix, Arizona 85015.

USABA Newsletter, Jim Duffield, Managing Editor, R.D. #3, Box 495, Felton, Delaware 19943.

APPENDIX D

Chronology of Development of Current International Governing Bodies in Sports for the Disabled

1924 — Comite International des Sports des Sourds (i.e., the Committee International on Silent Sports for deaf athletes) (CISS)
1957 — International Stoke Mandeville Games Federation (ISMGF)
1963 — International Sports Organization for the Disabled (ISOD)
1968 — International Special Olympics, Inc.
1978 — Cerebral Palsy-International Sports and Recreation (CP-ISRA). This replaced the International Cerebral Palsy Society, founded in 1968, which conducted international games.
1981 — International Blind Sports Association (IBSA)

Note. In 1982 the International Coordinating Committee (ICC) was formed with three representatives each from CP-ISRA, IBSA, ISMGF, and ISOD. This committee is to disabled sports what the International Olympic Committee (IOC) is to able-bodied sports.

APPENDIX E

Chronology of Development of U.S. Sports Organizations for Disabled Athletes

1945 — American Athletic Association for the Deaf (AAAD)
1949 — National Wheelchair Basketball Association (NWBA)
1956 — National Wheelchair Athletic Association (NWAA)
1967 — National Handicapped Sports and Recreation Association (NHSRA)
1968 — Special Olympics, Inc.
1976 — U.S. Association for Blind Athletes (USABA)
1978 — National Association of Sports for Cerebral Palsy (NASCP)
1981 — U.S. Amputee Athletic Association (USAAA)
1985 — National Les Autres Association (NLAA)

Note. Many other organizations have also been formed, usually to govern a single sport. The magazines *Sports 'N Spokes* and *Palaestra* are excellent sources of further information.

APPENDIX

Chronology of Events in the History of Sports for Disabled Athletes

1924 — Formation of the Comite International des Sports des Sourds (CISS, i.e., the Committee International on Silent Sports [for deaf athletes]) in conjunction with the first World Games for the Deaf in Paris.

1935 — First participation of U.S. disabled athletes in international competition. This was by two deaf students at the Illinois School for the Deaf in the IV World Games for the Deaf in London.

1939 — Publication of *Sports for the Handicapped* by George Stafford, professor of Physical Education, the University of Illinois. Contents encompassed all disabilities.

1944 — Creation of the Spinal Injuries Centre of the Stoke Mandeville Hospital in Aylesbury, England, and introduction of wheelchair sports as part of rehabilitation of war veterans by Sir Ludwig Guttmann.

1945 — American Athletic Association of the Deaf founded in Akron, Ohio. First president was Art Kruger, who held this office until 1980.

  • Earliest written record of wheelchair basketball being played in the United States. This was by war veterans at Corona Naval Station in California.

1948 — First Stoke Mandeville Games for the Paralyzed held with 16 ex-servicemen and women of the British Forces competing.

1949 — Beginning of Winter World Games for the Deaf in Austria. These are held every 4 years.

  • First Annual National Wheelchair Basketball Tournament held in Galesburg, Illinois, with six teams competing. Galesburg was site of a University of Illinois branch opened specifically to accommodate World War II veterans. Tim Nugent was director of the rehabilitation program there and is considered father of U.S. wheelchair basketball. Winning this first tournament was the Kansas City Rolling Pioneers.

- Founding of the National Wheelchair Basketball Association in the U.S. First executive director was Robert Miller of the Kansas City Rolling Pioneers. First officers (all disabled) were elected in 1950, and Tim Nugent was appointed technical advisor.

1950 — Charles Buell received EdD in educational psychology from University of California in Berkeley, thus becoming the first blind physical educator/athlete to receive a doctoral degree. His dissertation title was *Motor Performance of Visually Handicapped Children*.

1952 — First annual international sports festival for spinally paralyzed held with The Netherlands bringing a team of ex-servicemen to Stoke Mandeville.

1956 — First athletic scholarships were awarded to blind high school wrestling champions by Auburn University in Alabama, University of Maryland, and University of New Mexico. This appears to be the first athletic scholarships in U.S. for persons with disabilities.

1957 — First National Wheelchair Games in U.S. held at Adelphi College in Garden City, New York, with 63 competitors. Organizer was Ben Lipton.

- National Wheelchair Athletic Association was founded with Ben Lipton as chairman of its executive committee from 1957-1981.
- Founding of the International Stoke Mandeville Games Committee [Federation] by Sir Ludwig Guttmann as an equivalent to the Olympic Committee for able-bodied athletes.

1960 — First International Games for Disabled of an Olympic nature held in Rome for spinally paralyzed athletes under the auspices of the International Stoke Mandeville Games Federation led by Sir Ludwig Guttmann. Represented were 21 countries. This marked the beginning of the Paralympics held every fourth year in the same country (if possible) as the Olympic Games (1960-1980). After 1980, the International Olympic Committee requested that disabled athletes no longer use the term *Olympics*.

- British Sports Association for All Disabled founded by Sir Ludwig Guttmann.

1963 — International Sports Organization for the Disabled founded.

1966 — Publication of *Physical Education for Blind Children* by Charles Buell offers first comprehensive history of sports/athletics for a disabled population.

1967 — First Pan American Games held for spinally paralyzed athletes.

- Organization of the National Handicapped Sports and Recreation Association which governs winter sports in the U.S.

1968 — International Cerebral Palsy Society founded. This was replaced by Cerebral Palsy-International Sports and Recreation Association in 1978.

- International Special Olympics, Inc. was created by Eunice Kennedy Shriver with Canada and U.S. competing in the first meet in Chicago. Frank Hayden of Canada was first executive director.

1969 — The Stoke Mandeville Sports Stadium in England was officially opened and has been in full use ever since.

1972 — Classic book entitled *Games, Sports, and Exercises for the Physically Handicapped*, by Ron Adams, Alfred Daniel, and Lee Rullman, first published.

1974 — First National Women's Wheelchair Basketball Tournament held in U.S.

1975 — Bob Hall of Belmont, Massachusetts, was first wheelchair athlete to enter the Boston Marathon. Hall is a Class V post polio paraplegic. His 1975 time was 2:58.0 hours.

- First sports meets for U.S. cerebral palsied athletes held at Springfield College of Massachusetts under the leadership of Craig Huber and at Detroit, Michigan, under the leadership of Ray Clark. Documentation in *Sports 'N Spokes*, Nov./Dec. 1978.

1976 — Classic book entitled *Textbook of Sport for the Disabled* by Sir Ludwig Guttmann published.

- The Olympiad for the Physically Disabled was held August 3-11, in Toronto, Canada, with 38 countries officially participating and 100,000 spectators paying to attend. For the first time in history, blind and amputee athletes were invited to compete in addition to the spinally paralyzed. This event provided impetus for the formation of the U.S. Association for Blind Athletes (1976) and the U.S. Amputee Athletic Association (1981).

- U.S. Association for Blind Athletes founded in meeting of 30 leaders in Kansas City.

- UNESCO conference established that disabled persons also have a "right to participate in physical education and sport." This landmark meeting gave impetus to development of an international charter on physical education and sport and creation of an international development fund.

1977 — International Federation of Adapted Physical Activities founded with first meeting in Quebec, Canada. Meetings held every 2 years have been in Belgium (1979), United States (1981), England (1983), Canada (1985), and Australia (1987).

- First national championships of USABA held at Western Illinois University in Macomb with over 200 athletes from 24 states. Games director was Dr. David Beaver.

1978 — PL 95-606, the Amateur Sports Act, was passed which reconstituted the U.S. Olympic Committee and renewed its commitment to amateur athletes, including those with disabilities.

- National Association of Sports for Cerebral Palsy founded with Ray Clark as first chairman (for 1 year) and Craig Huber as second chairman/executive director. First international competition entered by CP athletes of U.S. was the 4th International Cerebral Palsied Games in Edinburgh, Scotland. Eighteen nations participated.

- Cerebral Palsy-International Sports and Recreation Association organized. International CP Games are held on even numbered years.

- U.S. Bureau of Education for the Handicapped awarded a 3-year federal grant to the National Wheelchair Basketball Association to provide inservice education on wheelchair sports at selected sites throughout the nation. Project coordinator was Ed Owen. This appears to be the first and only grant of this nature awarded.

1979 — Handicapped in Sports Committee organized by U.S. Olympic Committee to facilitate implementation of Amateur Sports Act of 1978.

1980 — Sled or sit skiing introduced for first time in Winter Skiing Championships at Winter Park, Colorado.

- The Olympics for the Disabled was held in Arnhem, Holland, on June 21-July 5, with 2000 athletes from 42 countries competing. For the first time, cerebral palsied athletes were invited to participate, but the invitation was limited to ambulatory CP athletes.

1981 — U.S. and International Olympic Committees issued formal statement rejecting the use of the term *Olympics* to describe competition by disabled athletes with the exception of Special Olympics, Inc., which is exclusively for mentally retarded persons. Subsequently, the term *Paralympics* was changed to VII World Wheelchair Games.

- United Nations declared this the International Year for Disabled Persons. As a result of the *Universal Declaration of Human Rights, Declaration of the Rights of the Child, Declaration on the Rights of Disabled Persons*, and *Nils-Ivar Sundberg Declaration*, all aspects of lives of persons with handicapping conditions have been greatly enhanced. It is the responsibility of *all* to assure that the education of individuals with handicapping conditions becomes an integral part of cultural development and that equal access to leisure activities becomes inseparable from social integration.
- First Annual World Wheelchair Marathon Championship was held at the Orange Bowl Marathon in Miami, Florida. This event also marked the first time a Class I NWAA athlete entered the 26.2 mile race.
- International Blind Sports Association organized.
- U.S. Amputee Athletic Association founded with Dick Bryant as executive director. First annual National Games held at Tennessee State University in Nashville with approximately 50 athletes competing.
- First crossing of the continental United States by wheelchair. Wheelers were George Murray (Class III) and Phil Carpenter (Class III).

1982 — First international meets held exclusively for *specific* wheelchair sports. Among these were the first World Archery Tournament for the Disabled in Mallorca, Spain, and the first World Table Tennis Championships for the Disabled held at the Ludwig Guttmann Sports Centre for the Disabled in England.

- UNESCO sponsored the International Symposium on Physical Education and Sport Programs for the Physically and Mentally Handicapped at College Park, Maryland.
- International Coordinating Committee formed with three representatives each from CP-ISRA, IBSA, ISMGF, and ISOD. This committee is to disabled sports what the International Olympic Committee is to able-bodied sports. First meeting was on March 11 at Leysin, Switzerland.

- Symposium on sport for the mentally handicapped held in celebration of The Netherlands—USA Bicentennial organized by Foundation Sports for the Handicapped, S.G.K., the Hague, The Netherlands. Proceedings published by B.V. Vitgerij De Vrieseborch, Jacobijnestraat 5, 2011 TG Haarlem, The Netherlands.

1983 — First International Women's Wheelchair Basketball Tournament held in Angers, France. Previously international competition had been held in conjunction with Paralympic or Pan American Games.

- Six wheelchair racers finished a mile run in under 4 minutes in Scarborough, Ontario, Canada.
- Seven wheelchair racers finished the Boston Marathon in less than 2 hours.

1984 — Neroli Fairhall of New Zealand was first wheelchair athlete to meet able-bodied eligibility criteria and participate in Olympic Games. She placed 38th in women's archery competition.

- For the first time, two wheelchair races were included as demonstration events at the Los Angeles Olympic Games. Sixteen wheelchair athletes representing eight countries competed. The Women's Wheelchair 800 m race was won by Sharon Rahn Hedrick with a time of 2:15.50. The Men's Wheelchair 1500 m race was won by Paul Van Winkle of Belgium with a time of 3:58.50.
- VII World Wheelchair Games (Paralympics), awarded in 1981 to National Wheelchair Athletic Association by the International Stoke Mandeville Games Federation, was planned for University of Illinois but changed to Stoke Mandeville site because of funding difficulties. This reflected an organizational change back to the 1972 structure when only spinally paralyzed athletes competed.
- International Games for the Disabled held for the first time in U.S., from June 17-29 on Long Island, New York. The 1800 competitors represented all disabilities except the spinally paralyzed, deaf, and mentally retarded, each of which holds independent games.
- Sal Ficaro received bachelor's degree in physical education from Springfield College, thus becoming first person with cerebral palsy to complete teacher certification in physical education.
- *Runner's World* became first commercial magazine to run a full-length article on a disabled athlete. The October issue featured Linda Down, a Class 5 cerebral palsied person, who first ran the New York City Marathon in 1982, requiring 11 hours, 15 minutes.
- The International Scientific Congress held in Seattle, Oregon, in conjunction with the Olympic Games included research and discussion sessions on sports for disabled athletes. This was the first time such sessions had ever been held.
- Plans for an international society on research for disabled athletes were developed at the International Scientific Congress. Robert Steadward of Canada was elected president, and a meeting was tentatively scheduled for 1986.

1985 — World Games for the Deaf held in the United States for the first time.

- James Mastro received PhD in physical education from Texas

Woman's University, thus becoming first blind person to receive doctoral degree in physical education.

1988 — International Games for the Disabled coordinated by the ICC scheduled for Seoul, Korea.

APPENDIX G

Addresses of International Governing Bodies in Sports for Disabled Athletes

Serving Spinally Paralyzed Athletes

International Stoke Mandeville
  Games Federation (ISMGF)
Stoke Mandeville Sports Stadium
Harvey Road, Aylesbury, Bucks,
  HP 21 8PP

Serving Cerebral Palsied Athletes

Cerebral Palsy-International Sports
  and Recreation Association
  (CP-ISRA)
A.J. Hessels, CP-ISRA
General Secretariat
6874 AJ
Wolfheze, The Netherlands

*Serving Amputee
and Les Autres Athletes*

International Sports Organization
  for the Disabled (ISOD)
Hans Lindstrom, ISOD
Secretary General
SHIF
Idrottens Hus
Storforsplan 44
12387, Farsta, Sweden

Serving Blind Athletes

International Blind Sports
  Association (IBSA)
Jan Molberg, IBSA
Secretary General
Hybratenveien No. 7C
Oslo 10, Norway

Serving Mentally Retarded Athletes

Special Olympics, Inc.
Eunice Kennedy Shriver
1350 New York Avenue N.W.
Suite 500
Washington, DC 20005

Serving Deaf Athletes

Comite International des Sports
  des Sourds
Jerald Jordan
Gallaudet College
Washington, DC 20002

APPENDIX H

Addresses of U.S. Governing Bodies in Sports for Disabled Athletes With Representatives on the Committee of Sports for the Disabled (COSD) of the U.S. Olympic Committee

National Wheelchair Athletic Association (NWAA)
Pat Karman, Chairperson
Andy Fleming, Executive Director
2107 Templeton Gap Road, Suite C
Colorado Springs, Colorado 80907
(303) 632-0698

National Association of Sports for Cerebral Palsy (NASCP)
Raphael Bieber
66 East 34th Street
New York, New York 10016
(212) 481-6359

U.S. Association for Blind Athletes (USABA)
Art Copeland
55 West California Avenue
Beach Haven Park, New Jersey 08008

Note. Each of these organizations has two representatives on the Committee on Sports for the Disabled of the U.S. Olympic Committee. Eligibility for this representation is sponsorship of two or more sports which are included on the programs of the Olympic or Pan American Games.

United States Amputee Association (USAA)
Richard Bryant
Route 2, County Line
Fairview, Tennessee 37062
(615) 670-5453

National Handicapped Sports and Recreation Association (NHSRA)
Ron Hernley, President
Capitol Hill Station
P.O. Box 18664
Denver, Colorado 80218

Special Olympics, Inc. (SO)
Eunice Kennedy Shriver
1350 New York Avenue N.W.
Suite 500
Washington, DC 20005

American Athletic Association of the Deaf (AAAD)
Richard Caswell
3916 Lantern Drive
Silver Spring, MD 20902
TTY: (301) 942-4042

APPENDIX I

Addresses of Other U.S. Governing Bodies in Sports for Disabled Athletes

American Wheelchair Bowling Association
Daryl Plister
N54 W15858 Larkspur Lane
Menomonee Falls, WI 53051

California Wheelchair Aviators
Bill Blackwood, President
1117 Rising Hill
Escondido, CA 92025

Disabled Sportsmen of America, Inc.
P.O. Box 5496
Roanoke, VA 24012

International Foundation for Wheelchair Tennis
Peter Burwash, International
2203Timberloch Pl., Suite 126
The Woodlands, TX 77380
(713) 363-4707

National Wheelchair Racquetball Association
Jim Leatherman, Commissioner
c/o AARA
815 N. Weber, Suite 203
Colorado Springs, CO 80903

North American Riding for the Handicapped Association
Leonard Warner, Executive Director
Box 100
Ashburn, VA 22011
(703) 471-1521; (703) 777-3540

Wheelchair Motorcycle Association
Dr. Eli Factor
101 Torrey Street
Brockton, MA 02401

Amputee Sports Association
George Beckmann, Jr.
11705 Mercy Blvd.
Savannah, GA 31406
(912) 927-5408

Canadian Wheelchair Sports Association
333 River Road
Ottawa, Ontario, Canada K1L 8B9

Handicapped Scuba Association
Jim Gatacre
1104 El Prado
San Clemente, CA 92672
(714) 498-6128

International Wheelchair Road Racers Club, Inc.
George Murray, Pres.,
Jeannette Parke, Sec.
165 78th Avenue NE
St. Petersburg, FL 33702

National Wheelchair Basketball Association
Stan Labanowich
110 Seaton Bldg.
University of Kentucky
Lexington, KY 40506
(606) 287-1629

National Wheelchair Softball Association
Dave Van Buskirk, Commissioner
P.O. Box 737
Sioux Falls, SD 57101

United States Quad Rugby Association
Tommie Willard
811 Northwestern Drive
Grand Forks, ND 58201
(701) 775-0790

Wheelchair Pilots Association
11018 102nd Avenue N
Largo, FL 33540
(813) 393-3131

For Blind Athletes
National Beep Baseball Association
James Mastro
P.O. Box 23717, TWU Station
Texas Woman's University
Denton, TX 76204

American Blind Bowling Association
150 N. Bellaire Avenue
Louisville, KY 40206

For Deaf Athletes
U.S. Deaf Skiers Association, Inc.
Donald Fields
159 Davis Avenue
Hackensack, NJ 07601

U.S. Deaf Tennis Association, Inc.
Robbie Carmicheal
3102 Lake Avenue
Cheverly, MD 20785

U.S. Deaf Volleyball Commissioner
Bill Davidson
3019 Halsey Avenue
Arcadia, CA 91006

American Hearing Impaired Hockey
Irvin G. Tianhnybik
1143 West Lake Street
Chicago, IL 60607

U.S. Deaf Softball Commissioner
John Miller
7111 Kempton Road
Lanham, MD 20801

APPENDIX J

Wheelchair Design

Several papers in this book have referred to advances in wheelchair design and the need for research in this area. This section briefly reviews types of wheelchairs and differences in design. For the history of changes in wheelchair design, the reader is referred to articles by LaMere and Labonowich (1984).

Medical Model or Regular Chair

This chair is the one most commonly prescribed by physicians. Its forebearer originated in 1700. King Philip V of Spain is believed to be the first wheelchair user. His chair had wooden wheels, with wooden spokes, adjustable leg rests, and a reclining back. H.A. Everest, one of the founders of Everest & Jennings Wheelchair Manufacturers, is accredited with the design of the contemporary compact foldable chair in the early 1930s, several years after a mining accident made him a paraplegic.

Sports Chair

Originally *sports chair* referred to those manufactured specifically for basketball. Now with the proliferation of wheelchair sports (tennis, racquetball, soccer, football, softball), the term refers to any chair built to allow optimal maneuverability, quick turning, and rapid acceleration. Over 15 sports wheelchair manufacturers offer distinctly different models. These are reviewed annually in *Sports 'N Spokes*, beginning in 1983.

Sports chairs are built for performance rather than comfort. They often have no handles on the seat back for pushing, no arm rests, and no brakes. Most have rigid frames and do not fold. They can, however, be disassembled easily and quickly for travel. Other differences between the sports and regular models include a lowered seat back, a cushion built into the seat, and a solid front bar for foot placement rather than the traditional folding foot platforms. Axle plates on the drive wheels are adjustable to permit different seat positions. By changing the axle location, the wheelchair's center of gravity is altered and maneuverability is improved.

Sports chairs have some safety factors not found on other types of wheelchairs. *Anti-tip casters* on the kick bar in the rear of the chair reduces the possibility of tipping over. The *roll-bar* (attached underneath the foot platforms) prevents the chair from folding in case of a spill.

Many athletes use the same chair for basketball and track. By purchasing several handrims of different sizes and taking full advantage of adjustable axle and caster plates, the chair can be modified for a specific sports event. Athletes whose major interest is track or marathoning, however, use specially constructed chairs.

Track and Racing Chairs

These chairs differ from sports models primarily in larger size of drive wheels, smaller size of handrims, and lowered seat position. Since 1975, when Bob Hall gained recognition as the first wheelchair racer to enter the Boston Marathon, chairs have changed drastically to permit greater efficiency in 26.2 mile and even longer runs. Improved pneumatic tires, often with over 100 pounds of air pressure, are used with as little surface on the ground as possible.

Camber, while built into some sports chairs, is a definite necessity in track. *Camber* is a characteristic of the drive wheel, describing a condition in which the bottom of the wheels are farther apart than the tops. The top part of the wheel is closer to the upper body than in the regular chair and is directed toward the arm pit. This makes pushing more efficient, lessens the chance that the athlete's arm will bump against the wheel, and permits a natural relaxed position for the elbows.

Overcoming air resistance in racing is done partly by forward bending of the trunk and partly by adjusting the seat. The front of the seat is kept higher than the rear and the seat back is reclined slightly backward. The goal is to minimize the angle of hip flexion and maximize the angle of knee flexion. For athletes with paralyzed or weak trunk and lower back muscles, however, the seat must be steeper to assist them in maintaining a forward trunk bend with thighs to chest.

Motorized Chairs

Motorized chairs (sometimes incorrectly called electric chairs) give severely disabled persons considerable independence. They move at high and low speeds and are generally capable of about 5 miles an hour. Most can climb inclines of at least 10 degrees. In keeping with its motto (Sports by ability . . . not disability), NASCP has designed competitive events in which Class I athletes utilize their ability to maneuver a motorized chair. NASCP wheelchair soccer also permits participation in a motorized chair. NWAA/NWBA rules, in contrast, do not allow motorized chairs.

The battery-powered chair is the most commonly used, with two 12-volt batteries which are mounted on a carrier at the back of the chair below seat level. These batteries must be recharged each night in order to supply power for approximately 8 hours of continuous use. Regular automobile batteries are used on most chairs. They are prone to the same problems that drivers experience.

Motorized chairs, which must have sturdy frames to support the weight of batteries and other special equipment, are very heavy. Without the batteries, a chair typically weighs 75 to 80 pounds. Folding the chair is impossible without removal of batteries. These problems in portability generally lead users of motorized chairs to purchase a second vehicle (manual) for travel.

References on History of Wheelchair Design

LaMere, T., & Labonowich, S. (1984). The history of sport wheelchairs—Part 1: Background of the basketball wheelchair. *Sports 'N Spokes, 9*(6), 6-11.

LaMere, T., & Labonowich, S. (1984). The history of sport wheelchairs: Part II, the racing wheelchair, 1956-75. *Sports 'N Spokes, 10*(1), 12-15.

LaMere, T., & Labonowich, S. (1984). The history of the sport wheelchair: Part III, track chair from 1975 to the present. *Sports 'N Spokes, 10*(2), 12-16.